I0297741

FOCUS GROUPS

A GUIDE FOR MARKETING & ADVERTISING PROFESSIONALS

JANE FARLEY TEMPLETON

PROBUS PUBLISHING COMPANY
Chicago, Illinois

Library of Congress Cataloging in Publication Data

Templeton, Jane F. (Jane Farley)
  Focus groups.

  Includes Index
  1. Marketing research. 2. Advertising—Research.
I. Title.
HF5415.2.T43 1987   658.8'3   87-4977
ISBN 0-917253-78-7

Library of Congress Catalog Card No. 87-4977

Printed in the United States of America

1   2   3   4   5   6   7   8   9   0

Preface

Focus Groups: A Guide for Marketing and Advertising Professionals is an expedition into the territory of focus-group interviewing: a comprehensive tour with a tour guide who speaks the language. Although they are "known" by marketers, media chroniclers, and even by growing numbers of consumers, what is known is the face of focus-groups, not the heart, the interpretive mind, nor the marketing muscle.

The book is addressed primarily to marketers—present and soon-to-be—and to those who translate marketing decisions into advertising, or who aspire to take up the cudgels of the advertising profession. It may be useful also to sales professionals, to those who now operate field facilities (or who plan to) and to the researchers who must work in tandem with focus-group interviewers and interpreters. Finally, for those who plan to become focus-group moderators/rapporteurs, it offers one point of view on mastering the necessary skills.

Any author must answer, if only for himself or herself, the questions "Why this book instead of another?" and "Why me, instead of someone else?" The answers to both are simple. Except for a book of readings published several years ago—a compilation of published papers that made no pretense of placing focus-groups in a theoretical or operative context—at the time of writing there *was* no other book of this kind. And the answer to "Why me?" is derivative: I am the one who broke the ground. Because the history of focus-group interviewing is so dispersed, my perspective does not encompass all possible perspectives. But twenty-five years of experience, if they have not made me a card-carrying sage, qualify me as an adept, at least.

ACKNOWLEDGEMENTS

I wish to thank first the clients who gave me permission to use report material, in whole or in part, for illustrative purposes and/or to reproduce preparatory paperwork (proposals, discussion guides, screeners, and such) used in research projects. My special thanks to General Foods Corporation for allowing the use of a full report, and to Jay Eckhaus, from that company, who patiently went over several versions of the report, and with almost Talmudic delicacy allowed all of the identifying text he felt would not hamper the marketing of the product.

Also to Vidar Jorgensen, of Computer Publishing Services, Inc., for permitting the use of the focus-group report on *Highwire Magazine*, in its entirety, many thanks.

For the use of their names and materials, thanks to Bill Communications, Inc. (*Sales and Marketing Management Magazine*), and to Charles Rhudy, for the use of preparatory materials and substantial report segments from his golf periodical project.

Thanks are in order too to those clients who paid me the compliment of proprietary concern about the use of reports and report segments, even when the projects were a decade or more past: both those who felt that they must decline to approve the inclusion of interpretive material ("...the report is still true, and the competition is still out there...") and those who approved the restrictive use of focus-group documents, omitting corporate identification. Many of these clients gave generously of their time and interest; I wish I could name individuals, but I cannot do so and ensure corporate anonymity.

Thanks to Robert Bengen, Research Director for Dunkin' Donuts, for his time and thought, for his resourcefulness in working out with me thorny client-moderator and client-rapporteur problems without compromising either party's interests and for more than five years of stimulating and rewarding collaboration as well. To the Pfaltzgraff Company for their invariable support in our work together, and for adjusting to my writing schedule, with special gratitude to Research Manager Jean Wolfe, for her time and enthusiasm. To Robert H. Albert, for his thought, time, and schedule concessions to this book, for agreeing to introduce it, for being a model of the "best possible client," and for giving me, as Editor of (then) *Sales Management Magazine*, my first assignment as a writer eighteen years ago. To the late Margaret Dangler of Nabisco Brands who, in the last fifteen years of her life, went beyond the role of model client and became my unflagging advocate and publicist, pressing me to aim higher (I did it, Margaret; I wrote the book). To Sam Guard, Claude Jeussemet, Lee Adler, W. Richard Mullan, Ralph Wemhoener, and Anita DeLesseps, among many, who saved me the unbecoming act of tooting my own horn, by tooting theirs in my behalf.

Thanks for the help of colleagues to whom I promised anonymity, and most of all, to one who extracted no such promise: to Dr. Barbara Swanson who—always and now—cheered me on, challenged my thinking, endorsed my premises, endured my funks, and delivered (rare but insightful) criticism, always in the company of support and agreement. Thanks, dear Barbara.

Thanks to you all. Thanks to you each.

Jane Templeton

Foreword

Focus groups may be the worst form of market research—to paraphrase a well known dictum about democracy—except for all the others, which is to say that each presents great difficulties and great opportunities. And, to pursue the similarities just one step further, both depend for the degree of their success upon the quality of leadership. Certainly Dr. Jane Templeton did not invent focus groups, but I think it's fair to say they would not exist in their present form and high degree of professionalism without her leadership.

Dr. Jane—as she has been known at our company for some 20 years—joined *Sales and Marketing Management* as a Contributing Editor not long after I became Editor. Her arrival was extremely significant to me because I'd been looking for someone with her talents to cover an area of great importance to the magazine: The human element. *Sales and Marketing Managment* (neé *Sales Management*) had an unassailable position in the area of market statistics—and our company, Bill Communications, now has a whole division with just that name—but was glaringly inadequate in the area of customer behaviour. After all, the *bottom*, bottom line of sales and marketing is: What do customers want, and when, how, why do they want it?

Through a mutual friend, I met Dr. Jane who, I was told, could turn the bare facts of behaviour research into lively, interesting, accurate prose. (Dr. Jane Templeton was then in charge of qualitative research at Ted Bates, a large, very successful international advertising agency known for its shrewd and savvy selling. Its success required shrewd and savvy customer information, which is where Dr. Jane starred.) Our mutual friend was right, and she's been sharing her facts and her fun with readers ever since.

Focus groups were at that time, as indeed they are now, Jane's basic source of the information she uses in her analysis of customer behaviour. She has brought this formless, shapeless, challenging tool to high perfection, and uses it with great skill and success. How and why, this book will tell you.

I'd like to tell you just a little bit about Dr. Jane, who is not only a professional associate but a good friend. One of her great abilities— which helps her enormously in her groups—is her ability to empathize. She's not only very bright but very human, and all of this shows through in a most unassuming way. I've been an observer "behind the mirror" at a number of her groups, and always marvelled at her skill in managing the seemingly unmanageable groups and delighted in reading her final reports.

Any truly successful communication, it was once said, must inform the uniformed without offending the sensitivities of the informed; in other words, both novice and expert can profit. That's certainly—and beautifully—clear in this book.

Robert H. Albert, Editorial Director
Bill Communications, Inc.

CONTENTS

PREFACE   v

FOREWORD   ix

CHAPTER 1 DEFINING FOCUS GROUPS   1

CHAPTER 2 THE FOCUS-GROUP INTERVIEW:
THE PHYSICAL EVENT   9
The Proposal   *11*
Planning A Focus-Group Project   *12*
Toplines And Full Reports   *33*

CHAPTER 3 THE TECHNICAL EVOLUTION   37
How We Got Where We Are   *39*
Starting From Where We Are: Ways To Mend the Situation   *44*

CHAPTER 4 THE THEORETICAL CONCEPT   51
To Buy Or Not To Buy   *59*
People Boxes   *60*
Mind Versus Body: Simplifying The Purchase Decision   *61*

CHAPTER 5 THE SOUL OF A FOCUS GROUP
(OR: "EVENTS INSIDE THE SKIN")   65

CHAPTER 6 THE INTERPERSONAL EVENT   81
The Moderator As Prime Mover/Participant   *84*
The Researcher As Contractor   *90*
The Moderator As Partner   *92*
The Focus Group As Microcosm   *97*

CHAPTER 7 CARRY-ON LUGGAGE   **99**
Dealing With People: 1. The Panelist   *103*
Dealing With People: 2. The Client   *108*
Dealing With Data   *111*

CHAPTER 8 WRITING THE REPORT   **117**
Framing The Report: Background And Purpose   *120*
Making The Data Accessible   *120*
Shifting Gears   *121*
The Predispositions   *124*
Reactions To Presented Materials   *135*
The Summary, Implications, and Recommendations   *137*

CHAPTER 9 THE FUNCTIONAL TOOL   **141**
Focus Groups As Tools Of Exploration   *145*
Exploratory Probes In Product Repositioning   *153*
Whats In A Name?: The Question Of Aegis   *155*
Translating Survey Questions Into Target-ese   *157*
Using Focus Groups For Show   *158*
The Use of Focus-Groups In Studying
  Creative Concepts and Execution   *160*
Qualitative Research Reified   *162*

CHAPTER 10 CHOOSING PANELISTS   **165**
A Mixed Bag Or A Matched Set: The
  Homogeneous/Heterogeneous Issue   *174*
Who's On First: The Question Of Multiple Interviewers   *180*

CHAPTER 11 HOW TO BE THE "BEST POSSIBLE"
CLIENT AND HOW TO BE THE "BEST POSSIBLE"
RESEARCHER   **183**
What Am I Bid? Getting Together   *187*
A Stitch In Time: Planning   *192*
Through A Glass Darkly: Doing And Viewing Groups   *195*
The Report Preparation Period   *202*
After The Ball: Best Possible Researchers And Clients
  Between Assignments   *205*

CHAPTER 12 COPING WITH PROBLEM GROUPS   **209**
  Coping With Moderator/Client Hazards   *213*
  Confronting Fallibility In The Field   *216*
  Grappling With Acts Of God   *219*

AFTERWORD   **229**

Appendix A: Six-Week Schedule For
A Focus-Group Project   **233**

Appendix B: Qualitative Research Proposal
For *Sales & Marketing Management*   **237**

Appendix C: Sample Screening Device For Selecting
Focus-Group Panelists—*Sales & Marketing Management*   **241**

Appendix D: Discussion Guide For *Sales & Marketing*
Management   **245**

Appendix E: Sample Introduction To Focus-Group
Panelists   **251**

Appendix F: How To Score The "Buzzword" List   **255**

Appendix G: Short Report Exploration of Consumer
Responses To Introductory Concepts For Cocktail
Mixers   **261**

Appendix H: Full Report   **277**

INDEX   **311**

Chapter 1

Defining Focus Groups

Focus-group interviewing is perhaps the most frequently used form of qualitative marketing research. But a precise definition of a focus group is hard to come by. This is not because nobody talks about focus groups—marketers and the media have been talking their heads off about them, especially of late. In fact, one aspect of focus groups that is frequently mentioned is their popularity. Case in point: a well-known marketing research text says:

> Marketing executives have been hearing a lot about focus- group interviews lately. (They are) so popular . . . that many advertising and research agencies consider them to be the "only" exploratory research tool. . . . A focus-group interview is an unstructured, free-flowing interview with a small group of people. . . .[1]

The text then goes on to describe what focus-groups are not (". . . rigidly constructed question-and-answer session[s] . . ."); lists possible *examples* (". . . women talking about hair-coloring, petroleum engineers talking about problems in the 'oil patch,' or children talking about toys . . ."); and, finally, lists "primary *advantages*" of the technique, in terms both objective (". . . fast, easy . . . , and inexpensive . . . " and subjective (the familiar S-list of qualifiers: Synergism, Snowballing, Stimulation, Security, etc.).

Aside from "fast, easy, and inexpensive," I can't really quarrel with anything in these statements. But after reading them, how much would you know about commissioning a focus-group interview? Or doing one? Or using one? Do you think that if you happened to stumble across one in progress you would recognize it instantly? ("Aha! This is a focus group.") Zikmund's description says *something* about *how* (focus-groups are loose and spontaneous), and in a categorical way, says *who* (women,

petroleum engineers, children), but aside from gender, age, and occupation, gives no particulars about the participants or *what* they are saying
about the product, at *whose* behest, and to *what* end.

You do get a pretty good idea of how Zikmund *feels* about focus-group
interviews—they're overrated. So maybe that's the problem. Unfortunately, apologists of the technique often don't narrow it down all that
much. Typically, an advocate of focus groups will introduce them historically, mentioning their earliest use, and alluding to their conceptual
lineage. Proponents, like detractors, are also likely to say a word or two
about their recent successes—though in a different tone. For example:

> Group interviewing—interviewing people in groups rather than in-
> dividually—entered the marketing research scene shortly after
> World War II, as part of "motivation research'. Like most motiva-
> tion research techniques, it was instantly condemned by the conser-
> vative research establishment as "unscientific' and therefore un-
> trustworthy. It has prospered nonetheless, and today in many
> marketing research organizations, group interviews are nearly as
> common as interviews done by the traditional survey question-
> naire.[2]

Notice that neither description names an exact moment of emergence.
This is not oversight, however: the "discovery" of the focus-group technique was unlike the discoveries in quantitative marketing research. In
the first place, it was not true and extant prior to its use, in the sense
that the normal curve was a true distribution of chance events, even
before it was recognized: a statistical verity, waiting too be found. In the
second place, the beginnings of focus-group interviewing were dispersed. Group therapy, T-groups, encounter marathons, and sensitivity
training, to name a few of its antecedents, were available as models, so
that slipping into the group method of exploration in the search for
marketplace truths may have happened almost accidentally—the time
was right for group techniques, in many contexts. It is likely that by the
time the new focus-group practitioners looked around for others to
whom they could introduce the tool they had developed, most of their
colleagues were "doing groups" too. Efforts to define focus groups at
this time would have appeared at best redundant, at worst pretentious.

And now focus-group interviewing receives more than its share of attention. (The opinion of the quantitative research establishment is correct in this regard.) It is an appealing approach in that it is persuasive, superficially direct and accessible, and presents much better photo opportunities than does questionnaire administration. It seems to have caught the fancy of marketers, the media, and the public. Indeed, it may now be all that is recognizable as "marketing research" to people outside the narrow citadel of the research community. Attempts to limit the appeal of focus groups by way of definition are therefore apt to look like sour grapes.

So all of us—practitioners, quantitative researchers, the media, and the public—think we know what focus-group interviews are. Like social acquaintances discussing a mutual friend, we use the same name to call up images of who knows what conceptual disparity. If M is Ruth's mother, L her lover, F her friend, E her employer, and R her rival, it can be said that each knows what "Ruth" means, but hardly that each has the same Ruth in mind.

My own best definition begins with the motivation which prompts "doing some groups" in the first place:

> An advertiser, advertising agency or a political entity (aspirant, incumbent, administration, party, etc.), feels that he/she/it needs help in selling a product, service, or him/her/ or itself.

It goes on to describe the essential character of the particular interview:

> A focus group, in essence, is a small, temporary community, formed for the purpose of the collaborative enterprise of discovery. The assembly is based on some mutual interest, and the effort is reinforced because panelists are paid for the work, leaving unspecified what the "work" is and the nature of the "discovery."

My definition concludes with a description of the interactive process involved:

> "Grouping" fosters the kind of interaction that penetrates impression management and uncovers more basic motivations, even

when the group is unaware of impression management or of the need to penetrate it.)

The following 11 chapters expand this definition, and expound upon it. But before proceeding, it remains for me to alert you to a few unresolved questions and editorial conventions which might otherwise perplex you.

Beware of Biases

The independent discovery and growth of focus-groups has produced a number of relatively independent and mature schools of thought about how to perform and evaluate them. Like everybody else who has grown up with the technique, I have strong biases about what makes focusgroups good and what makes them useful. Biases are not all bad in this regard. They cut through a thicket of snap decisions that must be made on-the-spot at every stage of a focus-group project: biases about planning, biases about how the interviews are best conducted and who is equipped to do them, biases about how focus-group data should be treated, and biases about what constitutes exemplary behavior on the part of three collaborators: moderator, client, and field staff.

A bias you can see cannot fog up your spectacles or distort your vision. By "seeing" I mean both the point-of-view that's espoused and the alternative view. Presenting both sides of arguments to which one is strongly committed is a tough assignment. I have tried to do this—to point out my biases when they come to light and to present the other side as fairly as I can. But I make no promises of equity. In most cases, my heart is really not with the opposition.

The three issues that generate the deepest feelings and the most inflexible biases constitute a real Gordian Knot. Though distinguishable, they are thoroughly interwoven. Their common strand is the seriousness with which focus-group data are taken or, if you like, the importance these data are given. The three subissues concern the *qualifications* required of a focus-group researcher; the extent to which focus-group research is considered *valid*—or whether the question of "validity" is even appropriate; and finally the characterization of focus-group research as *"quick, easy; and cheap."*

I do not propose to discuss these issues here, but merely to state briefly my own position on all three. In chapters 4, 7, and 8 especially, you'll find strong statements about how seriously *I* take focus-group findings (pretty seriously), and there are many other places in the text in which the importance of focus groups is assumed or implied.

References to the qualifications of focus-group professionals appear throughout the book, because I am not able to temper my strong bias that any attempt to make the field coherent can only succeed if two levels of expertise currently served by *interviewers* and *interpreters* are recognized and differentiated by function. The term "moderator" serves well enough to describe those researchers who *interview* only, or who interview and summarize, sticking to what was said in the interview. But there is another kind of focus-group researcher who not only reports the dialog, but interprets it as well. In this text, this individual is given the name "rapporteur." (The distinction is discussed in a more head-on fashion in Chapters 3 and 10.)

Recognizing these two levels of proficiency is especially important to current and future users of focus groups, who must determine which type of researcher to employ and how to evaluate the results that researcher delivers. At minimum, clients have the right—or the responsibility—of asking up-front *who* is doing *what*. Is the moderator acting as her own interpreter and report-writer? Is a *less*-qualified staff member doing the time-consuming and demanding work?

The myth of "quick, easy, and cheap" focus-groups is based on outdated facts. Focus-groups *were* cheap when we extracted less from them (working less hard in the process) and when neither we nor the recruiters knew much about qualification. It was still relatively inexpensive in the days before field facilities were pleasure domes, and before respondents learned that the traffic would bear more than $5 or $10 for two hours of their time.

"Fast" was always a relative concept. Focus-groups were faster from recruiting to reporting than a medium-sized quantitative study which involved creating a questionnaire, fielding, coding, and interpretation. But computers have changed all that. *Moderating* in a single location may be as fast as the *fielding* of a survey. But so far as I'm aware, there is not as yet a computer that interprets a unique event, requiring input from many communicative channels. Anyway, the information generated is not "more" or "less" valuable; it is just different.

Accounts of relationships between moderator/rapporteurs, clients, and the field staff (Chapters 6 and 11) are biased from beginning to end. But I think the biases are obvious—you can't miss them. The same is true for both "good and "less-good" dimensions of panel interactions. Besides highlighting the biases, I've attempted to give equal time to conflicting points-of-view (see Chapters 2 and 12).

There are other areas where bias intrudes, but those I've just discussed are the most important. Finally, I have adopted a convention of reference to avoid a string of bothersome "he/she" and "her/him" usage: I have, throughout the book, specified the gender of the moderator/rapporteur as "she," and that of the client as "he."

NOTES

[1]Zikmund, William G. *Exploring Marketing Research*, 2nd ed. (Hinsdale, Il.: Dryden Press, 1985).

[2]Wells, William G. "Group Interviewing," in Ferber, Robert, *Handbook of Marketing Research* (McGraw Hill Publishers, 1974).

Chapter 2

The Focus-Group Interview: The Physical Event

THE PROPOSAL

Whatever else a focus-group project is, it is most obviously a series of actions performed and documents prepared by the person who is responsible for the project—the moderator-rapporteur, sanctioned by the client.[1] Typically, the project begins with a request from the client for a proposal from the researcher. In some cases, when the two have a previous history of collaboration, a formal, written proposal may be replaced by a verbal pledge.

Time and cost are at the heart of the proposal. Even if the client's research budget is reasonably lenient and approval of the project seems certain, the client must have a fairly reliable estimate for planning purposes—say within 10 percent plus or minus, of anticipated costs. Focus groups are always something of a horserace, in the sense that you don't know what information you'll get out of them until you've gotten it. And accounting departments are notoriously low on gambling spirit. They insist on knowing approximately how big a bite a project is going to take, even if *nobody* knows for sure what the dollars are buying.

If the client is new, a formal proposal is usually necessary. It may tie up hours of the researcher's time, which probably will not be compensated. It may also involve a number of long-distance telephone charges for getting competitive estimates from facilities in each proposed location. Telephone charges *are* compensable, as "out-of-pocket" charges in the final bill, except in cases of *competitive* moderator-bidding: if the moderator is not chosen to do the research, it is customary for her to swallow both time spent and telephone costs.

Competitive bids for projects may be necessary when the client is unac-
quainted with the candidates, but I think it indefensible among known
moderators. If clients read critically the reports previously given by rapporteurs, there should be no doubt about who is "right" for a given
project. If exorbitant costs seem a serious possibility, researchers who
charge such should be taken off the eligible list. If a moderator is
eligible and "right," there's no need to make others spend time writing
proposals.

Occasionally even established clients require a written proposal as part
of the preliminary routine. I've been told by such clients that its importance is "somewhere between a ceremonial salute and the combination
to the corporate safe." This type of pro-forma proposal is a bit of a pain,
but only that.

A copy of a proposal endorsed by a client constitutes a contract of
sorts, which protects the researcher. The proposal is a capsule projection
of how well the researcher understood the project's goals, and thus
gives the client some protection as well. (A sample proposal will be
found in Appendix A.)

PLANNING A FOCUS-GROUP PROJECT

After the proposal is approved, the first official step in the project is
planning. Planning procedures are hard to gather into tidy bundles, because they differ so much from client to client and from problem to
problem. If the client is familiar and a veteran user of focus groups, and
if the project is a routine update of previous findings, planning can be
brief. If the client is marketing a brand new product, or is a newcomer
in an established category, or is contemplating a radically new marketing effort, or wishes to understand some totally unforeseen market reaction, and so on, then planning efforts should be given a couple of weeks,
or even more.

Planning begins in earnest when those who are commissioning the
project decide on what *kind* of focus groups they will buy (i.e., a
moderator only, assuming client responsibility for deciding what "happens" in the interviews; a moderator-reporter, who conducts the group
discussion and summarizes what has been said; or a rapporteur who participates in the interview in such a way as to elicit the factual and emotional raw material she will use in a subsequent interpretive report),

have chosen the particular *person* they want to do the groups, and have sat down with her to noodle it.

There is probably no factor more often responsible for disappointing results from a qualitative research project than inadequate planning. In particular, the first official meeting is crucial to the success of the project. It is the first opportunity everyone has to get an overall feel for the project objectives. It may also be the first chance for some client staff members to meet and interview the moderator. If one of the interested parties is having a baby or an income tax audit at the time appointed for the meeting, it is better for everybody else to find a more feasible day and hour than to *assume* that someone else can *represent* the absent person's interests in addition to his or her own. This illustrates one of the likely culprits in poor planning: the *quorum fallacy* (if six clients have an interest in the problem for which focus groups have been ordered, five, or even four, can represent all of the concerns).

The first conference is also the moderator's first look at—and may be her only chance to question—the preformed conclusions of some of the clients regarding issues addressed by the research. This tendency to adopt hypothetical presumptions as axioms—the *assumptive mode*—is the second major obstacle to planning a project.

The researcher may recognize these practices, and may fail to correct them. She *shouldn't* let them pass, having been through the process a few times already, but it is understandable that she doesn't want to:

(a.) Be seen as unreasonable in asking that the planning meetings—especially the kick-off—be fully attended, thus complicating everyone's calendar.

(b.) Look foolish by insisting on definitions for every bit of industry jargon and questioning every canonical assertion a client makes, motivations for purchases, brand positioning, or the target audience (which most clients know less well than they think).

In fact, the naive questioning of buzzwords and popular presumptions may be one of the reasons for the paradoxical truth that qualitative reports by rapporteurs who are relatively inexperienced in particular product categories are often richer and more insightful than those delivered by researchers whose experience has made them "specialists" in that category. It is especially difficult, if one has heard it all before, to approach projects or panelists as if for the first time, with the vigor and excitement of exploration.

Who's Invited?

Obviously, not everyone on the client's staff who is touched by a problem participates in planning the research that aims to advance its solution. In a well-run, closely knit company or agency, that would mean every employee. But those who should attend at least the first meeting include those who have discerned the problem (in-company or in-agency research people), those who feel it most keenly (production or/and marketing people), and those whose efforts must implement the solution (agency creatives, if the problem is communication; and marketers, new product or production supervisors, etc.). It would be useful if everyone who will attend the focus group interviews were "in" on some stage of their preparation. But certainly everyone involved in the use of the presented data should have a representative voice in the planning. When qualitative research fails to deliver the answers to key questions, it is more often than not because consensus has not been reached, before the project is underway, about the goals and subgoals of the study.

Rules of Order

Ideally, research planning for a focus group project should be similar in format to the interviews themselves, with the moderator's role shifting from speaker to speaker, so that each participant may probe or challenge any other. This form of interaction is useful because—unlike the more "orderly" planning of, say, a survey questionnaire—planners are not forced to answer questions with operational precision ("What exactly do you think is happening, and what will you accept as evidence that this is so?").

Qualitative research is more subjective, more "human," more informal than quantitative research. And the planning effort tends to reflect these differences. I say "tends to" because there are exceptions. Every now and again, a qualitative researcher is asked to address a problem that is properly quantitative, or to interface with a client who does indeed want to know which one of a universe of possible "outcomes" suggests which of a finite number of alternative solutions. An appropriate *response* in such cases is easy: the researcher, after making certain that she has understood the client ("I don't understand how you see focus groups as being useful for this problem. Please explain it to me again.") listens and considers again. If it *still* sounds to her like an inappropriate use of focus-group technique, she says "This is not the kind of thing I do well," and departs as quickly and gracefully as possible.

But the pitfalls of warm, friendly client interactions can be just as perilous. When client and supplier are charmed with one another, they may feel that they are communicating well, even though inferences have not been questioned, nor assertions challenged. The essential challenges—"How do you know that?" "What makes you think so?"—so familiar in the progress of a group interview can seem somehow distancing when client-supplier rapport is at stake.

More than friendliness is in jeopardy if goals are insufficiently clarified and plans for reaching them are not discussed as fully as possible in the earliest meetings. Each time the client expresses some aspect of the problem, the researcher must state her own interpretation—what she understands the gist of the communication to be—and wait for correction or modification from the client.

If both sides cooperate diligently, the researcher should have, at the end of the meeting, the raw material she needs to construct a *Discussion Guide* and a *Screener*. The ball is now in her court.

Paperwork: Constructing the Discussion Guide and the Screener

If time permits it makes sense to undertake the Guide first. In most cases, this is the more complicated document of the two, and the more likely to be elaborated or amended by someone on the client side.

A Discussion Guide serves several purposes simultaneously. It is ultimately exactly what its title says: a series of memoranda to the researcher-as-moderator, recapping the discussion areas she must be sure to cover.

For the client, the Guide is first and foremost a formal statement from the researcher of what she understands the project to be "about." Tacitly, it is also a kind of contract ("If I cover this territory, I will be doing what you have hired me to do."). Finally, it is a sort of preview of the way group discussions may actually proceed.

There is no one *style* of Discussion Guide that all focus group moderators adhere to. It can take the form of a skeleton outline or a full "narrative." I choose the latter, for two reasons:

- A narrative Guide allows the client to see not only what points I have understood to be crucial, but also the possible sequence and kinds of directional leads that will point our panelists toward those areas of discussion.
- For me, it is a working rehearsal of one possible "script" for the interviews-to-come.

A narrative Guide is also a working-through, for the moderator, of special "Lead-in" problems. In general, it is fair to say that many product categories are pretty low-voltage, from the purchaser's perspective. The decision to buy, and the brand choices a consumer makes, have been put on "automatic pilot" long ago. That is, having purchased the item many times, it becomes part of an invisible support-system for daily life, and surfaces again, briefly and partially, only when supplies are low.

A shopper puts "margarine" on her shopping list, but does not relive, as she walks through the supermarket, the nutritional debate she originally had with herself about *why* "margarine" rather than butter, lard, or any other of the many shortenings or spreads she might choose instead. She also "knows," without rehashing the decision, which brand is her brand, or which two or three are acceptable at a discount.

This is a necessary simplification. If every product or service were subjected to these original debates, the consumer would not have time to be an opera singer, a computer programmer, a female head of a household, a wife and mother, or any two of the above. Here the gender really *means* to be applied to female heads-of-household. Men, in general and in our society, tend to be more deliberate and less programmed in their shopping.

But when the panel is female heads-of-household and the topic is a low-ticket, frequent purchase item (which, if not *most* projects, is at least *many*), one way to elicit the first-choice freshness is to examine it from a different perspective. A handy label for this process is *making the familiar strange*. For example, a guide might begin:

[After the warm-up.] Bear with me. I am now going to tell you something, and I want you to believe it . . . at least for the next few minutes. We have discovered intelligent life on the planet Venus. It's intelligent, and it's benign, and it is as eager to know us as we are to know it. Our governments and theirs have decided to participate in a get-acquainted program. So a number of Gorks—that's what they are called—are being beamed down here to live with us for a couple of weeks, and the same number of us are vacationing up there. And *you* are all included in the lucky families playing host to a Gork. [Some words here about how tactful, considerate, and sensitive they are, and a physical description also here.] They don't speak our languages, but they have an extraordinary talent for mastering a language the second time they hear it spoken. Okay, you are in the grocery store with your Gork, and you approach the cooling bin where you find margarine. It's on your list. What other grocery items are there, by the way? [Here, we hope, the panelists recreate the relevant aisle and placement of margarine.] You reach for your brand of margarine, and the Gork tugs on your skirt and says: "What is that stuff, and how do you use it?" What do you say?

It's then possible to use "Gork-questions" to recreate the decision to use *margarine* and to place brand-issues front and center, without rousing antagonism. It is also possible at any point in the two-hour session to resurrect "invisible" decisions.

At the other end of the spectrum from overly familiar items are new products which must be phased into stable use-regimes. An example:

"Birthday Suit" : A proposed new product for a conservative health and beauty aids (HBA) company. A body lotion to be made a stable part of skin care routine. Priced and distributed for mass markets. The client was interested in discovering which women's age-group was most likely as a target, and where, exactly, Birthday Suit might fit into the current health and beauty aid products program for these women. Should it be pitched at skin- health, something a woman would do for herself, no matter who was around? Was it seen as a sexual come-on? A visible cosmetic improvement? The client, the agency, and I all agreed that women probably could not visualize it as part of their everyday lives, elbowing its way into their "beauty" regimens.

Eight groups, homogeneous for age (20–29, 30–39, 40–49, 50–59) are recruited. After the warm-up, the Guide says:

"Please go with me on a small fantasy trip. You have been commissioned to do a fascinating job, for which you will be handsomely paid. The catch is that you are going to a remote part of the globe [you pick it] where you will live, in constant phone and radio touch with home base; but you will be alone. A plane will drop mail and any other supplies you need, and will come after 6 months to take you home. Now, at the commercial airport where you had to meet the special plane that takes you to your destination, your cosmetic case, with six months of supplies, gets exchanged with a salesman's sample case. And *he* now has your beauty necessities, and *you* have his dog biscuits. The weather where you're going is ideal, and your living accommodations are all that you could ask. But you have to get hold of your employer or your best friend or your mother, to send you quickly whatever you'll need to nourish, protect, and beautify yourself— that you can apply from the outside. Please write the list you would make for whoever will shop for you, in order of importance or amount."

"Okay, same situation . . . *except*: This work you are doing is so important and so interesting that a national magazine is sending a photojournalist, a woman, to write and photograph the job and you. She keeps to herself, and there's no chemistry in either direction, but you'll be on display. What will you add to the list?"

"Same situation, . . . *except*: You are not going alone. You are part of a team. You have just met the members of the team. They each have private quarters, as you do. But there's a most attractive man on the team. What would you add to the list now?"

"Same situation as the first. You're alone, no photographer, no darling guy. Just you. *Except*: It is a hot, sunny island. Much of what you have to be doing must be done outside, and flopping clothing will be not only hot, but a hazard. Your living accommodations are air-conditioned. The humidity is 10% on a regular basis. What would you add to your lists?"

"Now let's bring back the team. Same as before, *except*: You have to share quarters with the gorgeous guy. What would you add? Would you get rid of anything?"

I believe the women in the group were *"there"*; a few in each group anxiously asked: "Will my husband/boyfriend know?" The discussion following the exercise made use of the things the women had *learned about* their own feelings and practices, and the rest of the discussion topics were raised by the women themselves, with little probing necessary and in a spirit of discovery.

Of course, a detailed Discussion Guide is not used in moderating a group. Once the narrative has served it's several purposes, I make a notational outline of topics, which is my best guess of the sequence of questions I must ask to learn what I must learn.

To be fair, there are also *dis*advantages to the narrative Discussion Guide:

• It's an extra step. It is easier to write at the outset the telegraphic notations that will accompany the moderator into the interview room. (If she knows herself to be creative, the moderator can improvise "Lead-in" strategies, and if disciplined enough, she may be able to do a run-through in her head, without writing it down).

• Because it is written as a script, with a plausible sequence, some clients may rely too heavily on a narrative Guide. When the group sequencing does not go according to the scenario, there may be panic behind the mirror (Even a carefully instructed client is apt to consider the events written in the Guide as set in stone).

• The concreteness of a narrative format may be for the moderator as well a *dangerously "safe"* retreat, if the group discussion is extra-difficult. The only right way to deal with surly, tuned-out, silent, or clamorous panels is to deal with them. But almost any collection of respondents can be coerced by a bullying moderator into following a planned program of discussion. And a narrative guide can tempt a harassed moderator to opt for following the guide, because it gives her a feeling of control.

• If the researcher-as-moderator has any special axe to grind (i.e., if under her research hat, she has *a priori* views about the "true" answers to the project's questions), the narrative guide may incline clients toward a belief in the hidden biases, and make the interview a proof of her hypotheses.

Of course the use of a narrative guide is a matter of personal choice, and presumes a certain amount of lead-time. (In a pinch, when time is extremely short, a skeleton outline is devised by either client or moderator, or preferably by both working together.) But to me, the value of the narrative Guide outweighs all of the extra work and extra caution it entails. It would be worth the price even if its only benefit was *communicating* to the client the problem as understood by the researcher.

The Screener is a simpler—or anyway, a *shorter*—document. It is a kind of purchase order for the types of people client and researcher have agreed should be interviewed. Once the researcher drafts the screener, the client agrees that these are the panelists he was thinking of (if he does), then reviews the cost bids which the researcher has gotten from several research facilities. The selection is made, and the researcher sends the screener to the field director of the chosen facility, who relays it to the recruiter(s). These are the people who interview prospective panelists, decide whether or not they qualify for participation, and elicit promises from qualified panelists to present themselves.

The screener is basically a set of discrete questions, of decreasing generality, with yes/no questions or multiple choice arrays, structured so that "unqualified" respondents are eliminated as quickly as possible. After a prospective respondent has replied to all of the questions, without being eliminated, all that remains is securing two hours (modal interview duration) of his/her time, commencing at an appointed hour and for some price within the estimated range of gratuities.

A screener is a *contract*, much more explicitly than a *guide* is, involving the research facility and the recruiter. A client and/or moderator dissatisfied with the recruits can protest that they are not the type of panelists requested. But if the screener has been accepted, and the individual respondents all passed the screener questions, client and moderator are bound to accept these facts:

• The recruiter and the research facility have discharged their obligations. They can't be expected to read a client's mind, and they must be paid according to the estimate mutually set.

• Luck has a lot to do with it. Unless some screener questions designed to test intelligence or stability have been included, an occasional group of "dim bulbs" is within the laws of probability. So is the occasional nutcase capable of stunning the other panelists into silence. (More on this in Chapter 12.)

• Low energy is another unpredictable respondent shortcoming. It rarely afflicts entire panels at once, but it's contagious if not reversed.

• The screened respondents may not fit the clients' expectations regarding the appearance, personality, or response to his product. But if two or more panels all refute his notions, this begins to be a "finding" that he'll be better off (if sadder) knowing.

Recruiters *can* be held accountable for lapses of ordinary common sense, like including in panels respondents with heavy accents, who need much help understanding English, or those with marked and distressing speech impediments. The prudent field director, in addition to apology, will sometimes offer to reduce recruiter charges and swallow gratuities for these panelists.

Screeners are not purely the purview of the client. The moderator, as researcher, is responsible for certain inputs as well. She has, after all, travelled this route often and recently, and may be sensitive to information about the general population, interactive considerations, and sampling probabilities that the client has not thought of, such as:

• *Broadening the sample*. Population trends in recent years suggest that "demographic spread" can no longer stop at 49 years of age, or even at 55. Unless the topic is age-limiting (i.e., hockey sticks) a "spread" panel these days is more representatively 18–65, or 21–65, although the bulk of respondents still falls into the 30–50 age group.

• *Narrowing* of panelists' ages may be necessary in the cases of children or adolescent youth. Ages 4–7 may seem like one group to clients. In reality, changes are so great at these ages that 4–7 must be split into at least two groups, if any interchange at all is going to happen. The same is true of other age groups—for instance, 12–15. Maybe truer. A psychiatrist friend once described a patient to me as ". . . between the ages of 14. . . ."

As a rule of thumb, the *communicative range* of panelists increases with time, after age 18. As adults mature, they become increasingly able and willing to tolerate and relate to greater differences between themselves and those they interact with.

The single exception is *gender*. Males and females can interact without distortion of responses only below the age of seven, if then. Older than that, respondents are likely to be so caught up in impression-management and gender-role defense that interview time is largely funneled into "border patrol" operations and lost to the purposes for which the panel was convened.

Of course, special cases override most of these general "rules." For instance, in the case of a product or service in which the research goal is understood to be *"finding out how best to change the positioning, to make the product (service) more appealing to the youth market,"* respondents will probably be limited to those under 30 or under 25, and reaching down into teen-groups.

Age cut-offs in some panels will also be broader than is usually tolerable in order to illumine the ways in which the product or service may serve pecking order rites between younger and older adolescents. And the moderator must get a grip on herself and undertake a few cross-gender panels as well, to identify gender-preserving, gender-relaxing, or downright sexual implications of the product or service.

At the other end of the continuum, in the case of new products or new concepts, demographic spread is apt to be as broad as feasible. And, excepting products whose usage and benefits are strictly gender-locked (vaginal deodorants, menstruation supplies, athletic supporters, etc.[2]), both sexes should be interviewed, with a couple of mixed-gender panels, if the exploration is to be exhaustive.

Rather obviously, where "couple decisions" are the mode, couple-interviews should compose the bulk of the panels. A prominent banking company has funded a number of couple-panels, some in each of several financial brackets. The stated purposes of the project are to create services which speak to the problems of, low, middle, and high-income depositors, and to communicate more directly with each group. The tapes and the findings belong to the bank, but I am free to report that gender tensions (such as arguments over which spouse writes checks and/or reconciles statements) correlate positively with increasing income levels across a number of panels significant enough to warrant attention.

In practice, few sampling decisions are this simple. Usually, in addition to the appropriate *demographic* specifications, particular *usage requirements* and sometimes *media habits* are specified as well.

For instance, I believe that some kitchen cleanser panels (which the research department privately coded as "the stainless steel bottom study") had the most exacting specifications I have ever been called on to deal with. The client could not be dissuaded from identifying as his target population only those female heads-of-household (HOHs) who:

• Had stainless steel sinks.
• Had two children or more, one of whom was in diapers.
• Owned cooking utensils with copper bottoms.
• Watched at least one hour of afternoon network television.
• Read *Family Circle* magazine.

The incidence of "qualified" panel members, was almost incalculably low, the recruiting estimate almost incalculably high (as were the gratuity payments necessary to free the women for afternoon and evening panels). Moreover, each of the panels was of such homogeneity that discussion was low in energy as well as in new intelligence. (Homogeneity/heterogeneity of panels is discussed in Chapter 5.) The client declared himself "very pleased," but from the point of view of the researcher, the completed project offered little more than confirmation of the client's existing biases about the narrowness of the target and his investment in the existing market strategy.

If screening is very simple or if time is very short (the client assigns the study a week or less before the panelists are to present themselves), the screener may be communicated by telephone. But in such cases it is always wise to follow up with a formal screener or a descriptive letter. Researchers do not communicate needs as unequivocally, nor do field supervisors listen as intently, as both believe they do.

A final word on screeners concerns the expectations communicated *by the recruiter to the panelists* in the course of screening them for eligibility. Most of the decisions about screener questions are made on the basis of communication in the other direction—what the recruiter learns about the prospective panelist. But it is a serious mistake to presume that consumers are dull-witted. For the most part, they are neither cretinous nor passive. While the recruiter gathers her data (most recruiters *are* women), the panelist will be asking—or/and guessing—what the interview is to be about. If the clues given by recruiters are easy to interpret, or if the recruiter answers the query, respondents will spend at least a part of the time between recruitment and the discussion reviewing what they *know* about the topic and deciding which of their *feelings* about it will prove most interesting or most socially pleasing. They'll *prepare* for the panel.

Prepared addresses by panel members are at worst misleading and at best a waste of precious interview time. To reduce this possibility it is prudent to include "blind" or misleading questions in the screener. These may be simply *broadeners*, like including questions about popcorn and potato chips to turn a soft drink screener into a more general snack food inquiry, or including questions on cold remedies and over-the-counter sleep medicine in a questionnaire on analgesics so that panelists may construe it to be about over-the-counter preparations in general. Or they may lead the prospective panelists' attention even further afield. In the case of soft drink interviews, questions about magazine readership help to fog the topic issue, while giving us some additional data on media habits. Inquiries about the drugstores where over-the-counter products are bought, or about pharmacist influence, could both handicap the panelists' topic guesses and enlighten us about the point-of-purchase. Some panelists will still guess right about the topic, but some won't.

In addition to the proposal, screener, and discussion guide, my own paperwork typically includes two additional pages; others may be necessary for particular projects. (Examples of all paperwork items are to be found in the Appendixes.) The two "regular additions" are a one-page *demographic* questionnaire and an *instruction sheet* for the *figure drawings* I regularly request of panelists. These are not for every researcher, and are clearly ancillary to the verbal and behavioral content of the interview; but they are so rich a source of confirmation and extension that I would feel the loss of them. The demographic sheet is a check on, and a concise statement of, the demographic data collected in the recruiting screeners. The drawings are extensions and delineations of the non-verbal communications of panelists, and represent, often in considerable detail, the "level of personal revelation" discussed in Chapter 5.

Scheduling Focus-Group Interviews

Choosing a site for focus-groups sounds a whole lot simpler and more straightforward than it is. The final choice depends on:

- Who's choosing. What inputs are considered.
- Who's going.

- Marketplace geography.
- Unpredictable contingencies.

Who's choosing includes everyone who has something to say about the location—all the voters—and also takes into account the relative heft of their votes. The client, who out votes everybody else, may begin with an expression of *preference:* "I was sort of thinking about four groups in the heartland and four in the Southwest—maybe Dallas"; or "We need something semirepresentative of our market: eastern corridor, South, Midwest, and far West." Or he may issue an *imperative:* "We'll do them all in New York so everybody can come." Or perhaps, "We're seeing fall-off in sales in the Southeast. Get us a supplier in Atlanta." Or there may be a client tug-of-war about which location is best.

The decision can be based on/influenced by who is to attend the groups; by what the product, service, or commercial campaign is doing in particular locales; by items of personal agenda ("If we do them in San Francisco, I can see my kid at Stanford."). It may also be influenced by the counsel of the moderator. This is sometimes formally requested ("We need to do groups of working women, homemakers, and single and married men. I'm afraid that with all those groupings the budget will only float one location. What suggestions have you?").

I warn clients, when invited to do so, of the perils of basing decisions on one city's response—especially one large metropolis, because of attitudinal skewing. The bigger the city, typically, the more professionally cynical the respondents. That observation is true in spades on either seaboard. A good rapporteur can correct for it, but clients can leave the interviews with a similarly skewed read-out. If only one location is feasible, someplace in the heartland is more likely to reflect national feeling and behavior than any other location. Cynical defensiveness is lower and so are interpersonal barriers. Interviews are likely to be livelier and more candid.

All of this is further complicated by personal preferences. Client votes and researcher votes—either or both—reflect each voter's personal "top ten" list of facilities, and are also affected by general theories concerning *types* of locations. (More about the supplier relationship in Chapter 6.) A client is likely to ask questions such as "Do suburban locations avoid the pitfalls of cities?" (The answer is Sometimes—it depends on the city and the suburb.) If the researcher and clients move to negotiation and compromise, the number of variables is multiplied greatly.

An established client had reason to believe that his product was shifting in impact on consumers. He also had a new product line, but was unsure whether or not to introduce it. Questions were:

• How does this year's attitude toward the standard product line compare with last year's?
• How does our consumer view the proposed new product line? If she buys it, will she leave our standard product line—switch within the brand—or will we draw switchers from competitive lines?

One of the locations was to be a repeat of the previous year's heartland setting. The other was to be a "high innovation" locale (i.e. metropolitan eastern corridor). But at the same time, the client hoped to avoid the professional cynics, frequently seen in metropolitan areas, because their responses might attempt to obscure the true appeal of the proposed new line.

For some product categories, the border between "Eastern Corridor" and "Heartland" appears to begin about 100 miles inland. For this study, the bulk of interviewing took place in the previous year's site, and a replication was assigned to a Philadelphia suburb. It could just as well have been a Connecticut or Maryland suburb, but there was a particularly cooperative and efficient supplier in the town we chose, which also happened to be approximately equidistant from each of our home bases. Also, the time was available and the estimate favorable.

Another client wished to check sales in California (since their product had been recently introduced there), and wanted also to update findings of the previous year. But the prior year's study included a *Northeast* corridor location (Boston), and the client had new survey data that suggested the product did especially well in the South. The two locations selected were Southern California and, as the Eastern Corridor/Southland hybrid, we had settled on Atlanta.

Problems of travel costs for client members to attend focus groups can be partially offset by lower facility charges—and (much) lower gratuity payments in Heartland locations.

Finally, chosen suppliers may be unexpectedly high in their estimates, may be booked for the dates chosen, or may be unwilling to promise qualified respondents in the calendar-time allotted for recruiting.

Where and When

In contrast, diurnal time scheduling often *is* simple and straightforward. The general rules are that:

• *Morning interviews* can only be recruited reliably among homemakers (though students, at certain times of year, young children, and certain entrepreneurs, who make their own schedules, are sometimes available then as well).

• Luncheon interviews with employed men and women are sometimes possible, if the participants are managerial enough to get away for a three-hour lunch (a half-hour each way for transportation and two hours for the interview) and if the promised recompense is sufficient to motivate them.

A financial client needed advertising input from the chief financial officers of a number of blue chip corporations. The recruiters for local research houses were unable even to get through the barbed wire of administrative staff to speak with the CFOs. I used academic title and media-credentials[3] to do the recruiting myself. And, with the client's permission, I offered lunch in a prestigious restaurant's special banquet room, transportation by limousine, and a $250 donation to the charity of choice. We talked during the champagne and lunch, and I showed them concepts and storyboards with dessert. They uncomplainingly completed figure-drawings and stories over coffee, and graciously stepped back into the limousines.

• *Afternoon* interviews are most convenient for students and night workers, and are a *second choice* for homemakers (who must leave the interview in time to meet their homecoming families).

• *Evenings* are prime-time for most employed adults. If two groups per evening are to be scheduled, those who must rise earliest, who live the farthest from the facility, or who would be most troubled by solitary, late-evening travel are given the "dinnertime" slot.

Any prospective panelists coming during lunch or dinner hours must be promised reasonably substantial food, not the usual "coffee and. . . ."

It is unwise—not to mention inhumane—to pack a day so tightly that the moderator has to interview three or more panels in any given day. Competent interviewing is intensive, energy-consuming work, and none of the principals (moderator, client, field personnel) are at their best after two two-hour interviews.

On occasion, I have undertaken three interviews a day. God help irritating panelists in the last group!

Final scheduling, within these parameters, is an intricate, flexible negotiation, reconciling panelists' availability, client availability, field facility "open" time, and moderators' free days. Cancellations and rescheduling are perilous. They antagonize respondents, who are then less conscientious about keeping appointments. A cancellation is always an increased risk if product samples, or any other requisite aids, are involved—there are always delayed shipments, mistaken addresses, and slow ponies to reckon with.

Field recruiters or other facility staff members are usually expected to check each recruited panelist on the day of the interview or the evening before. This permits last-minute substitutions, and prevents pre-interview histrionics.

The Interview

When the requisite number of respondents is assembled in the waiting area, the moderator is serene but "up," and the client is content with the audio level and the comestibles behind the mirror, it is time to begin the operation which is—for two of the three parties involved—the main event: the interview itself.

The best interviews appear to be seamless, spontaneous, and inevitable. But in fact a number of specific decisions have been made, rationally or subjectively, that will determine the energy level, mood, and cohesion of the interview. Of these decisions, the most apparent are the *setting* chosen for the interview and the *size of the panel*. These are not the frills they may seem. Some heavy debates on these issues among professional moderators have kept many an audience awake at marketing research forums, especially in the past 15 years. Before that time, the issues of setting and group size did not elicit much fire, for several reasons:

• Focus groups were still comparatively new to the marketing research toolbox, and we who did them hadn't been at it long enough to *have* strong feelings.

• Readily accessible facilities were even newer, so that choice was a rare luxury. We took the number of panelists who showed, and interviewed them wherever there was sitting-space, using whatever recording instruments we had.

• The marketing research community had not decided yet that focus group interviews were legitimate offspring, so nobody asked us.

The issue of group setting is basically an issue of mood or tone. Professional moderators who opt for a *livingroom style* of setting tend also to seek pleasantness and relaxation as their goal. I hope no one wants to conduct *un*pleasant interviews, but there are those who seek the more formal *conference table* setting and believe comfort and relaxation can be a good thing, but which you can have too much of when it comes to research.

Self-exploration is very hard work indeed, and putting it into words can be even harder. Arguably, a relaxed mood is wrong for intensive work. A livingroom setting, I think, communicates to the panelist that the proceedings will be the kinds of proceedings they are used to in livingrooms: polite or casual interchange, usually colored by superficial harmony and amiability, placing on participants no great degree of responsibility or motivation to labor. I believe too that the apparent "freedom" of cheerful social exchange is only a less visible constraint: it contains the expectancy of *agreement;* controversy rocks the boat.

"Livingroom" advocates further emphasize the "social" message by requiring panelists to wear, or sit behind, name tags or placecards, on which are traditionally printed only the respondent's first name. It is socially difficult to argue with someone with whom one is on a "first-name" basis, but whom one does not know on a more personal level.

One alternative—the one I choose—seeks to create anonymity comparable to the backseat of a taxi, or a similar temporary proximity, which is nameless unless closer acquaintance is sought. Panelists introduce themselves in whatever way they choose (usually *not* first name only), so that naming is available as a choice. Social warmth is not ruled *out* but it is not enforced either. As moderator, I signal a panelist I wish to address with a "spotlight" of eye contact, and address the panelist as "you." Some of the respondents do the same, while some request and use names. I have never felt that an address in the second person accompanied by eye contact, in any way reduced intensity or depth of communication. Quite the reverse.

The question of panel size is also an important issue. Proponents of small groups (6–8 persons) or mini-groups (4–6 persons) typically argue that large groups (9–12 respondents) allow too little "on" time for each participant. The argument implies something about the character of these small groups:

• They are usually orderly and controllable. People speak one at a time, each taking a turn.
• *Energy* in the panel is lower than in a larger group. Panelists do not compete to say things that they feel intensely, do not crosstalk and are unlikely to get excited (so that it may be difficult to judge what *does* excite them).

Neatness is an admirable quality in a panel. It is especially welcome if one is trying to listen to a recording of focus-group proceedings. But if asked to choose between order and excitement or energy, I wouldn't hesitate to choose the latter. And anyone who has ever had to deliver a ten-minute address might object to the assertion that ten minutes per person is not enough time.
Briefly then, my focus group interviews:

• Employ a relatively formal setting: a conference table in a research facility, in an advertising agency's home office or, in a pinch, a corporate conference room.
• Employ a one-way mirror and/or videotape, in addition to overhead microphones connected to an audio-recording system, and a loudspeaker in the observation room behind the mirror.
• Are conducted, typically, with 10–12 panelists, using the following format:

—After panelists seat themselves and are given refreshments, there is a short *Warm-up* period during which everyone, including the moderator, introduces her/himself, and the ground-rules of the interview are stated. (A transcript of a typical "Warm-up" is in Appendix E.)
—This is followed by a *Predisposition* discussion, which concerns itself with the contexts in which the product we are about to ex-

plore are bought, used, and thought about. This may include general reactions to advertising.

—Next, materials of one kind or another are introduced: products, concept statements, storyboards, (or other rough executions such as animatics), reels of finished, competitive, TV commercials, or any other marketing effort to which panelists' reactions are sought. If only the *client's* materials are shown, the exposure is preceded by a "focus-reveal," in which the moderator discloses the exact purpose of the discussion. If *competitive* materials are also shown, the focus-reveal is postponed.

Instructions to panel members at the time of introducing materials are, first, to write, privately, without consulting one another, their immediate reactions to each of the materials, and then to discuss them. This pattern of "write, then talk" is continued until all the materials have been exposed and discussed.

• After all materials have been discussed *separately*, there is usually a *collective and comparative* discussion of everything exposed to the respondents.

• The official close of the interview is a *wrap-up*, which is a prodding of the panel for their summaries of what was said. ("If you were sitting where I am sitting, what questions would *you* have asked that I haven't? What do you think the answers would have been?" or perhaps "When you leave here, and somebody asks you what you were doing here all this time, what will you tell them about the things we talked about? How do you think you will explain what the group as a whole thought?")

• Each panelist is given a packet of stapled papers: a *demographic* sheet, a set of *instructions for the figure drawings and stories,* and two blank sheets of paper. Each respondent is asked to complete the instructions before leaving the room.

The Post Mortem

After all respondents have departed, the client may come into the interview room, or may invite the moderator to step behind the mirror, so that both can discuss what has just taken place. This post mortem is sometimes a client mandate, sometimes a moderator request. The intelligence gleaned from this procedure can be vital, negligible, or a source of obfuscation.

As a rule of thumb, Post Mortems are advisable only if the original contract has been for "moderating only"; i.e., if no interpretive report will be written. In such a case, this will be the only chance the researcher will get to alert the client to any of the discussion which may be misleading: ("I know that most of these women *say* they sleep in elaborate and expensive sleepwear 5 nights out of 7, but listen for the section that starts when panelist 10 says 'I wonder how long we'd have to know each other before we tell about the flannel one-piecer we wear from Christmas to Valentine's Day,' and all the giggling that follows it.")

In other instances, researchers who will be reporting on the session(s) in another two or three weeks are well-advised to avoid post mortems. At the conclusion of a panel discussion, *nobody,* including the moderator, "knows" what happened. And it is unwise to commit to premature interpretations, which may have to be retracted at the time of report-presentation. Also more is jeopardized by the practice than the moderator's later discomfort. Enthusiastic or impatient clients can rush into action based on what everyone *thought* they heard, taking the bull by the horns only to realize, later, they got the wrong bull.

If the interview has been especially productive and the interaction exciting, the backroom contingent will be "nerved-up," while the moderator, however stimulating the group has been, will be wrung out. At this precise moment, moderator and viewers are galaxies apart emotionally. One has sat in enforced passivity and relative silence behind the barrier of the mirror; the other has been in the arena, confronting the lions without whip, chair, or gun. This unavoidable situation is frustrating for both parties. It is hardly the time for heavy discussion about events that will look different after the passage of time. If the client can't be dissuaded from such discussion, the moderator can honestly plead exhaustion.

There is an interview gambit that can ward off overly zealous clients. The moderator can select the most powerful viewer, or the one whose nerve-endings are closest to the top, and suggest that he participate in the *wrap-up* of the interview, saying something like, "I am the vice-president of marketing for the company that sells this product. I have been fascinated by the discussion. If I were to take one fact from it, what should it be?" This is only suggested when researcher and panelists have achieved a rapport that is practically familial. And it can only be at the very end, because even the warmest panel can be lost to the moderator *after* such an intrusion. Not every time, but sometimes, this kind of client-participation is useful. A client who can be taught to participate is apt to be more understanding of moderator fatigue and perplexity than the *same* client would be after two hours of fist-clenching and nail-biting on the other side of the glass.

TOPLINES AND FULL REPORTS

The most obvious difference between a *topline* and a *full report* is their length. (Sample topline reports and full reports are found in the Appendixes.) Toplines are shorter. They may or may not be less accurate, but they are necessarily less detailed. They are also cheaper and faster for clients, because they are less time-consuming and less draining for the rapporteur who will interpret them. Although she will *listen* to the tapes, she will not take a full shorthand transcript. Hence, there are no (or few) quotes in the topline to support or amplify interpretive statements.

Client and researcher should agree from the outset which type of reporting will best serve the needs—and not offend the budget—of the client. But the researcher is free to suggest a different arrangement—in either direction—after the group discussions are done, and the interpreting begun. Report-writing is slow, hard, and lonely. No rapporteur in her right mind would choose to present a full report rather than a topline, unless the complexity of the marketplace problem or the suggested solutions to it required the extra effort. But suggesting a topline rather than a full report doesn't invariably elicit the "Hallelujiah Chorus." Of course, one can't simply say: "That is a dumb problem, and the solution is so simple I don't know why you can't see it. . . . " But even put tactfully ("The panels were so vocal, and the agreement so universal, that I think for me to charge you for a full report would be highway robbery. I can do a good topline for $700 less, each group, and have it finished and bound by Monday."), the suggestion can fall with a thud. (The only explanation I've yet found to explain this is that importance equals bulk in some organizations.) Topline reports are much more dependent on the researcher's interpretations than are full reports. No (or few) quotes are included. The rationale for particular "findings" is not laid bare for clients to see and approve or quarrel with. In that sense, the topline is a more presumptuous document (it places the moderator-rapporteur in roughly the same position as the Delphic oracle). To compensate, the tone of the topline is usually breezy and egalitarian, and the format flexible.

When the groups are many, the sessions long, the panelists disparate, and the problem complex, the report may be lengthy. When the product is so brand new as to require elaborate "setting up" operations, or when a product has been rendered nearly invisible with familiarity so that it is necessary to "make it strange," and when, moreover, the materials to be shown are numerous, it is not unusual for a full report to run close to 200 pages, including appended drawings. But most full reports are probably no more than half that size. And very rarely, panelists are so univocal that no analysis of their differences is required, and the actionable solutions to the problem seem so apparent, that the full report will be perhaps 60 pages long, counting drawings *and* divider pages.

The substance of a full report, and its divisions can be viewed in two ways:

1. As a prepared *document*, with itemized sections, proceeding from the statement of the *problem* to a suggested *resolution*.

2. As a *process*, by which the researcher-rapporteur converts the often tangled or ambiguous verbal and behavioral amalgam recorded on tapes—plus any written reactions—into a systematic summary of what (in the researcher's judgment) the data meant: what was conveyed and intended, and the ways this intelligence *can be used* to achieve the desired results.

As a *document,* the full report has a standard, formal structure:

A *Table of Contents.*

A concise statement of the problem (*Background and Purpose*).

A *Methods and Procedures* section (which includes the major question areas and the discussion protocol).

A *Sample* heading, under which the demographic and usage profile of each panel is summarized.

The *Findings:*

Interactive Climate: Brief sketches of those facets of group activity which bear on the interpretation of reactions.

Predispositions: Inferences about how the panel members generally, or specific respondent *types,* orient to the product category. (The *Predisposition* section may be broken down into special predisposing factors like "Reactions to Advertising," "Brand-Awareness," and so on. Or it may separate special investigatory tools like the exercise of "Personalizing the Company," written questionnaires and such.)

Reactions to Materials: Responses of panelists—in tabular or/and narrative forms—to the marketing, advertising or product-samples exposed.

The *Summary of Findings*, which is a synthesis of the "finding's" information.

The *Implications* or *Implications and Recommendations* section, translating the findings into actions suggested by predispositions and the panelists' reactions to the material shown.

As a *process,* the full report is a total immersion: a period of days or weeks at a time when nothing happens except the report. It is listening to tapes, translating reactions into rough tables, and most of all waiting for *the organizing idea.* This idea is the principle that makes sense out of the jumble of thoughts and feelings and reported behaviors volunteered by panelists. The idea is unmistakable. And it occurs at its own appointed time: during sleep; on a bus or in a taxi; in the shower; in the midst of unrelated conversation.

The idea is obvious once it occurs, but inscrutable before that. It pulls all of the findings together, and it is tied to the motivation that makes the writing of the report worthwhile. The researcher's motivation is not (or is not strictly) based on the money that pays for the time a project takes. It is more directly the discovery of a secret which the researcher—and nobody else—knows. Because of the idea, the researcher comes to present the report with bright if weary eyes. It gives her an almost overwhelming desire to grab the client by the lapels and say: "Boy, do I have news for you!"

NOTES

[1]"Client" refers to the person or department who requests and ultimately pays for the project, and not—or not necessarily—the *advertiser* in an advertiser/agency interaction.

[2]Interestingly, I can think of no single additional category, this side of elective surgery, in which only one sex is the user, and only one sex has a voice in positioning, though my hunch is that women more often borrow male products and respond to male concepts than vice versa.

[3]My 16 years as contributing editor to *Sales & Marketing Management.*

Chapter 3

The Technical Evolution

HOW WE GOT WHERE WE ARE

By most accounts, focus group research emerged fortuitously when some resourceful qualitative researcher,[1] pressed by time and hampered by budgetary constraints, decided to replace a planned series of one-on-one qualitative interviews with a couple of qualitative *group* interviews, thus saving himself the tedium of conducting as many as 24 repetitions of the interview and saving his client or sponsor time and money as well. It may have been just that simple. But it was not out-of-the-blue. The time was ripe.

That apocryphal first (intentional) group interview probably happened sometime in the mid- to late-1950s, right after David Riesman[2] had pronounced the society "other-directed" and the new focus on the aggregate life of the individual had created T-groups, sensitivity training, therapy groups, organizational psychology and encounter marathons. Small wonder then if one qualitative researcher (or several simultaneously), oppressed by the task of reproducing a particular interview 20 times in a row, thought to combine rather than replicate. It was part of the zeitgeist.

Clearly, the first group interviews *worked*. But the reasons probably came later. It was as though a passing airplane had dropped a screwdriver into a remote and backward village whose buildings were held together by unsecured miters or bound with vines. Having discovered the screwdriver, the villagers had to invent screws and rethink joints. So with the focus group. Everyone connected with the marketing research community sensed that it was a useful tool, but exactly *how* and *why* it was useful had yet to be discovered.

39

Reports on the *applications* of focus groups began to appear in the 1960s, but they were sporadic and diverse. Each researcher in those early days thought of focus groups as his or her "discovery." There was not a concerted attempt to systematize the procedure. The fact that the same airplane had dropped dozens—perhaps hundreds—of screwdrivers on as many villages didn't stop each of the beneficiaries from presuming that hers was the one true way to use the tool, in terms of procedure, application, and interpretive significance.

The fact that the early practitioners represented such widely disparate backgrounds may account in some degree for the anarchic state of the art today. Some, like me, were recruited from academic research. Some were research consultants, with one tenured foot in academia and the other in marketing. Some were salaried research personnel in advertiser companies or advertising agencies, who scented a potentially "hot" new technique and moved over from the nose counting of quantitative research to establish new fiefdoms in the qualitative area. A decade later, research facilities began adding one-way mirrors and viewing rooms to accommodate focus groups and, seeing the field unclaimed, hung out *their* focus group shingles as well.

Symposia on the focus group and other attempts at collective identity did not commence significantly until at least a decade into its development. Perhaps it was already too late for accreditation or standardization of any kind. Today, "focus group research" is a motley designation, which may describe:

• Research practiced by highly trained rapporteurs sophisticated in psychology and sociology.

• A technique used by researchers whose main—or sole—training is in marketing research.

• An exercise by enterprising but untrained moderators who don't understand the interpretive scope of focus groups.

Caveat emptor indeed. Theoretically, anybody with reasonable deportment, a *soupcon* of charm, and clean fingernails can present herself as a focus group moderator. (More about choice of a moderator or rapporteur in Chapter 10.)

The confusion extends beyond the moderator's academic and professional background. Focus groups can be moderated with great rapport and sensitivity, or with virtually none. The moderator may be very familiar and comfortable with the dynamic properties of group interaction, or may consider "dynamic properties" intellectual puffery. She may or may not recognize her own biases. As rapporteur, she may or may not write some kind of summary report. (These days, even if a report is written, the moderator may have a subordinate or trainee produce it.)[3]

In content, the report may be no more than a collection of verbatim quotes of responses to each point raised in the guide. Or, at the other extreme, it may offer an interpretation of what *appeared* to happen in the group interview (verbally and nonverbally), a discussion of the *meaning* of what happened as the interpreter sees it, and reasoned hypotheses about the implications of these findings for marketplace behavior. Or it may be a more-or-less unsubstantiated *guess* about what happened and what it means. There is a place for at least the first two kinds of report, but it is not the same place.

So focus groups have had, almost from the outset, a certain uncontrollably gypsy air about them. This reputation has been enhanced by the fact that the technique attracts entrepreneuring gypsies to it. We can wonder whether the marketing research establishment could have contained and refined focus groups early on, but that is not what happened. The focus group appeared suddenly, the new kid on the block. Not that this was unique in the history of marketing research. Every few years a new technique comes along, promising to simplify some dimension of the problem of why people buy things. Each has flared up and blazed brightly, briefly. And each has passed into the research repertoire or been preserved by a cult of adherents who become the experts in the technique and the purveyors of its data to the marketing research community and its clients.

But focus groups were a new kind of kid. It was comprehensible to all—or apparently so. What's more, it was bright, attractive, and fun to be with. It made no promises of simplification; indeed, it emphasized the complexity of human responses. But it did so in such a way that the client felt as if he finally understood.

Clients found the act of sitting through market research meetings in which their consumer franchise became a faceless "target market," whose behavior was strewn with demographic breakdowns and numerical contingencies, tedious and belittling. Focus groups brought the client into direct confrontation with actual people, both those who bought his product and those who did not.

The complexity of the data was balanced by two new and beguiling attributes: the apparent *accessibility* of the technique and the data, and its *irrefutable persuasiveness.* Real people talked openly about their own needs and expectancies of branded products, or gave their own scenarios of advertising, detailing what they admired and deplored about each ad or commercial. Their words were understandable. What's more, they were *recognizable;* clients felt them to be people they had met, or perhaps to be *themselves.* No subsequent judge's instructions could persuade them to disregard the evidence or deny that the words they heard were spoken.

And there's the rub. Those two qualities—accessibility and persuasiveness—represent both the almost magical charm of focus groups *and* their major shortcoming. Because of the persuasiveness of the technique, unsophisticated clients may believe they have witnessed The Truth, and may make precipitous decisions on slender evidence, sometimes without even waiting for a more circumspect interpretive report. Because of the accessibility of the group-dialogue, clients feel as well qualified to judge the meaning and importance of the words they have heard as any ordained researcher. At last they envision themselves standing toe to toe with eggheads, and are not about to give researchers their proxy.

The initial, immediate response to focus groups by most market researchers was defensive. Focus group research was (and still is) decried because of what it is *not:* broad-based, quantifiable, incremental, exactly replicable, free from the taints of bias and misrepresentation, and so on. Instead of welcoming focus groups at the outset, the incumbent marketing researchers were more apt to pour hot lead on the practitioners' heads. As a result, the technique has served to widen rather than bridge the gap already existing between the nose-counters of quantitative research and the soul-searchers in the qualitative camp.

Today, it is typical of agencies or companies that frequently use focus groups to bring in as an outside resource, or install within the organization, a qualitative cadre administratively separate from the research department. In 14 in-agency years I have been associated with, but separate from, the research department. I was twice the research arm of the creative department, once the director of an autonomous qualitative department, sharing a floor with the research department (but not, I like to think, a ceiling), and once the research partner in a four-person strategy team. Never in those 14 years was I wholly integrated with the research staff.

Best Case Scenario: How We Might Have Gotten Someplace Better

A young patient of mine once described himself and his brother as being "bosom enemies." At the time it seemed to me a singularly felicitous phrase, and it has only gathered resonance with time. It describes any situation in which rivals for a common prize can neither resign the goal nor separate themselves. And it is not limited to the captive rivalry of siblings for the maternal bosom. It applies as well to the present day competition between the quantitative and qualitative camps in marketing research. At first glance, the contest seems only material: research budgets are tight, so the two contend over budgetary appropriations. But the stakes are actually higher than that. Each side is also seeking investiture by clients and by the research community as the legitimate holder of the book of answers. This contest is not regularly acknowledged because it rises from passion rather than reason, and neither side wants to bear the onus of pettiness. Dispassionate thought must lead to the recognition that the two disciplines are set up to answer different questions. What's more, the questions asked by each are essentially collaborative.

The marketing research tradition predates the qualitative evolution. Social scientists were invited in originally to enliven and illumine the paper and ink data of the market- researcher with flesh and foible and to offer communicators a point of address: Not "You are talking to a young, ambitious white-collar man," but "You are talking to Mathew."

Although I am partial to the social scientist, I think that it is fair to presume that social scientists came to the party out of enthusiastic curiosity. Certainly I did. Here was a brand new laboratory, a situation in which to explore human nature *in situ*, in a context novel to the academic researcher . . .and without the necessity of elaborate petitions for funds. A chance to investigate a behavior of *our* "laboratory animal," and maybe even check out our hypotheses, while being paid for the effort by those who would put it to use. There was and is no enterprise—commercial or academic—which spends as much money on the understanding and evaluation of human communication as the marketing-advertising industry.

At this point, how easy for the market researchers to set preconditions for letting the social scientists in: "You must learn *our* language as well. It may teach *you* as much about applying conceptual tools as it teaches *us* about how they are formulated." Again, I am biased, but I believe most of us would have received this as a double bonus. Conceptualizers are often vague and sloppy in devising rules of application.

But the fault is not all on the other side. I am certain that the fascination of clients with new data that did not require advanced calculations to understand was intoxicating. We took it personally. It is, after all, a human weakness to prefer adulation to travail. We gravitated to those who already "understood" us, rather than struggling to make ourselves understandable to researchers, in their established language. And established market researchers did not know us well enough to use the promise that would motivate us: a new rigor for application.

It is a tempting cop-out to look to constitutional differences as the culprit. It is probably true that those who invest their toil on the rialto are likely to be empiricists who translate their data into action because they must meet deadlines and effect improvements. Similarly, academic scientists are more prone to the slower gait of contemplation, and act only slowly and with great difficulty.

Still, both of us, in our different ways, are experimenters. We are also alike in being communications experts. Surely, with a little more effort at dialog, we could have arrived at a better working fraternity than today's border haggling about where our spheres of authority begin and end.

STARTING FROM WHERE WE ARE: WAYS TO MEND THE SITUATION

Focus groups are probably the main bone of contention today between the qualitative and quantitative camps in marketing research. I cannot speak for the scientific community, but only for my discipline. And the first step in improving our stalemate is to police our own efforts. Specifically, we need to clarify the uses of focus group research (the topic of Chapter 9) and specify those who can properly acquit the tasks.

I would propose two qualification levels:

• *Interviewing only* (or interviewing and a *summary* report of representative quotes from the interviews on each key question.)

• *Depth interviewing* (usually with an *interpretive* report in which the researcher details what panelists' responses *mean* in terms of conscious and unconscious predispositions, and inferences about probable behavior.) (See Chapter 5.)

Level One: Moderating Focus Groups

It may sound as if the moderator's role is simply that of a *facilitator*, who eases conversation. In some cases, that may be all that the assignment requires. But it is rarely all that gets done. In fact, "simply facilitating" may be a very difficult task for someone who is both untrained and unsophisticated. A dynamically inert and purposeless moderator may not exercise the discipline necessary for the panel to complete its work. But on the other hand, the line between being adequately *directed* and interviewing *directively* is a touchy distinction.

Direction must exist in the moderator's mind, as a series of exploratory goals, but the interviewer must not put words into panelists' mouths. This requires the exercise of some personal authority during the introductory phase of the group. (See Chapter 5.) It also requires that the moderator possess the capacity to understand her own biases.

A moderator's personal biases can seriously mislead both the moderator and the client. It is difficult to prevent bias from appearing, even in inflections or facial expressions. And groups are eager to give the moderator what she wants, especially if she is warm, enthusiastic, and charming. I am not knocking warmth, enthusiasm and charm, by any means. They make the work of panelist and moderator more fun. But they are as powerful in promoting false responses as they are in eliciting true ones. In discussions with clients after the interview, the moderator should know what her assumptions were going in, and should warn her clients to weight their interpretations accordingly.

A cautionary post-mortem comment will win the moderator brownie points for conscientiousness. An example:

"As a confirmed and steady dieter, I know that I usually assume an interest in weight control. So when the panelist mentioned 'playing the numbers game' with package labels, I might have jumped in too soon with 'Are you talking about the calorie count?' She could have been talking about ingredient weightings, which she did actually bring up later in the interview."

Along the same lines, in an interview that employs creative material (concept statements, story boards, finished commercials, and such), nobody can expect the interviewer to be passive, without feelings and preferences. But it is essential that a good moderator be able to make these preferences a part of the data presented to clients; for instance:

"I can't help favoring storyboard B. I just like it. I tried to be circumspect, but I may have given a little smile as I read it, or they may just have felt the vibes. The preference rating was actually pretty close, between B and C. I wouldn't want you to discard C without further checking. I may have tipped the scale."

Narrowly defined, a moderator's function is—or ought to be—under the direction of a marketing intelligence, which will be responsible for interpreting and applying data yielded by interviews. For this reason academic training in marketing would be helpful for would-be moderators. A couple of elective courses in psychology or sociology wouldn't hurt either. (Unfortunately, no specific courses in focus group procedures are currently available as far as I know.) But these are helpful background only, and the moderator can learn the necessary skills without them. Because focus group moderators have to be able to moor discussions among all classes and kinds of people, a college education of some sort is probably a prerequisite. That, and sufficient intellect not to be talked down by, or worse yet, made defensive by, super-bright or pretentious panel members.

Level Two: Moderating and Interpreting Focus Groups—The Rapporteur

The *rapporteur's* task includes expert moderating, but goes beyond it. She must have all of the social skills and the self-knowledge necessary for getting others to explore themselves. She must also know how to utilize interactional dynamics, to learn more about willingness-to-try, about newness panic, about motivational hierarchies, and so on.

Advanced degrees in psychology, anthropology, or sociology are essential for anyone intending to become a rapporteur. The rapporteur must be able to recognize underlying feelings under apparently straightforward motivational statements. And she must know instinctively how to improvise lines of inquiry which will allow panelists to discover at their own pace what she has perceived:

> In a study of shaving products, I was interviewing groups of men. After introductions, I *led in* to the context of shaving by asking them to say what they did between the time they woke and the time they left their homes for the day. There were, of course, variations, but each of the men spoke with loud groans of the weekday morning chore of shaving. I remarked that this seemed to be the most emotional part of the morning, and that they seemed to dread it. I drew more groans from the group. I then asked how long shaving took. Estimates varied, but none was longer than five minutes. I thought that I was hearing something unspoken under the slightly histrionic repugnance. Staying still on the conscious surface, I asked what could possibly make a task that took five minutes, tops, so painful. This surprised them a little, and I sensed that they were asking the question with me, were ready to explore. Improvising, I said: "You want not to have to shave. Okay. Scientists have now invented a one-time shaving machine. You can cover all the hair you want to keep—the stuff on your head, your eyebrows, any facial or body hair that's becoming, but any other hair, once you walk through this machine, is gone forever. Would you like to walk through it?" Of course not one of them was willing to use the "machine." In the next moment, they began to recognize—the more open panelists first—that shaving was an affirmation of masculinity, and that dramatic expressions of woe about the necessity of shaving were a way of pointing out to themselves and everybody else: "Look, I'm a man!" Supported by the group-participation, this examination of feelings was kind of fun, and the rest of the interview was lit with revelation.

She must also know what *not* to probe:

> The product was an OTC analgesic, for which the arthritic was the heaviest consumer, accounting for a disproportionate volume of sales. The *predisposition* section made clear to me that women on the panel were psychologically bound to their disease, which brought them great benefits of power and high martyrdom.

> We were using a reel of mixed commercials from the several OTC brands, including our own. The women were asked to write their reactions to each and then to discuss their feelings. One of the commercials lingered briefly over the pain of arthritis, and then with a burst of light promised that a cure for arthritis was near and that the maker of the analgesic was supporting promising research.

> They all hated it. What's more, although they seemed to have committed other commercials' promises to memory, they were amnesic for the message in this one. They remembered the visual, which they liked (a woman slowly, painfully climbing the stairs). But when I asked them what was happening while she

climbed, they "forgot" the voice-over message of hope, forgot even that there *was* a voice ("I think there was music"; "Nothing was going on"; "Maybe—was she groaning or sighing? I know *I* do. . .").

I reported to the client that a staircase was a great context, but that we had to leave the woman her arthritis. The client thought this was absurd, but the creative department of my agency was more receptive. They wrote a crude voiceover in which the announcer (one of the copy writers) read what sounded like a threat. The gist of the message was: "Sorry, but you're going to have to suffer for the rest of your life. If there is ever a cure for arthritis, expect it to happen roughly the same time the earth falls into the sun." We did some more groups, substituting this voice-over for the one on the reel.

They all loved the commercial now, and remembered every word. They felt that it understood them, respected their pain and courage.

The client bought the idea, and the agency went on to produce the commercial, which scored higher—by quantitative copytests—than any analgesic commercial on record.

In short, the rapporteur must move *comfortably* in the world of emotions, must know what to do with them. She must be sensitive and resourceful, without losing the thread of her client's marketing concerns. I don't know any other way to achieve this second-nature kind of deftness with psychodynamics than academic training: at least an MA, and better yet, a Ph.D. A clinical internship is a plus.

Should the rapporteur also study marketing? I'm not sure. At some point, the books must be shut and hands-on training must begin, but that point is different for different individuals. Forced to select between an MBA, on top of studies in the social sciences and a trainee's job inside a research organization, advertiser company or agency, I think the trainee position the better choice. But I know my biases. That's how I started. And I have never forgotten the answer of my first mentor, when I asked him whether or not I should take a few marketing courses. "No," he said, "Forget that. You take some marketing courses, and you'll know what you can't do. Learn that, and you'll stop *doing* it."

The one other increment of training I consider indispensable for both levels of competence (moderators and rapporteurs) is an *apprenticeship*. To be sure, we pioneers did not apprentice—nobody came before. And we learned from our mistakes, got bruised and got better. But learning by trial and error has nothing much to recommend it, if there's an alternative. I have trained a number of focus group researchers. Some went on to graduate work in psychology and became rapporteurs. Some were content to be good moderators, and some moved over into quantitative research or marketing. None felt their apprenticeship wasted.

When possible, the apprenticeship is gradual: behind-the-mirror viewing (which allows the trainee to get some feeling for the client-relationship), followed by a low-participation role in the interview process. During this later period, the trainee sits in the room with the panelists and moderator, takes notes, deals with creative materials and with the respondents' needs. Following this, the trainee serves as co-moderator, sitting at the table opposite the moderator and asking some questions of her own. During all of these stages the trainee and the senior researcher discuss each interview in depth. When the trainee has become a co-moderator, she is asked to draft her own version of- a report before seeing the senior's draft. If her insights are good they should be used, and the report listed as a joint venture. If time allows, a period follows in which trainee and senior alternate moderating/assisting functions.

One does not always have the luxury of such extended training. Whenever I have had to shorten or eliminate a phase, the omission has been felt. The trainee has been uncomfortable, or there have been gaps in technique or understanding which have deterred the trainee's subsequent progress.

Apprenticeship is by no means the standard route to a moderator's or rapporteur's career. But if focus group interviewing is to earn the respect it asks for, there is no better way than through apprenticeships.

NOTES

[1]Credit is frequently given to Paul Lazersfeld as the putative father of focus groups. I see no reason to dispute it.

[2]Riesman, David, *The Lonely Crowd* (New Haven: Yale University Press, 1950).

[3]A colleague reports flying back from a series of focus groups in California. She was listening to one of the recent interviews on her

Walkman tape-player, and transcribing the session, with behavioral notations, when she recognized another focus group researcher sitting near-
by, and waved. The other researcher answered the greeting by approach-
ing and saying: "What on earth are you doing?" My friend replied that
she was listening to interviews. The other was shocked. "What? You listen to your own interviews? Do you write the reports too?"

Chapter 4

The Theoretical Concept

Every now and then I'm called-on to interview marketing managers. In one such interview several years ago, the subject of marketing versus sales functions was raised. At this point I asked, "What are you saying is the difference between being a salesman or saleswoman and being a marketer?" The first person to reply said, "Marketing is the hardest subject there is to learn." He obviously had just received his MBA, which made his egocentrism tolerable to me and the other panelists. But I've thought about this response several times since. Marketing is not as vital to the public weal as preventive medicine or as remotely exotic as astrophysics. Quite a few otherwise unremarkable people tackle it daily. But it is perhaps the shortest and sturdiest bridge between the GNP and individuals' behavior, between producers and purchasers. As such, "hard" scarcely begins to cover its complexity. And marketing research, is no piece of cake either.

I don't mean to equate the complexity of marketing and marketing research with the sheer intellect involved in devising and testing equations in quantum mechanics. I mean merely that the *outcome* of marketing research—the individual or collective act of purchasing—is the result of so many antecedent influences that the act of deciphering it to estimate the effect of the particular variable being tested requires the impartiality of a scientist and the persistence of a bull terrier.

Consider the variance of human behavior even in situations in which the experimenter asks for nothing more than a yes/no response. You cannot say, "If I offer a person food, he will eat." Even if you control for the time since last repast, individual tastes, and the food's appeal, some will eat and some will not. And as if that were not enough, the *internal* behavior equations don't add up easily either. The subject's anticipated behavior—unpredictable from surface factors—is not a linear function

53

of his or her internal drive. In other words, you can't achieve predictability by specifying that the subject be hungry. The hypothesis "If I offer a *hungry* person food, he will eat," may be no more reliable than the original one.

You, the experimenter, offer food. The subject is hungry. He is also "feeling fat." Will he eat? If he is also discouraged about his ability to control his weight, or if he is angry (at anything), he may say, "Oh, what the heck" and eat—unless he is socially insecure and fears that you will think him a glutton. Of course, if he is still feeling fat (but less so than yesterday) and is relatively confident that his weight is a function of his will, he may refuse food—unless he regards your behavior (offering the food) as a challenge, and believes he would lose face by refusing. If he does take the food, he may eat little, some, or a lot. The coup de grace is that you cannot learn reliably, even from a subject who is trying to cooperate, which internal/external factors are determining his present response. Nor can he say what he is likely to do tomorrow or even an hour from now.

Further, eating when food is offered is a relatively primitive and simple response. Purchasing a particular product at a particular time and place is not. First, the gratification is anticipated, not immediate. Second, the purchase is motivated by whatever influences—word-of-mouth, advertising, point-of-purchase promotional efforts, seductive packaging—the purchaser may have been subjected to. Another part of the equation is what the subject may already know about the product or manufacturer. Added to all this are several contingencies—whether the purchase is a gift or for personal use, a spur-of-the-moment decision or the endpoint of a targeted errand, a habitual selection, or a first purchase, etc.[1]

The final decision to buy can be seen as three concentric decisions: the readiness to buy (something), the perceived need or desire for a particular product category, and the selection of a specific brand.[2] In each of these decisions, that intractable, capricious creature, the human being, participates in ways that are usually as mysterious to him or her as to an external observer. And even these schemata are reductions of the real complexities underlying a single purchase decision. Consider that each of the hundreds of millions of potential purchasers in this country has a brain that never rests. In this brain are an estimated 30 billion neurons, firing in more or less organized fashion according to *that* individual's unique perceptions of reality. The reality being processed is composed of moment-to-moment fluctuations of internal stimuli and remembered portions of *that* person's experiences, plus the external stimuli selected for attention. Some of these perceptual actions are conscious, and some are not.

When an individual enters a store (and performs an act of choice about *which* store to enter) the conscious part of his or her mind is constricted to some degree—focused on the matching of a shopping list, written or mental. The person may or may not have a conceptual map of the store in mind. Consciously or unconsciously, he or she may be recalling a social event, an unfinished work project, or the lyrics of a song. Even if the focus on shopping is relatively absorbing and the list well thought out—including brand selection—spontaneous revisions are possible. The store may be out of the selected brand. What basis does the purchaser have for choosing a substitute brand or store? Does the display trigger recall of a forgotten commercial? Does a brand name or product appearance suggest a feeling or happening from childhood or even from last night? How does the individual input price changes? Yet the aim of marketing research is nothing less than quantifiable intelligence about purchase and better-than-chance prediction—a tall order.

Events as complex as fully delineated purchase decisions are obviously too unwieldy to measure and tabulate. The summary table would have as many cells as observations. No research effort can proceed without simplifying the event in some way if it is to yield useful information. This sounds a little like the tail wagging the dog, with mathematical and statistical tools shaping the data on which they are to operate. In a sense, this observation is valid. Research was born in the "scientific method" and developed in the service of the physical and natural sciences, whose data can be construed in alternative ways (as, for instance, Ptolemaic and Copernican views of planetary motion) but need not deal with the unsystematic array of human caprice. Early on, research scientists appropriated the universal and precise language of mathematics for their own discourse. A bit later, to compensate for errors and approximations in their observations and improve predictability, they coined the concept of probability and invented the tool kit of statistics.

All of these instruments are available for use in the marketing discipline. But none can grapple securely with the many-splendored human decision process in its entirety. To advance the understanding and prediction of marketplace phenomena, the act of buying must be atomized, factored into its component vectors:

> If we want to carry out our program skillfully, we must state precisely in which of the infinite number of determinants of an action we are interested. Only when we make it clear to ourselves and to our respondents which groups of determinants are at stake will we get results which permit a sensible statistical treatment, which is, of course, the aim of every field study.[3]

In other words, to make unique behavior quantifiable and useful, we must settle for part of the truth it tells. The danger here is the possibility of forgetting the quirky reality that has been partitioned into statable, comprehensible fragments. These may be "true," but they can never be "the truth." Some "truth" invariably is lost when the entirety is decomposed into "characteristics":

> What is measured is not the object, person, state, or event itself, but some characteristic of it. When objects are counted, for example, we do not measure the object itself, but only its characteristic of being present. We never measure people, only their age, height, weight, or some other characteristic. A study to determine whether a higher percentage of males or females purchase a given product, for example, measures the *male-female* and the *purchaser-nonpurchaser* attributes of the persons sampled. It is important to remember that we are always measuring some characteristics of the object or event and not the object or event itself.[4]

Unspoken but implied is the loss of a range and richness available only in the "intact" event or object. This isn't a rebuke. *Acknowledging* the abridgment of things, persons, and happenings is all that a practitioner or teacher of marketing research can be expected to do. Examining a deceased purchaser's brain or heart would be clumsy and worthless, not to mention unethical. Even if there were some device for entering and measuring the mental or emotional undercurrents of behavior, it would be as partial and misleading as the more familiar dissection of "characteristics."

One of my clients wished to market a new fire extinguisher which, in addition to putting out the most common household fires, left residues that were easily removable with a vacuum cleaner. The client had determined that male heads of household were the most frequent purchasers but surprisingly few homes were protected by fire extinguishers in sufficient number or capacity. I interviewed two male panels, each covering a broad age range and qualified only by their status of married, male HOH. As this was an exploratory study, we were as interested in why they had *not* bought extinguishers as in why they *had*.

In both groups, I had the task of finding a way into the topic that did not involve naming names (so that the topic would be raised in the context in which they normally would think of fire extinguishers). In the warm-up introductions in the first group, one of the men gave "mountain climbing" as a hobby. Another panelist said (half-jokingly) that such a concept of "fun" was beyond his understanding: "After all, there's enough dangerous things to do. Like just driving to work. Why would you look for more?" When introductions were complete, I pursued this line: "Do you think of your everyday life as being dangerous?" When this had run on for a few minutes, I asked, "What is the most dangerous calamity that you can think of that is reasonably likely to happen to people?"

Almost to a man, the twelve respondents thought that fire was the most terrible thing that could happen to "regular," average people. At this point, I asked how many of them had installed fire extinguishers. Only two had, and one was "shopping for one now." I remarked that it was fascinating to me that they all feared fire and yet so few had taken steps to protect themselves against it. One of the younger men frowned an instant, taking this in, then smiled somewhat wryly and said: "It is interesting. When you said that, I asked myself why I haven't bought one, and I realized that I don't really think I'm going to die." A slightly older panelist asked him, "How old are you?" The younger man replied, "Twenty-eight . . . and a half." The older one countered, "When you still count the half years, you don't believe it. I'm forty-five, and I know damn well I'm going to die." The rest of the panel jumped in, and the discussion became serious. If all that was necessary was mental and emotional galvanizing, we had certainly located the hot button.

But what could my client have done with this? We could guarantee that the householder would survive the fire—after all, those who didn't would be in no position to sue. And setting aside the problem of how to devise copy without using a skull and crossbones, how would we develop a media plan? Would we aim for the younger HOHs who think fire is survivable, or the older ones, who don't?

Rather than pursuing this emotionally charged topic, I told the men they would have to postpone this very important discussion for "your own time"[5] and get on with the task at hand. Then I asked the men who had bought fire extinguishers what had prompted them to purchase. I learned they had done so because of property and insurance concerns, which offered a bridge to the new product's innovative edge: post-fire preservation of rugs and furniture.

Had I felt that emotional variables were somehow "better" spurs for buying, I would not have refrained from developing the life and death issues. These men were also property owners and had the additional fear of handling the potentially toxic debris that the popular fire extinguishers of that time were known to leave behind. (The ethics of arousing anxiety and not allowing it to be ventilated will be discussed in Chapter 6.)

The whole issue of *emotional* motivations—the messiest of human variables to summarize and tabulate—was (understandably) given short shrift by early marketing researchers. But when it was realized that probability tables failed to predict behavior reliably, consultants—so-called social scientists—were called in to help marketers understand more qualitatively those parts of consumer decisions that resist quantification. I suspect that this enlistment was undertaken with much reluctance on the measurers' part.

Qualitative/quantitative collaboration is no marriage made in heaven. After much consideration, the quantitative constituency had devised methods for estimating the probabilities of demographic and communicative inputs to consumers' purchase readiness and brand behavior. And now there was a new, unruly universe of behavioral promptings to understand and control. The data that social scientists revered seemed random and cumbersome to the quantifiers. The reductions that the measurers venerated appeared to the more holistic social scientists to let the human subject bleed to death.

The primary goal of both is to simplify the emotional/rational/behavioral equations to the point where they are *expressible* with a minimum of distortion. Beyond that, both sides seek to find causally *predic-*

tive relationships and, eventually, to devise ways to *influence* effectively behavior in the marketplace. The most obvious way to simplify the three-way juggling of *purchaser, purchase decision* and *purchase behavior* is to declare one of them irrelevant. This being impossible, the second choice is to *reduce* one or more of these into a finite number of templates. Throughout the course of marketing research, a large number of reductionist attempts have been made.

TO BUY OR NOT TO BUY

Purchase behavior surely is the most obvious candidate for simplification. It contains less theoretical baggage than either the purchaser or the purchase decision. In fact, there are only two endpoints: Purchasers either buy or they don't. This appealing dichotomy and the apparent ease of distinguishing one response from the other have led to a number of marketing test formats—from the Schwerin Test, which requires consumers to choose among competitive products before and after the viewing of commercials, to the more recent elaborate test market studies. But even here the simplicity is more apparent than real. The Schwerin format, for example, has obvious shortcomings:

• Even with more sophisticated store mockups available, the dummy "store" is not a supermarket, and the choices are less than exhaustive.

• The purchaser may have bought recently a closetful of "her" brand on a price-off sale and on this occasion may be getting some of her mother's favorite as a gift.

• The purchaser may have been meaning to try an alternative brand for some time regardless of the commercial shown.

• The purchaser is fully aware that purchases are being recorded and may be trying to choose what the researcher seems to want--or what the researcher does *not* want.

• The purchaser is fully aware that purchases are being recorded and may also be quite conscious of the status implications of competitive brands (e.g., *The New York Review of Books* versus *The Inquirer*).

• Brand choice in purchase number 2 may be influenced by purchase number 1 ("I already have that one. What else do I want?").

Most confounding of all, there is no clear way to distinguish the purchase *decision* from the purchase *act*. In a study on bathroom tissue a

couple of years ago, I asked what seemed to me a straightforward purchase *act* question: "You've nearly run out of bathroom tissue, and you
are in the supermarket. Which brand do you buy?" Panelists have been
told that "there are no wrong answers" and that "we really want your
best assessment of what you would do." The first respondent refreshed
my memory about the complexity of buying behavior: "Where am I running out?" she asked. "Because if it's in the master bathroom, I will always look for White Cloud. If that's not there, I may even ask for it. If I
can't get that and I'm in a hurry, I might take a pack of Cottonelle. But
if I'm running low in the guest bathroom, it's strictly color. If the blue
towels are up, I'll get whatever is blue."

Did commercials count for nothing? Her next reflection suggested
otherwise: "Except for one: I will never buy Charmin. Even if I have to
change the towels. There's something tacky about the name, and Mr.
Whipple makes me want to barf." Commercials do count—but both
ways. And the mind that decides is the one that deploys the hand and
arm. The purchase act may be simply a mindless reaching. But more
typically, the decision informs the act in a convergence at the point-of-
purchase (POP).

PEOPLE BOXES

Looking at people categorically is another reductionist method that is
valiantly tried every decade or so. In the seventies, it was
psychographics and *lifestyles*, both of which were built on AIO (Activities, Interests, and Opinions) questionnaires, which in turn were constructed from Likert scale questions. By today's standards, both of these
efforts were modest enough, content to assign names to the various
mutations of Likert scale "clusters." Psychographics presumed nothing
about intrapersonal dynamics, nor did it make pronouncements about
that interpersonal entity, the society, In its pure form, psychographics
also failed to predict shifts in the dominance of particular lifestyles.

The people boxes of the eighties fall into the VALS (Values and Lifestyles) categories. The Stanford Research Group, which parented VALS,
has traveled further afield, and fully fleshed out the categories with
dynamic sinews. Population weightings are assigned for each category,
and a direction of evolutionary change is proposed. Furthermore, the
parent group has a value system of its own. For example, the "inner-

directeds" are the true elite and are thriving, while the "lower" categories, like "belongers," are diminishing.

I have a personal bias against typologies in general. By this I mean not the *user personality* categories that arise from particular projects and apply only to user groupings, but the sweeping partitioning of "all Americans" or even "everybody in Duluth." I have trouble cutting out people to fit patterns. The reverse is not only more reliable; it shows complete, real people in the actual purchasing act.

Stronger than that is my bias against hierarchical typologies that classify one "type" as superior to another. Moral judgments of individual equality aside, I don't think marketers or advertisers can afford this kind of elitism. In my (deliberately) limited experience with such graded systems, the client somehow always falls into one of the "higher" groups and the consumer into one of the "lower" ones. This affects the advertiser's perspective on his or her client. I believe that this subtly disguised contempt shows through the advertiser's communications. I have seen many cases in which otherwise brilliant copy was unsuccessful. Copy-test panels are often puzzled about why they dislike the material. "It makes me uncomfortable" has become a signal to look closely for buried contempt. It is also an unwelcome red light. Of all the sins an advertiser can commit, contempt is one of the hardest charges to level. "Bad" clients grow defensive; "good" ones become melancholy. ("Goodness" and "badness" from the rapporteur's perspective are discussed in Chapter 10.)

MIND VERSUS BODY: SIMPLIFYING THE PURCHASE DECISION

Of the three purchase components, the purchase decision is the most complicated. It contains the decider's complexities and portends the purchase act. It can also be viewed as the most important factor, as it is interwoven with the immediate purchase act and also acts as the basis for predicting future purchases once its contingencies are sorted out. In this light, the recurrent popularity of mechanical, electrical, and most recently, computerized reaction measuring devices is understandable. Hooking people up to PGSRs (psychogalvanic skin response), plethysmographs (blood volume from capillary dilation), and pupillary cameras, to name a few, is an effort with a good cause.

The problem addressed here is that the "respondent" is a sealed box with no means of entry—and even if there were one, one wouldn't know what to record. These devices are all direct measures of some part of the response. They are usually unconscious and independent of the subject's introspection. In brief, the rationale is that emotions have physical consequences or accompaniments that are automatic, i.e., not subject to voluntary control. Because these responses are involuntary and usually minute, they can be elicited without the person's being able to suppress them—often without his or her being aware of them at all. Collectively, these are the *autonomic responses*, governed by behavioral areas of the central nervous system that lie beneath the cortex: the thinking part of the brain. The endpoints of autonomic effector impulses occur in body areas that may also serve voluntary promptings: muscles, skin, eyes, etc. But the autonomic reactions tend to be more indirectly concerned with gross emotional behaviors, such as approach and flight. They are involved in preparing the body for action and are, in a sense, "readiness" reactions (increased blood supply to the muscles, heightened blood pressure, dilated pupils, etc.).

The autonomic reaction pattern can be measured either as activation of the mobilizing reflexes or as suppression of the "conserving" reflexes—those that *prevent* us from exhibiting massive emotional reactions to pinpricks, mildly pleasant odors, and so on. Of the possible measurable reactions, the suppression measures are the more accurate (which accounts, in part, for the longevity of the pupillary cameras). The most familiar measure, however—and the most popular in nonclinical settings, because it is easy and not uncomfortable for the subject—is the measure of palmar resistance (sweaty palms)—the PGSR. It has gained popularity not only because of its ease of use, but also because of its high sensitivity. In fact, its sensitivity is one of the problems—it can be elicited by a variety of stimuli, not just those intended by the experimenter. It is thus hard to focus interpretively. It also fatigues very quickly, creating the danger of a judgment of "no response" when the reflex is simply refractory. Also, I know of no way to distinguish between autonomic measures elicited by strong attraction from those resulting from strong aversion. In practice, this may mean little (presumably no thoughtfully presented product or commercial message will be strongly offensive)—but what if the *experimenter* is highly personable or the subject really hates the *wallpaper?*

Finally, with respect to the usefulness of gadgetry in general, it has not been demonstrated that involuntary changes in interest, attention, and feeling are better predictors of buying behavior than are conscious, voluntary, controlled responses. The heyday of the "gadget" was probably the late sixties. It was ingenious and enterprising, but the disrespect implicit in this somewhat cloak-and-dagger approach to human responsiveness was probably transmitted to the subjects. Inferring molar responses from molecular response parts was an admirable but largely fruitless attempt.

Focus groups—and more generally all qualitative techniques—are not better ways of solving the same problem. The goals of qualitative exploration are different from those of quantitative testing. Though clients frequently "choose" to use one method over another, the true choice to be made is that of the problem and its most useful resolution. Focus groups do not result in numbers—or at least they should not. Focus groups can deliver working hypothesis of a causal nature. Quantitative research usually does not deal with causes, although this is its ultimate goal. The quantitative research professional assembles intact people and events from the measured "characteristics" discussed earlier. They work with inductive precision toward the whole.

Qualitative research is not reductionist; it does not aim at simplification or measurement. The qualitative researcher must not merely tolerate complexity, but actually *hunger* for it as the hallmark of his or her subject—the behaving human. Different kinds of individual researchers make up the qualitative and quantitative enterprises—and for *my* money, it is the qualitative researchers who have all the fun.

NOTES

[1]Roughly equivalent to Lazarsfeld's "influences toward action," "attributes of the product," and "impulses of the purchase." *See* Paul F. Lazarsfeld, *Qualitative Analysis: Historical and Critical Essays* (Boston: Allyn & Bacon, 1972), p.184.

[2]Earnest Dichter, *The Strategy of Desire* (London: T.V. Boardman, 1960), Chapter 7. Dichter uses five concentric circles.

[3]Lazarsfeld, p. 186.

[4]Donald S. Tull and Del I. Hawkins, *Marketing Research: Measurement and Method* (New York: Macmillan, 1980), p. 215.

[5]They did. They left *en masse* for the building coffeeshop, at the end of the interview.

Chapter 5

The Soul of a Focus Group (or: "Events Inside the Skin")

A faithful map of any territory can provide an individual who proposes to visit the place with useful data about what the territory is like. If, for example, it is a relief-map, the traveler can find out from it whether the area is mountainous or flat, barren or intersected by rivers. If it is a road-map, he can find out how to get around in it. If a meteorological map, he will anticipate its weather with some accuracy. But no map can really tell the traveler what it will be like to *be* there. Atop a mountain, he may say "Oho, the air is thin at this altitude.I should probably take it easy the first few days." But the topographic map cannot convey how it *feels* to breathe oxygen-reduced air. The road map cannot tell him what he will *experience* driving on an interstate highway or a dirt road. The meterological map will not dictate how he should dress or what activities he should plan.

I have outlined some of the basic assumptions and major choices that guide me in doing focus-groups. I would like now to take you a little farther into the process of the moment-to-moment decisions made in the moderating and interpreting of a focus group project, so that you can understand better how the data are gathered and how they are used.

First, you should understand that mapping a particular focus group is not possible. Nobody has ever visited the country of this exact group of individuals, at this place and time. True, the discussion guide offers a course to follow from the warm-up to gathering the best information the panelists can offer bearing on the goals of the project. But a typed transcript of any actual interview has about the same relationship to the guide that a 36-inch snake has to a yardstick: it's hard to line up and check off.

The topics suggested in the guide are raised, but not sequentially. Topics also tend to be interwoven and to reappear, sometimes with very different implications, throughout the interview:

A particularly vivid example happened in an airline interview with male business-flyers. The group had been unanimous in denying that advertising had anything what-soever to do with their choice of airlines, which was based strictly on rational business considerations. When I asked them for the "messages" in current, competitive commer-cials, the group was unanimous in reporting that they "just turned off" when commer-cials for airlines came on, because such trivia was unrelated to choices they might make. One of the men reported particular impatience with the "dumb jingles" used in some of the airline commercials. This detail suggested to me that he, at least, had not been *completely* "turned off." I asked him to be more specific about the jingles. He was in the act of obliging when one of the other panelists interrupted loudly. "Hold the phone! I sat here telling you that commercials had nothing to do with which airline I fly, and I've just remembered. I took the train into the city last Wednesday, and that crazy _____ airline song was running through my head. I was annoyed with myself, but even when I was careful to turn my head away from thinking about it, I heard it, and realized I was whistling the tune. When I asked my secretary later that day to make a plane reservation for Chicago, I suggested *that airline*." Here, the rest of the group began having similar hypermnesia.

What did it mean? This particular man had more than a little charismatic pull in the group. His initial derisiveness had seemed influential in the group members' disparage-ment of airline commercials. Were they *really* remembering their own behavior . . . or merely emulating his? I went back over the same ground covered not ten minutes ear-lier: What airline "messages" did they remember specifically? What had caused them to react positively to each? The fact that most of them were able to answer the questions said that at least some part of the previous response was untrue: Specific recall sug-gests that the recipient is at least not "turned off" or tuned out.

But had my client taken the earlier statements as true and quit the backroom to go get bombed, or done some "tuning out" himself, he'd have had a quite discouraging—or at least incomplete—picture of advertising impact. Not to say that the group's denial of in-fluence was untrue. It represented a need to legitimize the influence of advertising. But it told us the lines of communication were still functioning.

Further, the written material may contradict the verbal transcript, or both verbal and written reactions may be belied by the behavioral obser-vations, by the projective data, or both (more about this below). One reason for the nonsequential, interweaving flow of discussion is the avoidance of *direct questions* throughout the interview. This kind of in-terchange ("Do you like doughnuts?" "Yes.") happens as near to never as conversation permits. Obviously, direct questions would be simpler to moderate, to answer, and to interpret. But I feel that the answers to questioning of this sort are often useless, or worse: dangerous. They cannot give the rapporteur some of the kinds of information (motivational, causative) that she is seeking. But more importantly, they tend to provide answers which can seriously mislead.

I can offer at least four reasons for avoiding direct questioning:

1. Partly, I avoid direct questioning because the kind of interaction it produces is *boring*. The immediate result is emotional disengagement from the topic, for everyone concerned: panelists, moderator, and viewers. Such disengagement leads panelists to *automatic, unsearching answers* to the questions. Feelings would still be going on, because feelings operate all the time. (Some of the feelings might even be strong-- like the urge to leave the room or to gag the moderator.) But the feelings experienced by panel members in a direct question-and-answer interview will have *low, intermittent, or no relationship* to the stated topic. Put another way, their minds will wander. A clever and funny moderator can of course make even this format entertaining. But responses then will be centered on her cleverness.

2. Since direct questioning is necessarily one-on-one, each question will be directed in turn to each panelist. And parallel questioning of the individuals in a group is a very efficient antipersonnel weapon, in the sense of group dynamics. As noted above, respondents tend to become disengaged from the topic. But that is not the only loss. They also become disengaged from other members of the group, so that interpersonal *provocation, influence,* and *drift* are no longer discernible.

3. Also, asking a question directly does not permit the issues to emerge spontaneously. This deprives the moderator and the behind-the-mirror audience of the opportunity to gauge the relative saliency of the topic, or to weigh and consider the mental and emotional company it keeps: the ideas immediately associated with it, the feelings that accompany it, the language which would naturally be used by panelists to express it, and so on.

4. Finally, there is a less obvious reason for avoiding direct questioning: less obvious, but central to the precise kind of interpretive responsibility which is assumed by the focus group researcher. She avoids direct questioning because of the difficulties it leads to in *willingness to respond.* Not that the panelists are *un*willing to answer direct questions (providing the questioning hasn't put them to sleep). Rather, they are too willing: in fact they are willing to answer *regardless of whether or not they know the answers.*[1] I am not suggesting malicious intent on the panelists' behalf. I have found most group members to be most willing and cooperative. Nor am I falling into the trap of underrating the intelligence of panelists. It's true that they don't know the answers, but, to compound the problem, they *don't know that they don't know.*

Remember that the kinds of questions typically addressed by this type of research, if expressed in direct form are uncommonly complex. The rapporteur goes into her groups attempting to answer a brain-buster like: "If this storyboard were to be developed and produced as a commercial, what reactions would the people in this panel be likely to have to it, and what would they then do about their reactions?"

Questions like this are not merely complex. They also require attitude-projection and behavioral conjecture that I'm not sure any panelist can manage accurately by introspection. Simple past, present, and future tenses are hard enough to handle, heaven knows. A question such as the example above, if asked of a panel respondent, would have to be set in some obscure tense like the pluperfect conditional: "If such-and-such were to happen, in the following situational context, then would you. . . .?"

Direct questions just like those given *are* asked—they are asked of the researcher, about the panelists, by the people who requested and will pay for the answers. And the questions are duly set down in the "Background and Purpose" section of the final report. They are also, more often than not, answered by the person responsible for the project, with limitations and caveats reflecting the size and probable skewing of the sample. But they are neither asked of nor answered by the panelists themselves, directly. Because if we asked, they would answer. And (it bears repeating) they not only don't know the correct answers. They don't know that they don't know.

That statement and the claim which is implicit in it bear some thinking about. Assuming that panel members want to be cooperative (and that is a tenable assumption). and that they have had 20 or more years to get an accurate fix on themselves, it is a tall claim to say that a focus group researcher can learn things about them in a two-hour group-interview that they themselves do not know, that not even the brightest of them, with the best intentions in the world, can tell us. But we can—and do.

The things that focus group researchers principally seek to learn about respondents are things that they rarely think about very concentratedly: buying, brand-choice usage, and product attitudes, for instance.

These things are negligibly important to *them* as ordinary citizens in the real world. But they are the very essence of *our* real world. Most people interviewed in focus groups either shop impulsively, giving brand selection only a few seconds' thought, or have put brand choice on automatic. They have other, more important things to think about, and little motivation to search themselves for better understanding of this sphere of their lives. *Our* motivational stakes in understanding these things, on the other hand, are very high indeed. So we try harder to uncover them.

Furthermore, a professional rapporteur brings to the interview situation two kinds of expertise which the panelists probably don't have. We use our expertise in *human behavior* and our familiarity with *marketing strategies* to figure out how internal events like feelings, attention, and memory, combine in the act of making a purchase.

When a qualitative researcher talks about interpreting consumer reactions to get the answers to specific questions or to make specific recommendations, she means something different from the "interpretations" of a questionnaire survey. Survey interpretation treats respondents' verbatim statements as facts which can be measured and compared across different populations. In the case of group interview data, however, what respondents *say* may be amended or modified—or in some cases even totally contradicted—by the researcher's interpretation.

I don't mean that the panelists' responses are ignored; quite the contrary. *All* of each panelist's communications are taken into account, from minute-to-minute and in aggregate. As I perceive it, at least three communicative channels are open throughout the interview, providing three kinds, or levels, of information:

The Level of Public Affirmation. This is what panelists actually say. It is *their* interpretation of what they think and feel, shaped by the social role they are trying to maintain, and in conjunction with the expressed views of other panel members. Since they have not been asked to go on record with a flat yes or no, they are not greatly concerned with consistency (or can't keep track of it). The interviewer *is* concerned with consistency, but not with promoting it. She watches motivational drift closely because an about-face is as useful as an unassailably consistent stand.

The *language* panelists use in discussing a topic is also a part of public affirmation. Since the panelists themselves have introduced the topic (assuming the moderator has done her job well), their language is relatively uncontaminated by our expectations of it. A marketer of expensive cosmetics, chiefly targeted to women over 35, was initially shocked by the *appearance* of user-panelists and even more profoundly shocked to hear the user refer to that line's quintessential moisturizer as "grease." Subsequent data revealed to the client that this apparent disrespect was the women's fear of yet another huckster's pitch. They *wanted* to believe the efficacy story, but didn't want to be disappointed yet again and didn't want to appear foolish. Answers to the question "What would you need to know about this product, to make you stop referring to it as 'grease'?" provided raw material for a new, medical-scientific product strategy.

The Level of Private Acknowledgement. This level of information derives from the various written tasks the panel members are asked to do according to the particular goals of the discussion: self-descriptive exercises for the warm-up section of the interview; product and/or brand-usage information during the predispositions section; evaluative notations for the presentation of materials; section; votes; brand personality descriptions, and so on. A written assignment, where used, always precedes the public discussion. If your eyebrows go up about the assumption of some independence between these two levels, it is true that the public discussion cannot be kept wholly independent of the written responses. I do often ask respondents to turn their written sheets over before open talk commences, and I do begin discussion with a question put some other way than the question asked in the written task, so there is no exact parallel. But I can't erase the written answers from their minds.

I'm really not sure exactly how or why it happens, but written reactions very often sound as though different groups wrote them. They are nothing like the group interchange. Evaluative notes or even voting often do not track with the open discussion. Sometimes they are so different as to lead me to check handwriting. My guess is that written material reflects what panelists honestly think as opposed to feelings they subsequently "own" when they are under some degree of social pressure. Perhaps their spoken contributions reveal what they want to be seen and heard to say. When the time comes to fit written statements or comments into an interpretive scheme, I use the content plus indications of *intensity* of opinion or feeling (underlining, heavy pressure, exclamation points) and *involvement* (how much is written, personal projections of product use, etc.).

The Level of Personal Revelation. This is, primarily, what is learned from the panelists' unspoken communications: vocal range and variation, postural changes, facial expressions and constrictive or expansive demeanor, to mention a few.[2] Three respondents can say exactly the same words and express quite different inner states. Consider the phrase: "Frankly, it leaves me cold." Assume that one respondent making this comment spits it between clenched teeth, leaning forward with hands gripping the edge of the table; that a second says it in a low voice without inflection, suppressing a yawn, leaning back, with hands slack; and that a third says it almost laughingly, sitting forward, with arms hugging (or perhaps with one hand over the mouth), eyes sparkling and chair swinging.

It is up to the interviewer to be aware of such behavioral distinctions, not only in the person speaking at any one time but in the group as a whole. For instance, she may note how quickly a group warms up; and whether (and when) they react autonomously, or look to one another or to the moderator for guidance. She is aware, too, of the intensity of controversy and of the panelists tendency to return to, or avoid, particular topics.

Besides the vocal and behavioral clues, the figure drawings and stories I regularly ask panelists to produce are also sources of the "personal revelation" level of data. They are used to elaborate, to substantiate, to explain, or to reconcile sketchy, ambiguous, or contradictory impressions.

It may have occurred to you that when a moderator shifts her attention from one level of response to another during the interview, she is confounding the distinction between *moderating* and *interpreting*. The line between the two *is* a little fuzzy. Some clearly interpretive operations may go on—out loud—while the interview is in progress. Decisions about when and whether to interpret are a matter of the interviewer's judgment.

Interpreting, even if relatively superficial, is almost certain to raise the emotional intensity of the group. It may also generate a certain amount of anxiety. The balance is difficult to describe. Placidity, comfort and consensus are by no means the only, or the most ideal forms or outcomes of a focus group exploration. But the moderator assumes an obligation to keep the intensity of feeling and interpersonal contention within tolerable bounds and to hold rein on behavioral chaos. If she judges that the group is cohesive enough to contain stress, and that the individuals in question are sufficiently comfortable with introspection not to become intolerably anxious, then she is justified in offering interpretive probes which can be extremely productive. For example:

"You say that it leaves you cold, but I'm getting a very different message from your voice and manner—that you really *dislike* it very much." (Or ". . . That something about it amuses and delights you.") "Can you clarify those different communications for me?"

When a respondent can assimilate the degree of internal conflict which probes such as this create, and has enough self-awareness to resolve it; or alternately, when the climate of the group is so supportive that another panelist will rush in to help the challenged respondent achieve self-understanding, these interpretive interchanges are salutary from every perspective. They are helpful to the moderators and to the viewers trying to understand what is happening. They also provide the respondents with the uniquely heady achievement of insight. This may explain the apparent paradox that interviews which have seemed to be charged with ambivalent or unpleasant feelings, and beset with interpersonal strife, are frequently perceived by respondents as joyous, uplifting experiences. It is a common experience of moderators to wind up exhausted and drained from interviews which have wrung them like washcloths with their factionalism and contradictions, only to have the facility's field supervisor comment, "That must have been a super group. Everybody's begging to come back."

In the closing minutes of the interview wrap-up, it is a good idea for the moderator to invite additional questions ("If you were sitting where I am sitting, what would *you* have asked?) or summary interpretations ("If you had the job of summarizing how the whole group felt about_____, what do you think you'd say?") from the panelists. Since sessions are often up-tempo, interpersonally active and sometimes tense and factional, respondents usually seek a closure, and are more than willing to jump in at this point. And wise moderators will gratefully accept the things group members have spotted which neither they nor the viewers have picked up.

After the conference room door closes on the last panelist, the process of interpretation really begins. If there is to be a post-mortem, it is held immediately after the interview. Those in attendance at this debriefing are (at minimum) the moderator and viewers who have been there from beginning to end. (It may also include viewers who arrived late or those who took recesses.) In this informal session, the researcher notes conspicuous themes of the discussion, mentions spontaneous impressions of the behavioral flow, perhaps glances at the written responses and the drawings, and charts the general direction of the group, using the contributions of everyone present.

Interpretation is the hardest, yet the most rewarding, part of the project. Obviously, the final interpretation will depend on the purpose for which the groups were convened and the form which has been agreed upon for communicating the results (e.g., full report or topline, written report or verbal presentation). But whatever the purpose and intended format of presentation, the act of interpreting group interview data consists in bringing together disparate material—written reactions, interactive discussion, observed behavior, drawings and stories—weighing and sifting it, and finally organizing the multiple clues into an articulated set of premises and speculations.

To use one example, a frequent goal or subgoal in a focus group project is to explore panelists' reactions to creative material. The researcher will expose them to several comparable concepts, layouts, rough copy, storyboards, animatics, rough commercials or other materials. She may do this to assess the pros and cons of each, to choose among them, or compare them with familiar presentations of proven appeal. These are frequent assignments for quantitative methods as well, but the way the moderator collects her data is different from classical copy-testing. The written, private comments are roughly comparable to a quantitative assessment, but of course they are discursive rather than categorical.

An important premise of quantitative polling is that the interview is free of the artifact of social influence. The focus group researcher, on the other hand, explores the influence of the group as a primary datum. In the gathering and evaluating of responses to copy, qualitative practitioners do not attempt to measure increments of memorability or interest. No scales are constructed, nor are respondents asked to estimate the likelihood of purchase. It follows that the kinds of answers given to these questions will be different (from the copytest categories) in meaning if not in labeling. For instance, in a copy-exploration, I attempt to summarize responses in the following categories:

Comprehension. Superficially, this is like the category of the same name in conventional copy-testing. I include in reports some estimate of how well panelists seem to *understand the message* of a concept or an execution, but with one important distinction: I assume that in any communicative event, the message that is transmitted is no more valid than the one that is received. This is the principle of *negotiable truth*. It dictates that the weight of truth, in any interpersonal situation, is directly equivalent to the relative power of the participants in the situation. In a scholastic examination, a student's answer is graded "wrong" if he has misunderstood (failed to comprehend) what the professor said. Similarly, if a gunman says: "Get over against that wall," failure to comprehend *which* wall he means might have disastrous consequences. These are simple cases. A married couple—assuming both parties have an equal stake in the relationship—might find the resolution of "I know what I said"/"I know what I heard" arguments all but interminable, since the negotiating power of each is equal.

"Comprehension" of a promotional message is in the professor/gunman category since consumers have the all important power. They buy or refuse the promoted product at least partially on the basis of the message *as they understood it*. What the copywriter or vice-president of sales and advertising *intended* to say, or *thought* he said, is of relatively little importance.

One would think that clients and creatives would be relieved by the simplicity of this concept, and the certainty with which comprehension can be evaluated. Oddly, they're not. One of the hardest points to communicate in a report or presentation is that, if most of the people in the groups have a positive reaction to what they "comprehend" the message to signify (and most of them "comprehend" the same message), comprehension is high, even when the message they understood is *not* what the copy meant to say. If we want to have any control of input, we should examine the slippage between the intended communication and what is communicated to the audience.

Persuasiveness. I also search the data for anything it may reveal about the extent to which respondents are convinced by the materials shown that they should try the product (or continue to buy it). Precisely because I *don't* ask them directly: "Would you buy it?", I feel free to place some weight on spontaneous statements of buying intention. I take these especially seriously when they are supported by indications that the respondent has projected the buying or using of the product into his future expectations, e.g., by *incorporating it into a larger plan.* "I would buy it, and use the money it would save me to go to the movies." I also watch for and use things like *switching from the conditional mode to the declarative mode:* "I would buy it so that I *will* be able to save money and go to the movies with it."
Facial expressions and behavioral responses bear on the state of being persuaded as well. So does the factor of social plasticity/resistance: how strongly respondents who *are* persuaded of the message will argue with those who are not, or how stoutly they will resist the arguments of confirmed doubters. If these responses do not emerge spontaneously, I may fan the contention ("How would *you* persuade her of what you believe?"; "How would *you* answer that argument?" Though they may be subtle or fleeting, these behavioral signals are at least as reliable in gauging persuasion as are conventional, static indications.

Importance and Recall. I generally combine these categories in a concept I have privately labeled *"Embeddedness."* This refers to the extent to which other, subsequent life events which respondents are likely to experience will tend to *evoke, rather than to bury,* their recollection of the message. For instance, if the next time the respondent gets into a lather about rising prices, she seems likely to remember our product, and if she is further the kind of person who padlocks her purse, and lathers about inflation often and intensely, then for this respondent, the message is highly "embedded." Embeddedness also includes the quality of *identification* which panelists may feel with the idea, the situation, or the people depicted in a creative execution. Someone who gets a genuine shock of recognition—"Hey, that's me!"—when he looks at a commercial featuring attendence at a baseball game is likely to be reminded of that commercial every time he watches live or televised baseball, thinks of a particular player, or perhaps even when he "pitches" a crumpled sheet of paper accurately into his wastebasket.

Believability. Is something that shifts significance according to the *product*, the *degree* of belief (or skepticism) and the *reason* for which it is believed (or not). I report on this when it seems to me important, but I have no permanently assigned evaluation for it. Clearly, a cosmetic product that is considered "too good to be true" may have created a very positive impression. On the other hand, a response like "It's some of your damned advertising double-talk," in response to advertising of a bank's services, or a food product's freedom from additives, indicates that a product hasn't been very well received. Cosmetics are *supposed* to be magic, to stretch belief; food and banks are not.

Liking. The romance which panelists have with the creative material is by far the untidiest of the responses-to-executions that we consider. Presumably, an ad or commercial that isn't sufficiently liked won't be allowed to deliver its message. But everyone who has gone a few rounds in the business has seen "adorable" campaigns that didn't move the product, and "outrageous" ones that did. I have to address liking in reports, because it is something that people talk about in panels, but there is no one standard rule for interpreting what, if anything, liking a commercial or advertisement has to do with purchasing the product. I tend to think that strong feelings in *either* direction register more clearly and last longer than the most benign low-level response. A comment like: "It's short and to the point and no-nonsense"—whatever pejorative connotations are intended—is nearly always a kiss of death.

As for how I combine the three layers of interview material mentioned earlier into estimates of "persuasiveness" or "embeddedness," or whatever other judgments I have been asked to make, there are, again, no invariable rules. When written reactions are at odds with publicly aired opinions or feelings, I can't assume, *a priori,* that one or the other is more true. I have to take into account the type of product, the experience of using it, the probable impact of social pressure on the product category, and so forth.

If the written comments are more positive than the beginning of the discussion, it *may* mean that respondents are drawn to the product but feel compelled to pay lip-service to consumer cynicism. If attitudes expressed in the group become more positive as the discussion continues, I would probably assume that this was true.

On the other hand, initial private acceptance followed by public rejection *may* equally well show a quick disenchantment with advertising claims which are perceived as superficial or irrelevant. Such a pattern could indicate more intense net aversion than when both written and verbal responses are moderately, uniformly negative.

There are no formulae. There are, alas, few precedents. Sometimes long familiarity with a product or product category will give me a reassuring feeling of solidity and even some ready made hypotheses for explaining contradictions. But here too I must be alert for signs of change.

There is also a kind of cumulative serendipity by which an experienced researcher recognizes in one product category attitudes that are familiar from another. For instance, she may speculate about whether a product that used to be seen as almost purely cosmetic seems to be shifting to a medicinal image (because attitudinal patterns suddenly seem to resemble those habitually seen in drug product interviews).

By and large, once the interviews are done, the tapes reviewed and the various responses of the respondents sorted through, I am alone with the data and with whatever tools I have acquired to organize them into a final report. When I am asked what goes into a project report, I always have the impulse to offer a resume. Focus groups have astonishing flexibility, and can absorb whatever a researcher brings to them. The interviews themselves—and the reports that interpret them—are as they are because of my academic and clinical background, and have gotten better as my marketing background expands and deepens.

Having started off with the declaration that I was setting forth *one* way, and not *the* way, to use group interview research, I find I do have something to say about how one "ought" to approach group interviews. They should be approached with as simple and clear an idea of the objectives as possible, and with an equally clear (though perhaps less simple) inventory of one's skills, blind spots, biases and expectations. This will instruct the professional as to what she can do very well, where she must exercise caution, and—when the data are before her—how to recognize moderator skew when she sees it.

NOTES

[1]The observation that autobiographical recall of such material as purchase-behavior can be undependable is not uniquely mine nor even particularly new. A review of the literature on this point can be found in: Bradburn, Rips, and Shevell, "Answering Autobiographical Questions: The Impact of Memory and Inference on Surveys," *Science,* 10 April 1987, 157–61.

[2]If you were worried about the independence of verbal and written responses you may also wonder about the behavioral baseline against which interview behavior stands out and can be interpreted. This is established, informally, for individuals and the group as a whole during the warm-up. They are checking me out, and I feel it perfectly fair that I take their measure as well.

Chapter 6

The Interpersonal Event

A focus group interview, as an existential and interior happening, expresses and depends upon at least four concurrent interactions. It is a "good" group (useful, rich, provocative) in direct proportion to the integrity of all of these four collaborative elements:

• The interaction of the panelists with the moderator.
• The internal reciprocities of panel members.
• The relationship—immediate and long term—between researcher and client.
• The relationship—immediate and long term—between researcher and the particular facility-supplier.

Two auxiliary interactions are also involved, which can enhance the value of the group outcome but more often act to undermine it. These are *client-to-client relationships* (representatives of different departments, proponents of different theories, advertiser and agency representatives, etc.) and *supplier-to-client relationships* (supplier plying client with food, drink, small gifts, etc.). Both relationships are apt to distract attention from the purposes for which the groups were contracted. Serving good and interesting food *can* reduce the tedium of inactivity in the back room, and client-to-client interchanges during lulls in the group discussion—when panelists are writing, for example—*can* be constructive. But in practice they more frequently serve to dilute or confound the research process, because suppliers may be more interested in soliciting repeat business and clients in advancing individual status than either party is in discovering the new areas opening up in the interview room.

The researcher is directly involved in the four primary relationships:

- As a *member* of the group and participant in the discussion.
- As the *instigator of*, and *cohesive force in*, the community formed by panelists.
- As the *responsible agent* of the client, and the client's *liaison officer* with panel-members.
- As a *partner* of the field staff, in securing the best possible respondents—an enterprise that makes both "partners" look good.

One of the challenges of being a focus-group moderator is in attending to all four of these relationships concurrently. She must be concentratedly present for and with the panelists, but must also be alert to whatever communicative signal has been agreed on with the client for redirection of focus. She must be aware of the sensitivity or obtuseness of the facility staff in such matters as tuning in to the discussion, so that they will know when to reverse a tape, refill coffee pots, ferry messages from behind the mirror and so on. Each duty is important.

At times the concurrent responsibilities of the moderator may be further elaborated. The client may have requested videotaping, which adds the presence of a videotape camera and the responsibility of cueing the cameraman for zoom shots of particular panelists. In terms of priorities of what will best advance the goals of the research effort, the first two relationships—those inside the interview room—are the most critical. And although they are conceptually distinct, in practice these two relationships—between panelists and moderator and among the panelists—tend to fuse.

THE MODERATOR AS PRIME MOVER/PARTICIPANT

The delicate balance of being both leader and participant is developed very carefully by experienced moderators, who begin well before the convening of the first panel. For most projects the moderator will probably travel to a community different from the one she lives in. There is the question of what clothes to take: they must be appropriate to the climate, but even more so to the attitudes of the panelists in a given locale. Regardless of the age or sex of the panelists, the following dress code is appropriate:

• Stylish enough to convince respondents that they are participating in something important, but not so much so as to make them feel under-dressed.

• Conservative in cut, rather than trendy.

• "Ladylike"—covered up. Gender and attractiveness not denied, but underplayed.

• Loose-fitting, permitting comfortable movement.

• The single concession to conspicuousness is *color,* which should be light enough or bright enough, close to the face, to invite attention, and encourage eye-contact.

It is important that the moderator provide for unexpected travel hazards. If baggage is checked it can be lost, so the foresighted moderator carries with her in the cabin a change of clothing, at least one copy of every form to be used in the interview (so that copies can be made), cosmetic "first aid," and an emergency tape recorder. She also carries the flight numbers of clients and the telephone number of the supplier.

On arrival, she reports to the supplier's field staff and checks on reconfirmations. She is usually one hour early in arriving at the facility on the first day of interviews, to check last minute cancellations, examine the room, and to serve as an anchor for clients to moor by when they arrive.

About 15 minutes before the interview is scheduled to start, she runs through the discussion guide, and does whatever "focusing exercise" is useful for her. For me, this consists of reminding myself that I am about to meet 12 people I have never met before, in whose minds lie the answer to a puzzle I am trying to solve. Also that this is the only chance I will ever have to crack their particular codes. And finally that they are as eager to tell me what I want to know as I am to receive the intelligence. This arms me with the principal instrument of effective moderators: *intense—but respectful—curiosity.*

In general, this is the same instrument used in clinical interviews, with the intensity and tempo stepped up. A clinician has the time to wait for a patient to reach insight at his or her own pace. Focus group moderators do not have this luxury. The curiosity, then, is intensified, but the rules of respect are the same. Even if I am very confident about what a panelist is "really" feeling or thinking, I cannot impose a judgment. I can merely inquire about it, using behavior and verbal report.

Nobody has a right to walk about in someone's head unless invited to do so. I make the same assumption in the moderator's hat that I do in the therapist's chair: that the person I am interviewing tells me the truth as he or she perceives it. If any deeper "truth" is to be revealed, the respondent and I go searching for it together.

Luckily, the other panelists—like other members in group therapy—are not similarly encumbered. And insight is frequently speeded by other members of the panel. A moderator concentrates on building a feeling of anticipation and excitement about the new human terrain which is about to be explored, and goes into the interview warmly open to all expressions of the participants, prepared more to be informed than to inform. It is important to remember that the *topical* experts in a focus-group interview (like the patients in early stages of psychotherapy) are the participants: they know all that is known about their feelings and reactions.

The *procedural* expert is the moderator, who knows how to engage attention and interest, encourage self-observation, fan controversy and provide the confident acceptance that makes confrontation (of the self and of others) easy, safe, and fun. The essential framework of a well conducted interview is composed of the moderator's *emotional approach*, an inquiring mind-set, and the *interactive* climate initially set up in the warm-up and introductions by the moderator.

There are a few "naturals," who almost *cannot* be bad group moderators, since the necessary characteristics are semi-instinctive. However, there are some basic tools and techniques which can help less favorably endowed moderators.

These include reasonably comfortable quarters, social lubricants (like food and preliminary small-talk), and the moderator's *presented self*. Of these, the latter is by far the most important, and is not a chance or haphazard matter. A highly skilled moderator has a fully-developed, consistent, clearly perceived "interview self" which she assumes as the role to be played during the interview. The interview self need not be strikingly different from the interviewer's everyday self. But it must be distinctive enough to permit disciplined control during the interview, and objectivity during the later interpretation.

This may appear to contradict the need for warm, sincere enthusiasm and interest, but it does not in fact. Warmth, involvement, respect, and the desire to understand are indispensable facets of a useful interview self. They cannot be counterfeited successfully. But these feelings are expressed through the unique filter which is the moderator's *presented self.*

Developing and assuming an interviewer role helps the moderator to understand more clearly what signals she is transmitting, and therefore to understand more clearly the responses she receives from respondents. It also makes it easier for the moderator to take risks. If, for example, the topic under discussion is likely to arouse some degree of anxiety in panelists, the moderator risks responses of anger, rejection, or defensive uncooperativeness from the panel. If she is functioning as her interview self, however, she is free to operate purely within the bounds of panelists' tolerable anxiety, without the further restrictions of her own anxious discomfort. She will not be squeamish about the group's affection or acceptance, because disaffection and rejection are aimed at the interview self, rather than the actual self.

As this assumed personality becomes more habitual and comfortable, it can operate without specific effort. It is put in place before the interview begins and remains for the rest of the two or three hour discussion.

It will have occurred to you already that there are some unspoken but essential activities performed by moderators frequently during the interview. These include *scanning* and *reviewing* to check which topics listed in the guide have been discussed thoroughly, touched on but dropped, or not mentioned at all; *tracking the nonverbal responses* to be considered for direct interpretation; and taking *time-checks* of discussion minutes remaining. But the interview must "flow," it must appear easy, natural, and seamless. This is not a purely aesthetic requirement. The moderator has made it clear to respondents during the warm-up: "We are going to do something exciting. It may be unfamiliar to you, but you can trust me. I will be interested and considerate, and I know what I'm about, so nothing unpleasant is going to happen to you. I am holding the reins loosely, but I can tighten them for security, whenever necessary." A loss of control (such as being unable to ease a transition) makes panelists feel unsupported.

In an ordinary conversation, it is difficult or nearly impossible to reconcile constant checking operations with uninterrupted fluency. Time is needed for checks and reviews—and there *is* no time for mental recess during an interview.

Obviously, while panelists are writing their introductory biographical notes, their record of brand use or their reactions to materials, the moderator can disappear for several minutes behind her *interview self*. But there are not many such idle moments, and the scanning goes on. The solution is that the *interview self* finally becomes habitual enough to run by itself for as long as a minute or two, smiling and secure (or with the puzzled look that invites explication), *even speaking*, while the moderator is consciously searching for an earlier remark which can be used as a transition to the next topic.

To repeat: the moderator's *instrument* consists of her actual self, with whatever skills she brings to the task. It is driven by *curiosity,* regulated by *respect,* and expresses itself through her *presented (or interview) self,* which performs other tasks throughout the interview with other tools. It may help to think of this multiplicity as being similar to a vacuum cleaner powered by electricity, aimed by a nozzle, with one master-hose or wand to which are attached an array of tools used to perform particular tasks.

This analogy is accurate as far as it goes, but it is mechanical, not relational in nature. While the panelists and the moderator are in the room together, the bond between them is first of all *contractual—a quid pro quo*. Through the recruiter, they have been promised a gratuity in return for two or three hours of their time. The moderator, after introducing all of the participants (including her interview self), sets the tone and then leads in to the topic the panelists are about to discuss and consider.

Whatever the persona assumed by the moderator—and this can be anything from boldly theatrical to nearly invisible—the focus always remains on the panel members. As the individuals become a group, the moderator-as-participant moves out of the action, so that the discussion can be *between* respondents rather than parallel and isolated moderator-respondent interaction. Thereafter, her activity as a panel member is limited to liaison between a shy or inarticulate panelist and the rest of the panel, or to playing devil's advocate to test the solidity of a consensus feeling. When a question needs exploration, she "fields" it, as often as she can, by referring it to another respondent to answer.

Facilitating group interaction presumes the moderator's ability to recognize when the group is floundering; the ability to distinguish for instance between a real exchange and "semantic ricocheting" (when two respondents appear to be addressing the same idea because they are using similar words, but are truly talking past one another). In such cases, the moderator does not charge in and explain, but again refers the problem to others in the group: "Isn't it funny, you both seem to be saying the same thing, but you appear to feel—and I certainly agree with you—that you are not exactly in agreement. Can anybody else figure out what's being said here?" If the group does not then jump in, or joins but fails to clarify, the moderator might then say something like: "I may not be picking this up right, but what I hear *you* saying is that a lot of advertising means a lot of money spent, which comes out of your pocket; while *you* are saying that if the manufacturer has enough faith in the product to invest that much in advertising, you are more apt to have faith in it yourself. Am I reading you both right?". She then again sits back and encourages the two respondents to settle the matter.

Topic bridging is another way in which the moderator participates with the group, making a smooth, subtle transition from one topic or focus of interest to another. If she is a sufficiently experienced scorekeeper who can remember not only which topics have been raised but who raised them, the moderator may find it convenient to rein in discussion of a potential bridging topic, hold it in reserve, and return to it at the right moment.

If, for example, there is a transition coming from advertising influence to purchase habits, the moderator can reserve a comment on point of purchase display, mentioned earlier in the discussion, and use it for transition: "You were saying earlier that you often go into a department store intending to buy something quite different, and walk out with a new perfume. What happens, at one of those shopping trips, from the time you enter the store until you hand over your money or charge card?"

When an imperceptible transition is impossible, when respondents don't make the move spontaneously, and when the bridge cannot be built from respondents' comments, the switch is made cleanly and swiftly, with the moderator directing. "This is almost too fascinating, and we could stay with it until next week. But you know we are interested in advertising. After all, this is a room in an advertising agency. So I am now going to show you. . . ." No feeling of string-pulling or manipulation filters through to the respondents.

Resolution is the last participatory responsibility of the moderator. In panel discussions (as in real life, for that matter) participants are better at "Hello" than "Goodbye." Some discussions move so clearly that only the most perfunctory kind of summation is necessary. But others are riddled with contradictions, and tangled with afterthoughts and disagreements. Especially when an interview has been emotional, contentious, or just very complex, respondents will need help in reaching some kind of closure: at minimum, a mutually agreed upon log of where the interview has taken them.

The moderator begins by asking the panel, as a group, to propose a summary. If this direct request draws a blank, the moderator can sometimes elicit a group summary nonetheless by beginning a summary but leaving a dangling sentence: "Let's see, if we had to describe to somebody what happened this afternoon, we could say. . . ." The tension of an unfinished sentence is very often enough to mobilize a rescue by some respondent, in the form of a tentative completion: "Well, I guess we said that insurance wasn't our favorite topic. But then it seems like we all had very definite ideas about it, and we were intrigued by most of the ads, especially that one with the serious hippie."

THE RESEARCHER AS CONTRACTOR

No accurate description of the relationship of the researcher to the client exists. The client of course contracts with the researcher for the delivery of a finished product. The researcher in turn subcontracts with the facility and/or the recruiter. Indirectly, she also subcontracts with the panelists. If *moderating* is all that is bought, the term "contractor" becomes a more accurate description of the researcher's role, but even so, it is incomplete. A moderator always hopes that there will be little client-input during the interview, but she never *forgets* that the client is there, behind the glass. (More about client deportment in Chapter 10.) That presence shapes some of her interaction with the respondents. She is likely to think many times during the interview, "I hope you heard that," or "Don't misunderstand what he is getting at," or "Please be insightful and recognize that this is all the response I can wrestle out of them on this topic." That is, she is aware of being the client's *agent* as well. But she is also a client-to-panelist and panelist-to client translator. She performs a *liaison* function.

Along the way, she has learned a good deal about the client's business. In the planning that precedes a focus-group project, she has immersed herself in the creation of the product (or service) of which the panelists are actual or potential consumers. She has identified with it, and thinks of it not only as the clients product, but as *hers* as well: her task becomes "How best to persuade consumers to buy what *we* are selling?" In the part of the discussion known as the "focus reveal," (when the moderator reveals the brand or company) panelists tend to identify with the client also, and to think: "It is X company that has sent this person to consult us." An effective—if somewhat cumbersome—way to increase sales would be to hold focus groups in every city in the country. Participants invariably feel complimented when corporations solicit their opinions.

And then there is the *personal* side of the client-researcher relationship. The moderator has made the enormous effort and taken the considerable risk of expressing exactly her thoughts and intuitions to the client. In an ideal arrangement, the client has done the same. For the duration of the project, the two are thereby bonded. If the project involves travel, they'll probably travel together, eat together, and together analyze each new intelligence that the panels provide. And in the end, the report (if a report is called for) is not written for posterity, or for a general audience, but this client alone.

Questions of accountability and authority are infrequent, but troubling when they happen. Who prevails when a client decides that it would be interesting to use a procedure he has heard about, but the researcher believes the procedure to be useless in or destructive to her relationship with the panelists? I have only once been called on to do something in a focus group interview which I felt could subvert the group process and antagonize the respondents. I explained that the procedure in question was not a qualitative process and neither belonged in the group format nor could adequately be performed and interpreted in such a setting. The client persisted. I could not move him. Because I felt sure the panelists would not be harmed—only turned off—by the procedure, I agreed to do it once I had covered everything else in the guide. I said that I did not consider it to be interpretable and would therefore leave it out of the report, but transcribe it for him separately.

I would not undertake a project with that client again; not because he pulled rank but because we had a major difference in our perception of what focus groups are and can do, and our preliminary communications failed to reveal this. Now during the preliminary talks with new clients, I ask each to describe his idea of a "good" group interview.

And what should a rapporteur do if she has been asked to answer a question—and agreed to address herself to that question—but finds in the process of interpreting the interview that the wrong questions have been asked? A major snack food manufacturer had decided that more of his product would be sold if it could be promoted as acceptable (healthy, parentally approved) to eat. This seemed plausible to me too. We planned a project in which snack eating by children and adults was explored. I talked to snackers, both children and adults, and to the parents of snack-eating children.

It soon became clear to me that lifting the taboos on consumption of this snack would rob it of much of its seductiveness. We had tested alternative advertising for the notion of *acceptability,* so that I was able to answer their original question (What is the best presentation of acceptability?). But it would have been misleading to restrict the interpretive report to the best expressions of a premise that, to these panels, made the product less, rather than more, attractive.

The client agreed, and added two new storyboards to the ones I was already showing. These restored some images of secrecy and of the hoarding of the product. But in one of them the parent is aware of, and easy about, the child's consumption of the snack, and in the other the parent is oblivious. These additions gave us three *degrees* of acceptability, which made clear which of the positionings should be tested quantitatively.

A moderator with no interpretive responsibility can have no say in what the client makes of her data. But if a report is to be written, the rapporteur is bound, not by the client alone but by her commitment to truthful reporting. If she senses that her interpretation will be unexpected and unwelcome, she should make plain the bases of the interpretation. The client should be allowed to dispute the interpretation and, if he is able to make a substantive case for his view, the report should be accommodated to include both interpretations.

THE MODERATOR AS PARTNER

"Partnerships" with the field staff can be more or less satisfactory, more or less friendly and close, more or less intricate. The existence of such partnerships is too new for the mores to have become established. The readily accessible focus group facility is a relatively new development. There were few before 1970, and the first were rudimentary. Some enterprising research houses sensed the promise in the focus-group business when there were relatively few of us doing it. A handful of them made minor adjustments to their existing facilities: e.g., took down a wall and utilized the small window previously used by a single client spotchecking research activity, such as questionnaire administration.

I realize that many focus-group researchers today can hardly imagine the time when there were no full-scale facilities. There are now a number of well established focus-group facilities whose staffs are professionally older than the moderators they service, so that defining the relationship frequently devolves onto the supplier rather than the researcher.

The researcher who is less than satisfied with the recruiting rigor of a facility has no recourse except to discourage the use of the facility in the future. But even this exercise of power can be sabotaged by a supplier who does not wish to pay for expert recruiting or doesn't want to work hard. Facilities sometimes attempt to side-step the moderator. Too frequently, they succeed. In their efforts to please the final bill-payer, the client, these suppliers offer "gourmet" spreads and plenty of alcoholic potables to the viewers, and provide takeaway souvenirs (pens, luggage tags and desktop utensils, among others). Or they may offer on-site diversions, like television games, to keep the clients amused and ensure their return.

Since researchers frequently compete for client business, word-of-mouth warnings that a once responsible facility has become client-oriented come late, if at all. Once the discovery has been made, there are three choices open to the rapporteur:

• Find a new facility hungry enough to be conscientious and support this supplier to clients, but guard the secret in the way connoisseurs hoard the names of new and fine restaurants.

• Resign oneself to the situation and trust to one's charm or to throwing oneself on the supplier's mercy. Or submit to outrageous over-charging.

• Try to negotiate ways to continue the relationship without hardship to either partner. Obviously, if this doesn't work, she can return to one of the other options. But it *may* work. Sometimes, the supplier has come to the conclusion that excellence on their behalf is not appreciated, and that everyone is there for a boondoggle and a movable feast. In such cases, a concerted effort to correct the perception of the field supervisor, plus credit given where due, may be all that's required.

The researcher who feels totally dependent on the facility and thinks that focus groups can only convene in such places will eventually learn otherwise. There are still many areas of nonmetropolitan America where no such niceties exist. Usually there are *recruiters* not far off, who can line up respondents and can assemble them in what is sometimes euphemistically describable as a "central location." If no trained recruiter is available, a quick canvas of churches in the area, or of schools and colleges, can generally turn up a talented amateur who can be pressed into service for recruiting. This is the way most focus groups were arranged no more than 30 years ago. The researcher may find such situations initially enervating, but they will build her confidence in her ability to work under adverse conditions. Less than a dozen years ago I was given a memorable project which is a case in point. A manufacturer of winter vehicles was dissatisfied with a proposed new advertising campaign. The manufacturer consented to retain the current agency if they would accede to and be guided by fresh exploratory research. I was asked to talk to the core user/buyer of these vehicles, and the client was sure he knew where they were to be found: in rural Canada and in the nonurban wilds of Minnesota and Michigan.

I located and telephoned two recruiters and a socially influential community hub, all willing to guarantee the presence of 10–12 qualified respondents at the chosen times and places. All the interviews were scheduled (impractically, as it turned out) for a two-week period in January. I set out on this project, accompanied by a management rep I'd met the day before, to interview whatever panelists had been recruited.

Actually the willingness of the men to meet with us was never a problem. There's not a whole lot to do in January in rural Canada and in nonurban Michigan and Minnesota. In Canada, we met in the homes of panelists, using a portable tape recorder to capture the interviews. Again, no problem. But the next set of interviews was a little more trouble.

Our plane out of Toronto was canceled because of weather. The management rep had a solution: he was a licensed navy pilot who still flew and he suggested we charter a plane.

Frequent travel doesn't necessarily result in the *sang froid* necessary to view as deliverance a plane trip in a private plane out of a socked-in airport, in January, with a stranger who flies as a hobby. By noon, the weather had lifted little. The first interview had been set for 7:30 that evening, and we had slim pickings among connecting flights in Chicago—if anything other than birds were flying—and a forty-mile cab ride from the Minneapolis airport. I called my supplier.

"Let's not give up," she said. "The men would be so disappointed. You keep calling me. I don't have to cancel before 6:00, because I can still reach the furthest one then, he's only fifty miles further north."

By one o'clock a small commercial plane had been found for "people who *really* have to get out today." We got seats and, to my surprise, reached Chicago safely—fifteen minutes and two buildings away from our originally-booked connecting flight. I had called the recruiter from Toronto, to say that things were, if not hopeful, a little less hopeless. Her reply, as before, was bracing. "Good," she carolled, "We'll expect you. You don't have to call unless you hit more delays."

There was no time to call from Chicago. We took our bags and ran to catch a plane which taxied out promptly, then sat on the runway for an hour deciding whether or not to take off. It finally did, landing us in Minneapolis at eight o'clock. There was a long line in front of every available telephone. We ran for a cab, found one, and instructed the driver on how to reach the church in whose basement recreation room there might or might not be a dozen men waiting. It took an hour to get there. We arrived at 9:30, two hours later than scheduled. They were there, and there were still sandwiches and coffee enough to last the night—luckily, as it turned out. We were all there for most of it, despite the fact that the wife of one of the men was in labor, and he (apologetically) made several progress-report calls.

Things were going so well that the president of the agency decided to join us at the two Michigan locations: the first was one town's library (after closing).The second location was the *least* urban area I have ever interviewed in. The only "central" room was the back room of a bar. The seasonal motel was opened for us with bare-minimum service, which included fireplace heat. The trip there had been grueling, over largely unmarked and very slippery back roads. We had no time to remove our coats; once behind the bar, we shed them and I saw for the first time that the agency president was wearing a fawn-colored suede suit. Fearing that this might get us off to a bad start, I suggested that he go in search of food for all of us. So when the panelists arrived in their

earflap-caps and mackinaws, they were not put off by the casual clothing the account rep and I were wearing. By the time the president
returned, his apparel caused no more than a brief gasp, audible on the
tape, but the look on their faces was an experience I shall never forget.

This is not merely a chronicle of endurance. The report presentation
for that project won me the only standing ovation I have ever received
from a client. And the agency kept the business two more years.

There is still adventure out there for anyone who wants to know what
groups *used* to be like. But nobody needs more than one such experience to appreciate the part played by a superior supplier. Like every
other professional I have a private map of most areas of the country representing good facilities, those which can be okay but can also be less
than okay, and those I have lately found nothing but poor. There are
very few facilities so bad that I have refused projects for which the
client insisted on using them. Any employer who is committed to
facilities that poor either does not know good recruiting from bad, or
may be on "commission" (getting a "cut" of the fee). In neither case do I
wish to participate.

What makes a supplier-moderator relationship a good one is hard to
describe, beyond agreeing on an operationally specific contract: "You
will be paid for panels for which all respondents are truly qualified. I
will *not* pay, either for recruiting or gratuities, in the case of non-
qualified panelists. Assuming that recruiters cannot always recognize
real nutcases or people with speech defects or language problems, I'll
pay for all of these, whether I use them or invite them to leave; but if
this happens often, prepare to miss me." And being up front: "If I *ever*
catch one of your recruiters packing a panel (instructing panelists to
respond in a particular, false way, in order to make quota), such
panelists will not be paid for, and you get *one* chance to discipline
recruiters. The second is the *last* time."

Beyond the mutual acceptance of this contract, there is no one interaction climate that can be defined unequivocally as good. There are a few
(fewer than a half-dozen) field supervisors I am personally so fond of
that I frequently make social time for them outside the facility. There
are probably fewer that *seek* this kind of interpersonal warmth. There
are a couple of first-rate facilities at which all parties keep their distance. Most are somewhere between. This is a matter of personal style
on both sides, and interferes minimally in the selection process.

Complaints are easier to make when no friendship is at risk. Indeed, one of my favorite suppliers is cool on personal relationships, but on the rare occasions when I have questioned *anything* about the panels (energy level is one such complaint, and this is hardly the fault of the recruiter) has immediately offered to convene a second group, at no charge other than the gratuities.

THE FOCUS-GROUP AS MICROCOSM

There is one additional interaction that deserves comment: the one *between* panelists, which exists beyond moderator-respondent reciprocity. It is not present invariably, and is always incomplete. But even in rudimentary form, it is often interpretable. It involves the role assignments, the process of diffusion of ideas, and the interchanges among the panel members acting as a small but distinct community. In cases where qualified panelists define a real-life population, distinct from the "average consumer" (for example, sufferers from headaches, arthritics, or those over 65), the interpretations of interaction processes within this segregated population can be critical in forging communication aimed to reach a parallel segment of the larger community.

Finally, when strong emotion intensifies the "grouping" process (as in the fire-extinguisher panels mentioned earlier—see Chapter 4). The context of the discussion is more truthful and has greater relevance to behavior than can ordinarily be found in any such artificial grouping. In the best case, the challenge of curiosity and discovery can effectively deepen the communication. The times when this happens are the times each rapporteur hopes for, waits for and rejoices in.

Chapter 7

Carry-On Luggage

I would be astonished to learn that "focus-group researcher" had become a frequent choice among those who are making career decisions. It seems unlikely that the children of today's moderator/rapporteurs would want to follow in their mothers' footsteps; unlikely because this vocation lacks both the saliency and the crisp functional distinction of, say, a fireman, a teacher, an entertainer or a nurse. When these children enter college, it remains an unlikely choice. No college curriculum I know of offers courses in it. It doesn't pack the promise of power or wealth.

Even granting the premise that a fully qualified rapporteur should have an advanced degree in one of the social sciences, few social science majors, at best, have focus groups in mind as the ultimate expression of their education. It is too nebulous a career goal to identify as a five- or six-year objective. It does not occupy an important place in society. In the narrower sphere of business, it is still off the beaten track, though by no means as esoteric as it once was. When polite strangers ask: "What is it that you *do* exactly?" the reply, "I do focus groups," is a sure conversation stopper.

Typically, the first practitioners went into focus-group research because the opportunity was there and they were curious. Also, as with all pioneers, the field was attractive to them partly as an uncharted frontier. Even today the conducting and interpreting of focus groups is especially appealing to those who have found other work simplistic, routinized, or unchallenging. My bet is that it is a second or third career choice.

Practitioners of focus-group research come to their calling not only carrying the intellectual equipment they were born with, but also with whatever additional knowledge and proficiency they have accrued on the way to matriculation. They carry, too, a history of the ways in which they have learned to use both their innate and acquired toolboxes. Focus-group research accommodates a wide range of styles and presumptions. It thus retains its original idiosyncratic and expressive repertoire. And because flexibility is still important in recruiting new blood, regulation of professional activity—beyond the setting of credentials for competence—has very low priority. Each convert to focus-group research brings along a different valiseful of interviewing techniques and interpretive principles. The short lifespan of focus-group interviews as a career option, plus the methodological flexibility which has accrued to it, haven't encouraged standardization of either the moderating or the interpretations of focus-groups. There is, to date, no single code of behavior. Each individual practitioner must accept the responsibility for establishing and following her own bylaws and rules of procedure, based on her capabilities and on what she endorses as "right"—meaning both efficient and ethical—behavior. The following account of how and from what sources *my* behavioral code evolved is offered more as an instance than as a pattern.

Assume that the rapporteur has had a prior career in another field. She probably has some code of professionalism and propriety in the context of her previous work history. Her first step in transposing her standards of performance is to become aware of the attitudes and practices which made her expert and ethical in discharging her earlier obligations. For me, the first step was to analyze the behavioral choices I regularly make in the clinical situation, to see which attitudes and actions are directly applicable to dealing with the people I encounter in focus-group interviews. Making the transposition successfully requires that I understand, too, the ways in which the focus-group situation *differs* from clinical interactions.

In addition to interactions with people, the other part of what I carry in my "overhead rack" is a set of conceptual tools for handling data, only some of which are readily transferable to focus-group data. In my six years as grantee and chief investigator in research of my own design, the scientific rigor—or lack of it—which characterized the six-year term of the research grant, was totally my responsibility. Whether or not the

habits and values appropriate in that situation fit this one, it's an inescapable fact that this kind and degree of accountability, once assumed,
is very hard to put down.

Perhaps basic research is uncommon in the backgrounds of focus-
group professionals, but those who *do* come to focus-groups with some
"scientific" background will save time and confusion by understanding
at the outset that there is nothing in the focus-group method *per se* that
engages or meshes with scientific consideration. Whichever of the
scruples of scientific discipline that may be applied to the interview itself, or to the interpretive operation, are brought to it by the rapporteur
and reside in her head. If concepts like independence of variables,
reliability, or validity are brought to bear on a focus group project, they
are brought there by the researcher. They are no part of the theoretical
foundations of the technique, but are strictly artifacts of the individual
who performs it.

DEALING WITH PEOPLE: 1. THE PANELISTS

Chronologically, the moderator's first dealings with panelists are indirect, mediated by a recruiter who asks the questions the moderator has
set down in the screener. The screener usually begins with a question
about the panelists' previous experience as participants in other groups.
The ideal panelist is generally thought to be a focus-group virgin: someone who is not merely a first-time panelist, but who has never *heard* of
focus-group interviews. But because certain demographic slots are targeted by many products, and because a 50 mile radius from the field
facility is the widest trawl a client can reasonably hope for, a virgin
panelist these days is nearly a creature of fable, like the unicorn.

This doesn't mean that we have depleted our stores of qualified respondents. At least it doesn't mean that to any researcher with a clinical
background. Clinicians learn that retests are valid if retesting is done
after an interval of at least six months. This applies even to fairly
straightforward tests like those used to estimate intelligence: tests with
right and wrong answers, many of which can be researched in the interval. Clinical testing also prescribes a pretty tight set of interpersonal ex-
changes between tester and subject, which do not give the subject much
flexibility of role participation. Presumably it would be a snap to learn
how to be a good test taker.

In focus groups, there are no right and wrong answers that can be found in an encyclopedia. Furthermore, the role of *panelist* is infinitely more complex, and thwarts learning because there is a different panel mix each time, and probably a different moderator too, for each consecutive panel participation. Also, the panelist will probably be discussing another topic for which her previous panel participation has not prepared her. Considering all these factors I conclude that even if the birthrate should drop to zero, we have the life-span of most moderators to go, at the very least, before we run out of usable panel members.

The degree of freshness I find useful in panels is, by clincial reckoning, recoverable in no more than six months. But to be on the safe side, I usually require that panelists have had no prior experience on other panels in the preceding six months, and none with the product category we will be discussing within the past year. I have found this convention to be perfectly satisfactory for discouraging the development of "professional" panelists (who are in any case more annoying than destructive of group climate, providing the discussion guide is sufficiently novel). The *blind screening* discussed briefly in Chapter 2 further hinders panelists who are trying to be "good at it." It's hard to write an interview script if one is not sure what the topic will be. (Panel selection is more fully discussed in Chapter 10.)

Panelist eligibility, as judged by test-retest validity, is only the first place *chronologically* at which my clinical training enters the picture. It is far from being the first in *importance*. Much more central to the ethical handling of groups are issues that involve mutual trust: the panelists' expectation of *confidentiality*, the *credence* given by the moderator to what the panelists say, the attitudes of mutual *respect*, and finally, the *tone*, or ambience of the discussion.

Confidentiality

In the clinical situation, the promise of confidentiality is promptly and cleanly made and scrupulously honored. In the interview situation, complicated by the mirror, by audio recording, and sometimes by a video camera, promises of a similar degree of confidentiality are impossible to make. The best approximation I can offer is to inform panelists, as speedily as possible, of these obstacles. (See warm-up transcription, Appendix E.) Telling the truth about the mirror, the recordings and the video cameras is probably no longer optional. Many panelists know or guess their presence. Before the advent of comfortable viewing rooms and mirrors big enough to accommodate the Mormon Tabernacle choir, we often used TV monitoring and adjoining hotel rooms. I elected to tell respondents about this set-up as well. Moral or ethical questions aside, it was and is a good idea on a purely practical basis. A panelist in search of a bathroom could stumble into a viewing session and, on returning to the panel, blow the participants' focus as high as an elephant's eye.

And, feeling as strongly as I do about the ability of most people to interpret nonverbal signals, it is virtually certain that panelists would pick up from me that they were being unfairly asked to tell the whole truth and nothing but the truth, while I as moderator was withholding important information from them. Although it is a remote possibility, this kind of invasion of privacy without informed consent may be legally punishable.

Strangely enough, I have only twice, and only from a single panelist in each instance, met with any objection to the mass-eavesdropping. The first instance was the beginning of a panel discussion on foundation garments. The woman expressed discomfort, but volunteered to stay when I offered to excuse her. The second occasion was a male panelist who, on learning that the product to be discussed was a moist cleansing tissue, to be used after evacuation, said "I can't possibly talk about that with people watching." He was excused. In neither case did other panelists exhibit discomfort. In fact, the expression of discomfort seemed to bond the panel more closely. In the first case, the panel became warmly supportive of the woman who gamely stayed. In the second, the remaining men felt comparatively stronger and braver than the exiting one.

I have sometimes felt uncomfortable *for* panelists. One such project required women to discuss vaginal deodorants, which they did, complete with demonstrations of usage—and cheery waves to observers behind the mirror. Panelists have removed false teeth, acted out attacks of hemorrhoids, discussed the ways in which upper respiratory infections interfered with their sex lives, and debated with each other over which of them experienced the more embarrassing effects of flatulence. It is not uncommon for a panelist to preface a confidence with the query: "Is this confidential?" In such cases, I say that *I* will not talk about it, that it is "confidential, given the presence of viewers" or ". . . of the camera." Such remarks have never discouraged the confider.

I liken such potentially embarrassing disclosures to the volunteering of similar material, and to truly searing confidences, in the clinical interview. The panelist, like the patient, is trying to live up to the promise of telling the whole truth, and simultaneously is testing his/her acceptability as a unique individual to the moderator/therapist or to the rest of the world, as represented by other panelists. When this happens, I feel it would be much more damaging to say something like "Are you sure you want to tell us this?" than to treat the sensitive material as a proper and interesting subject of discourse. The panel invariably either supports—or in some cases anticipates—this attitude.

Credence

Credence in the focus-group situation, as in the clinical interview, is an act of will on the interviewer's part. Specifically, the interviewer makes the assumption that panelists are telling the truth. The assumption is frequently tested in the course of most discussions, and must hold fast even when a panelist's statement is empirically improbable ("I have never bought a soft drink because of advertising.") or internally inconsistent ("I never watch a single commercial, because I hate those awful jingles like . . ."). The moderator can press for qualification ("You may be the only living American who is never swayed by advertising when you are choosing soft drinks. On what basis *do* you make your choices?"), but must not waver in her belief of what the panelist says. Disbelief shows. It usually results in sullen withdrawal, which turns a respondent to stone for the remainder of the interview, or in angry insistence on the statement, which colors and distorts that panelist's future responses. Sometimes the panel disciplines a member ("If you never listen to commercials, how do you know about that jingle?"). More often the panelist sets the record straight himself.

Respect

The attitude of respect includes acceptance of panelist responses as true. In addition, it includes another assumption: that each respondent's contribution is important. It is exhibited by thoughtful consideration of every serious expression of a participant. No response is dismissed as misperception or wrongheadedness. The interviewer stimulates discussion of such points ("You look as if you disagree with that idea. Why and how?"), but does not, verbally or nonverbally, ignore or disdain it.

Respect does *not* include tolerating panelists who use the interview to make jokes or to ridicule another's contributions. A direct address usually stops repetitive sniping, and it often brings back into the discussion a bright and productive panelist who had emotionally wandered away. For instance: "You've had your fun. You know that you are here to work, and that's what you are being paid for. There's no harm in enjoying the discussion, and if you can think of some way to make it more enjoyable, I'll listen to suggestions. But you're all here because we need some answers to our questions. If you can't help us, I'll excuse you, but maybe the others in the group *can* help."

Not that the atmosphere must be grim or solemn: a humorous observation injected into an otherwise weighty conversation can sometimes ease tension in the discussion of a difficult subject or a problematic product. A group of women, in an interview about condoms, had their consciousness raised more than was comfortable. One woman had talked about her fears of uterine devices. ("You hear about infections from IUDs making women sterile.") Another had discussed the perils of "sponges" and diaphragms. ("The sponge is a little like a tampon. You can get toxic shock from it. Or even a diaphragm I think, if you leave it in the way they tell you . . ."). The women, as a group, had raised the issue of condoms. ("It's the only safe thing. Well, not safe because it can slip off. And if you make it tight, couldn't it cut off circulation?") One of the panelists, outraged, summarized the interchange: "An IUD can kill you or sterilize you. You get toxic shock from sponges and diaphragms. You suggest a condom and he says: 'That's not good for me!' Make it tighter. If they die, they die!" There was a sharp intake of breath from the group, followed by two full minutes of relaxing laughter.

Respect includes providing support when a panelist really needs it, but this is seldom. However tender the moderator may feel toward a shy or anxious panelist, she should never allow the respondent to evade the task. It is apt to be a disservice to rush in with succor. It is *always* a disservice to do so prematurely. When the panelist says "I can't," a moderator's friendly but firm "Try" keeps the respondent anchored in the group, preserves the purpose, and may give the panelist the heady experience of being better than he or she thought. Allowing a shy person to drop out—accepting his or her evaluation of what's "impossible"—implies that the moderator too thinks the panelist's contribution is unimportant, or the panelist weak.

Moreover, it fails to respect the *other* interpersonal commitment the moderator makes: her responsibility to the client.

Tone or Ambience

The tone (mood, ambience, color) of a panel discussion ultimately depends on the temperaments of the panelists, individually and collectively. It also reflects the spirit in which the products or services which are the interview topic are seen and used by panelists. The moderator is tuned to these eddies of feeling and thought during the interview, and responds to them.

Her own contributions to the tone of the group are predetermined in some degree by the attitudes described above. But in addition, her demeanor reflects her own perception of the task. My own intentional contribution to the group ambience of any discussion is a feeling of purposive excitement: there is work to be done, which has direction and accomplishment, and that work is also an uncharted adventure. This attitudinal bent has two advantages. First, empirically, it seems to work well. Second, phenomenologically, it fits. It is the way I really feel.

DEALING WITH PEOPLE: 2. THE CLIENT

In terms of the formal therapeutic contract, the client relationship actually resembles the clinical situation more than the panel relationship does. For one thing, the problem I am engaged to help solve is the client's problem. For another, the bill is his too. To a clinically naive client, such an observation might be offensive. Even today, people who have never experienced therapy (either as therapist or as patient) misperceive the therapeutic process as a "sick" or "crazy" patient being treated by a "well" or "sane" therapist. Worse, they may view the process as a dialogue between two lunatics, one of whom has an advanced degree.

Since this is not my perspective it is difficult for me to keep in mind that some clients would be insulted to be treated like, or likened to, a patient. I must constantly remind myself not to work with clients as I work with patients. (I suspect that other clinical rapporteurs will recognize the difficulty.) What this means, among other things, is that the researcher who is at other times a clinician must keep the partition up in client relationships. She cannot afford to deal with clients in the free, clear, non-euphemistic manner she has learned in dealing with patients.

A quantitative researcher with whom I have shared a number of projects, and whom I greatly admire for his unfailing lucidity - and for his methodological resourcefulness, had set up a planning meeting for a problem we were to tackle jointly. Accountability for the project was his. He had sub-contracted with me for exploratory group inter-views and so had become my client. As the meeting progressed, it became clear to me that he was uneasy with the fact that I could not forecast what the results of the focus group interviews might be. I was right with him there and said that the unpredictability of the method was frustrating to me too, especially at the outset of a project. I further promised to post-mortem with him after each of the interviews.

He was still miserably tense and uncomfortable, and reminded me that no secondary plans could be undertaken until we knew "where the groups are going." This is a feel-ing I have experienced before myself. Plunging into focus-group discussions, in blind faith that I will ask the right questions to get the answers that will light our darkness, I still wonder sometimes if the parachute will open.

And now I couldn't bury *my* anxiety at letting control of the problem pass into the hands of panelists I hadn't yet met, although I was in a position, as moderator, to sal-vage disastrous panels. I suddenly realized how much more anxious and powerless *he* must feel. Sympathizing with his problem, and with the best of intentions, I forgot myself and asked him directly: "What is there that I can do that will give you the feel-ing of control you need?"

His response was electrifying. He was outraged. He had heard my question as pejora-tive and presumptuous. If I had intended to suggest that he was "a controlling person" or in fact intended *any* diagnostic speculations, his reaction would not have caught me so by surprise. As it was, I understood—too late—both the outrage and the several months it took to cool, and was circumspect enough not to try to repair it by explaining.

Clinicians are actually the least likely people to offer diagnoses when they are not asked to do so. Not only because they are bound to respect the privacy of others' thoughts, but also because a clinician, maybe bet-ter than people in other fields, knows humbly that the human behavioral repertoire is . . . the human behavioral repertoire. We all have matched sets of feelings. If therapists are quick to recognize their patients'—or anyone else's—feelings, it is because they have felt that way too. Others' feelings are accessible to a therapist because they are familiar to her. She is not likely to treat expressions of feeling condescendingly.

But this is not common knowledge. It is prudent for clinicians to be-ware of commenting on clients' feelings unless the client has formally acknowledged them. Otherwise, even a feckless and good-humored remark like "Here's a report that will really lift your spirits," coming from her, can be received as: "You're a depressive."

The analogy of client dealings and dealing with patients is, in any case, incomplete. It is true that the client's problem is the one we are engaged in solving. And the client, like the patient, pays for the help. But in two basic ways, at least, working with clients is very different from working with most patients. Patients possess a degree of *motivation* to solve their problems, and a degree of *commitment to the therapist* which should be no part of the rapporteur's expectations in client dealings.

A patient experiences his problem as *pain*. And he *owns* the pain. It hurts him. The degree to which a client experiences his marketing problem as personal anxiety or depression varies considerably. But it is most uncommon for a client to feel that, for instance, his career or his authority is dependent on the outcome of a project. He *knows* the problem, but neither embraces it as his nor essays the introspective work necessary to solve it. If he locates the problem at all, he places it in the minds of the consumers. He is only the victim of their unfortunate attitudes. In clinical terms, he would be like the man who says: "I have a problem. My wife thinks she's an aardvark. I want you to talk to her and to some of her associates, to find out how it affects them. Then come back and tell me what is the matter with her and what I should do about it."

A secondary effect of the client's feeling little or no pain and eschewing introspective work is that he is likely to resist a change in perspective. *Newness panic* is very nearly a universal malady. But when a patient resists a new idea or prescription for change the therapist simply offers it again, as often as the opportunity presents itself. The rapporteur has very limited access to the client's mind and must therefore make an effort in each meeting to get innovative ideas accepted. Her input must be persuasive or downright compelling.

Now consider the degree of a patient's commitment in the clinical enterprise. A patient characteristically comes to a particular therapist he has chosen asking not: "Can I be helped? And how much would you charge me for it?", but "Can you help me?" A client usually has selected the "cure" already: focus-groups. He comes to one, or several, researchers and asks how quickly and inexpensively he can get the work done, much as he might ask a physician to "give me an antibiotic." And often it is the generic remedy he asks for.

Oddly, the *better* a client's experience with focus-group projects the *less committed* he is likely to be to particular moderators or rapporteurs. The more accomplished the moderator he has observed and the more persuasive the reports he has read, the easier the whole thing looks to him. Like something he could do himself, if only he had the time. Good interviews don't sweat, and good reports don't strain. There are no mysterious instruments used or computer printouts to be interpreted. The assumptions made deal merely with the workings of human beings, about which he is as qualified as the next person since he is one.

In fact, the client might define the "best" interview as the one least taxing to him, as he sees and hears it behind the mirror. This would be the orderly and slow-paced format of sequentially interviewing each panelist on each question in the guide. No crosstalk, no contradictions, no struggling to follow the proceedings, and no doubt about what has happened.

Much more demanding, for moderator and viewer alike, is a discussion led by a moderator whose expertise enables panelists to generate the excitement they need for exploration, who is able to elicit and use the volatile, unpredictable, effortful, communicative escalade of focused interaction. Such an interview, with overlapping responses and bewildering turn-arounds can be hard for the eavesdropping client even to penetrate. To add to his perplexity, the client often realizes that his perception is quite different from that of the rapporteur who triumphantly assures him the interview was "very rich," but answers his query about what it means with an airy "I don't know yet."

A therapeutic journey begins with a dialogue between therapist and patient about how each perceives what they are about to embark on. Surely a focus-group project, to which the client brings less personal commitment, should include some discourse about the data-gathering phase—at least tactful instructions on how to listen.

DEALING WITH DATA

In the world of marketing research, it is unusual for qualitative techniques—especially focus-group interview studies—to be mentioned in the same sentence with "scientific." The convention among marketing researchers is to divide the realm, like ancient Gaul, into three provinces: *exploratory* research, *descriptive* research and *causal* research. These three denominations, in the order given, refer not only to different data sources and data-gathering operations, but are also hierarchical in the sense of chronological progress ("exploratory" precedes "descriptive" and both precede and prepare for "causal") and also in the sense of increasing scientific rigor. Exploratory research is the least "scientific," causal research, the most. Convention further specifies that focus group interviews are modally or solely within the province of exploratory research, since exploratory studies are the least rigorous.

But a rapporteur who has previously packed scientific scruples with her change of clothing and emergency moisturizer cannot dispense with them just because nobody expects her to have them. The problem is that there is no consensus about where and how such scruples fit, no precedent at all for the existence of scientific pretensions.

Reliability

The question of *reliability* is relatively easy to address. *Reliability*, understood as the likelihood that an infinite number of similar projects will yield similar results, is best approached by *replication of group interviews*. Replication is essential within interviews at one location, to guard against the possibility that a particular panel of twelve people are recent emigrants from remote space, whose contributions will not be seen again in this galaxy. If at all possible, replication should also be undertaken in two or more locations, to guard against the possibility of local aberrations.

The importance of multiple group interviews increases with chronological age from legal maturity to legal retirement. These are not arbitrary designations. Adolescents are more peer-centripetal (more conforming as a group) than adults between the ages of 21 and 65. An accurate study of the feelings and behaviors of a few adolescent groups is apt to be broadly applicable. So far, people over 65—at least those in cluster-communities—seem to be more peer-centered as well. Though as there come to be more people who survive retirement, and survival time also increases, they may evolve more options, and more individuality.

Validity

What on earth does a science-minded focus-group researcher do about the question of validity? Even within the same interview, the four kinds of input (verbal, written, behavioral, and projective) may suggest contradictory interpretations. (Relationships between these four kinds of input are discussed in more detail in Chapter 5.) This would be easy enough to handle if we could impose some system of ascendancy by which one of these data sources is "more true" than another. But such an assumption could not be acceptable to a social scientist whose beliefs are even moderately holistic. And if we *could* come to terms with simultaneous contradiction, that still leaves untouched the question of validity over time. Is it safe to assume that an individual's immediate reaction (allowing that one's interpretation of that is valid) would still apply at some time in the future? Or is it only a momentary truth that would be altered by time? If the response would change with time, have we any formula for guessing in what ways it would change? Finally, if the ultimate criterion of marketing research is marketplace behavior, can any degree of *predictive* validity be claimed for a focus-group project?

Since the focus-group method is both too new and too flexible for any significant accretion of theory, users must build their own scientific structures empirically to accommodate the degree of such structure each one personally needs to function comfortably. I find that I need quite a lot, but most of it remains internal. Everyone *else* is uncomfortable if I sound scientific.

Starting at the beginning, one classical article of scientific faith is that you can't measure everything at once. You need a place to stand. The givens I rely on are left over from my clinical research and have mainly to do with people.

Two axioms I accept without question. The first is that all people draw their responses from the same collection of possibilities. I need not ask, then, whether a given reaction which has appeared in one or two groups will or will not appear in the population at large. It has *already* appeared in several individuals, and if it is possible for them it is possible for everyone. The only question to be answered is what the weighting of the response will be. I will make a general guess, but *counting* is not my proper business. That is for quantitative research to decide, once I have described the reaction as faithfully as possible.

The second axiom is that people are truthful. That is, every message they transmit—verbally or not, consciously or not—is a true piece of information about the sender, if only I am adept enough to decode the message. Moreover, I believe this kind of honesty to have *resilience*. I perceive that humans are communicators by evolution and by choice; if I am *not* adept enough to read the message right the first time, *and if the senders understand me to be both respectful and interested*, they will keep on transmitting until they are satisfied that the message has been received.

Beyond these two articles of faith, it has always seemed to me an inescapable fact that any research with subjects at least as advanced as the rhesus monkey (and maybe back as far as the paramecium) must eventually base its theories on the individual as an organic whole. The dualism by which certain neuronal functions are falsely abstracted and called "mental" or "psychological," while functions of other parts of the body are called "somatic" or "behavioral," are simply conveniences for the researcher. Such compartmentalizations become reified and spawn theoretical gibberish. The "mind" is located in the brain, which is in the head, and the head is only one part of the organism, albeit the primary part, or at least the part which interests us. Moreover, the actions of the left hand are, in fact, registered in the brain, so the right hand may know what the left is doing.

More to the point, the way in which a person does behave or intends to behave in the marketplace is registered too. Or at least all of the skeleto-muscular directives ever sent—including those in the marketplace—are registered as something analogous to carbon copies stored at command headquarters. The switchboard there is busy, make no mistake, and the stack of carbon copies is high. But the message is there, for anyone willing to take the time and make the effort to find it. I guess that this boils down to the cheery assumption that "Truth" is available in any respondent, and that it can be discerned, without the violation of the subject's black box, if one is ingenious enough and persistent enough to break the code.

If truth is indeed there maybe I can uncover it. Truth includes not only large and lofty ideas, but also the humble truth about whether these individuals will be persuaded by whatever I present to them to buy the bread or antiperspirant or ballpoint pens my client is selling. This belief drives the qualitative researchers who subscribe to it to extract from panelists as much information as possible during an interview, and then to scrutinize what has been extracted without oversimplifying or discarding one kind of expression in favor of another.

In more scientific terminology, this means that I am willing to run more risk of *alpha* error than *beta* error. That is, I'd rather "find" something that isn't there than miss something that is. Once a hypothesis has been articulated, it can be checked. You can't check hypotheses that are never made. The worst thing that can happen if a researcher makes an alpha error is that she has been wrong or silly. The perils of beta error are that the researcher may miss something important, and mislead the client. Deciding that beta errors are the more serious of the two types has some implications for the method of interpretation of the complex raw data of focus-groups. (More about interpretation in Chapter 8.) Since it is a given that all of the respondents' communications are valid, the question asked of the data is not "Which one is true?" but "What is the truth that contains all of these expressions?"

In a beauty aid study in Mexico, all of the men and women interviewed said flatly that they never thought about skin color (lightness/darkness) although it was clear from the way they talked about skin care that color was related to attractiveness and was also an indication of perceived social class. Equally unanimously, they said that the way skin looked was one of the most important elements of attractiveness. Asked what one problem they would request a "fairy godmother" to solve, each solemnly said that he or she would ask to get rid of the "manchas" (spots), and each with deep sighs, would tap several facial areas on which (you've guessed it) the skin was unmarked and the coloration even.

The final report informed the client that although skin color was very important, it could not be directly addressed in copy because these individuals truly "did not *think* about skin color." Nothing could be done about it, and thinking about it was only painful. It further informed him that although important emotional issues cannot be easily denied, the mechanism of symbolizing general anxiety in localized fashion is a kind of repressive compromise familiar in hysteria. The final paragraphs of the predisposition section read: "Bleaching creams are not much used by our respondents. They feel them to be too irritating, and think they may be damaging to the skin if used steadily. Also, it is easy to infer, a bleaching cream exposes too frankly and uncomfortably the light/dark issue. Of the several skin creams they use for the spots none is formulated as a bleaching cream. The best formulation to be made of all of these conflicting statements is that imaginary "spots" are best removed by the power of imagination which created them. Therefore, the fact that A [the product] is not itself a bleach is not a promotional disadvantage. Direct confrontation of the question is offensive. The words "white" or "fair" or "pale," or homonyms, buried in the copy or juxtaposed to defensible claims, may motivate to purchase. Moreover they may provide fulfillment for the hopes they arouse. For example, a popular idiom here for "hitting the bulls eye" is *dar en el blanco*.

Initially, many hypotheses are developed, to fit all of the conflicting facts. Their number is only limited to those for which established psychological and/or physiological mechanisms can be found as possible substantiation. Subsequent data then confirm some hypotheses and contradict others. Those which remain when all the data have been taken into account become the hypotheses on which implications are based. The method of systematic reduction of hypotheses is familiar to psychological testers.

Finally, I bring with me to my research my personal views about the meaning of the work I do. Probably all other researchers do as well. It is fashionable these days to regard advertising as the worm in the apple, "creating needs" where none existed and obliging consumers who do not need the goods advertised to imagine that they do. I've never been able to swallow that one. Consumers do not seem to me to be such empty-headed dopes as cynics suggest. I believe that consumers (including myself and all my ilk, advertising copywriters and account managers and the advertisers they serve) have enduring needs for things there are never enough of to go around, like beauty, power, and wisdom.

We live in a materialistic society, like it or not. The good news is that in a country where material goods can be purchased but power, wisdom, and beauty cannot, it is possible for those who are talented to create emblems. Good advertising can persuade people who may never be able to credit themselves with those valuable characteristics that for instance, owning a particular kind of car will endow the owner with (some) power, or that possessing a particular set of books will bring the possessor (a kind of) wisdom, or that use of a particular beauty aid will increase (to an extent) the user's beauty. What's more, in a materialistic society, it *works*. If that is not a service, I don't know what is.

Chapter 8

Writing the Report

Writing a report, I believe, is as intimately unique a process as writing anything else. I've always admired those who outline and keep index cards for noting down interpretive ideas as they come. My own reports are always explosions into written form from a head in which everything has fermented to the bursting point.

I identify as the *writing* of a report everything that intervenes between the gathering of the data and the presentation of the final report. Purists are welcome to point out that *two* processes actually fill that period, that the various materials which contain the information for the report must first be interpreted, and that it is this interpretation which is rendered as a report. In practice, the processes of interpreting and writing are so tightly interwoven that they are nearly impossible to separate.

The rapporteur on the brink of writing an interpretive report is now burdened by the same axioms that seemed to simplify the interview phase of the project. In particular, she is slowed in making her choices by the assumption that all of panelists' communications, written, oral and behavioral, at any level of consciousness are equally true communications. While the discussion is in progress, this assumption lightens the moderator's task by relieving her of the necessity to ferret out lies, and simultaneously increases her discernible respect for panel members. In a sense, it also simplifies interpretation in the same way. Everything communicated is fully and equally true—she need not scan for lies.

But the bad news is that she is left with a puddle of truth. There is no pattern in this data until the interpreter imposes one. It is a little like putting together a jigsaw puzzle before the picture has been glued on to it. The picture—the final report form—is in the bottom of the box. The rapporteur can glue it in place when she has put all the pieces together. A stable and coherent design will then be made of the scattered fragments.

FRAMING THE REPORT: BACKGROUND AND PURPOSE

In the introductory "Background and Purpose" section of the report, the large, general questions addressed by the research are presented. The rest of the report will be oriented to these questions. In theory, the earlier the background and purpose section is in place, the better. It is a tremendously good idea for the researcher to write this section *before* moderating the groups and have it waiting in the typewriter when she returns from the field.

• This is the *coolest* and most stable part of the report. It does not require the creative heat from the pressure of the deadline. There is no *need* to delay it.

• At the point of starting a report, the interpreter's mind is crackling with random fragments of data. *Any* visible ordering is balm.

• If she has even a draft of the Background and Purpose section to toss into her suitcase, the rapporteur can use time with the client in the field to check, yet again, their agreement on the goals of the project.

However, there are always last minute problems—forms to assemble, plane and hotel reservations to synchronize, crises in the field—any one of which can eat up pre-interview time. The time necessary to reflect on and construct a "Background and Purpose" statement, is a luxury that even a moderately busy researcher can rarely afford before the interviews begin. The closest I have actually come is drafting a few "B and P"s on boarding passes and ticket envelopes.

MAKING THE DATA ACCESSIBLE

Once the statement of purpose is in place, both in written form and in the rapporteur's mind, it is time to systematize both the data and the intellectual apparatus that must decode it. I suspect that the options for "next steps" at this point are chosen idiosyncratically, depending on unique individual patterns of problem solving. The most congenial procedure for me is to convert written responses into charts, and audio (or video) tapes into transcripts. These become the worksheets for the act of writing the report.

Specifically, all the personal information on the demographic forms and from the self-descriptive statements which each panelist writes preparatory to introducing him or herself to the group is "charted" on ledger sheets (11" x 17" or larger), broken out by group number and headed "Sample." (See transcript of sample "warm-up" in Appendix E.)

Similarly, panelists' notations on brand-usage, brand personality, occasion for usage or any other predisposition topics assigned for panelists' writing will be charted by group and headed "Predispositions." Chart entries are made for written responses to each of the materials presented, and labeled "Reactions to Concepts" (or "to Product," or "to Storyboards," etc., according to the material presented). Behavioral notes on attention, intensity, discomfort, and such, inferred from postural, expressive, vocal, and other nonverbal observations, are inserted as reactions to materials or to predisposition topics.

The working transcripts of the taped discussions differ from detailed *verbatim* transcripts in two ways:

• Each topic or question addressed by the panel is *summarized* verbatim (excerpts are used for illustration).
• Vocal modifiers (pitch, tone, cadence, timbre) are noted (for the moderator's contributions as well as panelists').

Clearly, interpretation has already begun. Summarizing interactions entails making judgments about which contributions are germane and pivotal and which pertain to personal goals like ingratiation or image-management. Writing has also begun with the selection of *verbatim* responses to be included in the final report.

SHIFTING GEARS

The process of readying data serves an internal function as well. In any accelerated learning program, *total immersion* in the subject to be learned is recommended. If the project has proceeded well, the rapporteur will have collected a substantial, if disorganized, primer of potential information bearing on the client's particular problem. But she must understand that the intelligence contained in her mind and in the charts is potential, or better, preliminary. Before the client can use it as a basis for further activity it must be translated: decoded and then recoded. As translator, the rapporteur must totally immerse herself not only in the topics to be included in her report but in the mood and expression of each panel as well.

Listening to the tapes, rather than trusting memory, is an important part of this immersion. It is spendthrift of time and energy, but it is an activity whose value can be proven to any thoughtful researcher using a single project for illustration. No matter how promptly or how carefully an interview is reconstructed from memory, listening to tapes will provide a few surprises, and can sometimes totally shift the weight of feeling attributed to the group's responses. This is so for at least three reasons:

• As indicated in earlier chapters, the moderator is very *busy,* during even the blandest and tamest of interviews. And the number of simultaneous observations made and tasks performed increases algebraically with the complexity of the questions, the disparity between panelists, the energy and tempo of the group, the intricacy of any product sampling or demonstration, the demeanor of the client, and the emotional loading which attaches to a product, or advertising communication, or to a manufacturer's image. Because her mind is sent on a bewildering number of errands at any given moment in the discussion, she is bound to miss turns of phrase, softly made comments, shiftings in persuasion, feelings expressed during crosstalk, and so on.

• Trusting to memory also requires that the moderator's recall be exact in a number of modalities. To remember accurately, she must reach backward cognitively to understand the *sense* of what has been said. She must remember sequence accurately (which of two comments came first may affect the persuasive vector of the group). Her *auditory* memory must also be infallible. Long before creating language, human beings understood each other intuitively, emotionally, by tone, pitch, cadence, and all of the other nonverbal aspects of vocal production. These remain throughout life as *carriers* of the intellectual *content*—the "sense" of the words—in spoken interaction. They can totally alter the thrust of the message. But auditory memory is apt to be unreliable, possibly because the *carrier's* message is "understood" at an unconscious level[1] The tapes act as a megaphone for the often-neglected carrier information.

• Memory has a general *direction.* Never perfectly conforming to the remembered event, it is systematic, not capricious, in its deviations. The memory of complex events tends to be *simplified*. There is no question about the complexity of group interview data. Contradiction is commonplace, and some degree of interpersonal conflict is as close to a sure thing as human dealings permit. Moreover, the desire to understand what is happening reinforces the natural tendency to remember events as being simpler than in truth they were. Both moderator and client will erase from their memories the puzzling discrepancies of the discussion.

The immersion begins, then, with the assembling of raw data. Here, the very problems which most tax the rapporteur are also the hooks which pull her more deeply into her research. No one who can pass a puzzle or a paradox without wanting to solve it can ever be a good focus group researcher (and perhaps not a dedicated social scientist either).

Once immersed, concentration is narrow and intense, like light through a burning glass. Wherever the rapporteur looks, she sees people behaving in illuminating ways with respect to the product or service, the company or the medium, which is the focus of the project. Her world has become for a time monothematic, bounded on all sides by the questions she is asking of the data.

My assignment once was to find the different ways people interacted with coffee personally or socially. I had come as far as the use of coffee as a social (friendly or romantic) pretext for a *tete a tete*, and the use of coffee as a ritual of intimacy before parting. I had already hypothesized about the use of coffee as a magic carpet of solitary focus, which enables someone to isolate and distance him/herself without ever leaving the room. But I was puzzled about business uses of coffee. The shared break was, of course, one obvious use. But I sensed that there was something more, related to the romantic rites of coffee, in which the cup was actually shifted according to the degree of intimacy. But I could find no bridge into this topic.

Becalmed, I took a coffee break (what else?), and went downstairs to the coffee shop in my building, intent on letting up on the cramp in my head. As I looked about the room, I saw two men seat themselves. Although I could not hear them, it was obvious that "A" was an operator, and that "B" was his target for tonight. The waitress set cups down in the middle of the table. "B" placed his cup directly in front of him. With more cleverness than I would have accorded him, "A" put *his* cup directly opposite, setting his own boundary.

The little hedges of cups and saucers stayed where they were through the first filling. "A," I could see, was warming to the sell. When the waitress came back, both men signaled that they wanted seconds. "B" took a swallow, and made gathering movements as though preparing to get away. At this moment, before my fascinated eyes, "A" extended his right hand in an arc that moved both cups to one side and leaned forward.

"B" was a gone goose. I understood the choreography behind coming in for the kill, and went back upstairs to try it on for fit.

Incidents of this kind are extremely common. Rapporteurs I have interviewed report it too. It's enough to give the stablest of researchers paranoid delusions, the way the universe plays out the human scenarios which illuminate whatever project she is working on.

Other Preliminaries

In addition to the Background and Purpose section, the Introduction to the report includes 2 other sections: "Methods and Procedures" and "Sample." The Method and Procedure section simply states whatever one has to say to this client about the focus-group method generally, and recapitulates what in fact the moderator, working with these panel members, actually did. This includes the sequence of topics and of presented materials. The introduction concludes with a description of the "Sample." This includes demographic and usage variables and, when the recruiting has been notably good (or notably bad) notes the resemblances or disparities.

THE PREDISPOSITIONS

Clients frequently request that a "Summary" or "Implications" section appear immediately after the introduction. I find this disturbing—not because I don't understand the request, but because I *do*. Many of those who will receive copies of the report are not as caught up in the problem as the particular individuals on whose behalf the project was requested. Or they are too highly placed to bother with unnecessary details. They can read the problem (in "Background and Purpose"), what was done to solve it (in "Methods and Procedure"), and the final outcome, without cluttering up their in-baskets with minutiae. The project is the client's, after all. If he were to pitch it into a file unread, a rapporteur might find herself "too busy" to take the next project from that client, but has no cavil if the bill is paid.

Clearly, the client's attitude, if known in advance, affects the zest with which report-writing is undertaken. In a sense, the client who does no more than read the summary section has taken the rapporteur entirely on faith. I personally prefer a little resistance to conclusions I have spent weeks building—it's a sign of active interest. And I take more readily, in a busy period, a project offered by a client who is flammable if the issues are exciting. But that's not everyone.

However the report is sequenced in the binder, it is probably written like a suspense novel: the scene is set, the problem stated, the characters introduced, respondents described, and then the action begins.

The "plot" of a report begins with the Predispositions. This section quite literally explores (as fully as time permits) the whole complex of opinions, attitudes, feelings, beliefs, prejudices, and habits which together shape the readiness of these panelists to buy and use the product/service; the way each will receive communications about the item itself or the company that supplies it; the attitudinal residue of previous experience with this product/service category; the social and emotional values it abuts on; particular concerns of familiarity or innovation in the category; gaps in the product spectrum which suggest new product opportunities; and so (unendingly) on.

It is probably in this section that the rapporteur needs the greatest discipline and the greatest objectivity. Just as it is true that moderators must rein in their initial curiosity about the elements that predispose for or against product acquisition, so it is essential to the usefulness and vitality of the report that the rapporteur make firm and circumspect decisions about what to include and what to discard—and stick with the decisions. Everything she learns is interesting to her, and much of it is brand new, even if she is familiar with the category. But chances are that predisposition findings which are not 100 percent germane to the problem at hand will not be new to the client who, remember, lives with this product and its attributes for nearly a third of his waking life. And they may no longer even be interesting to him. The rule is that information that is probably germane and truly surprising—outside the reach of any of the possibilities suggested in client-researcher conferences—deserves some (brief, at least) mention.

The content of the predisposition section will be determined by the overall reason for doing the groups in the first place. As a general rule, new product explorations, reactions to concepts, corporate image studies and the like, will carry a heavier weighting of motivational description and speculation, than will exploratory probes of proposed creative executions. However, if the executions to be presented are based on a substantial re-positioning of the advertised product or service, the interpretation

of the predispositions may well be even more elaborate than for a totally
new product, since account should be taken of the attitudes which must
be *unlearned*, as well as those proposed to *replace* them.

Interviews conducted primarily for creative purposes usually emphasize reactions to presented materials. The predisposition section of
the report in such a project needs only enough exposition of the respondents' pre-existing mind-sets to explain and nail down their attitudes
toward subsequent presentations of creative offerings.[2] "Creative" folk,
as clients who request such groups, typically want more verbatim quotes
in their reports, since they need to know how their target consumers talk
about using the product/service and how they feel about current and previous commercials. It is important, too, to trace in some detail the
relationship between what is said, what is felt, and the unrecognized
sources of feeling (if the client will sit still for it). Creative clients do
not always know what it is they want to know, but if the rapporteur can
present the visceral underpinnings that result in enthusiasm for or rejection of a promotional communication, and if she can do so arrestingly
and simply, the creative client can grasp the principal with lightning
speed and run with it far beyond the specific commercial or ad campaign.

A client of mine, a familiar health and beauty aids company, wanted to introduce a
new over-the-counter (OTC) medication. Not only was this a product new to them, but
also it would be the first OTC product to enter the market against an existing product
which had so far *owned* the category. A large number of groups was requested (the
client didn't want to be misled by an "unrepresentative" sample).

After moderating the groups and interpreting the results, I presented a report to the
client and agency creative staff which could be boiled down to two major findings:

1. The only direct benefit claim we could make affected the purchaser's wallet, rather
than any part of her/his body.

2. There was an unmistakable personality constellation associated with the using of
our competitor's product, which I delineated in the report, and which was clear enough
in my mind for me to hypothesize specific attitudes and behaviors for most situations.

A tug of war ensued between research and creative factions that lasted nearly a
month. The creative stance was that a lower price claim was inherently unexciting.
Hadn't I urged the client to up-price the immediately preceding product introduction? I
pointed out that the last new product was in the cosmetic category and that beauty aids
did not conform to the rules of medications, marketing wise, and vice versa.

I explained, too, that the other concepts which they preferred to the claim of a discount price on a parity product would not fit with this unique product situation.

Creative: Why can't we claim product superiority?

Research: Because these users wouldn't believe it and would label our campaign as deceptive (specific references to topics in the discussion guide).

Creative: How about a believable endorsement from somebody impressive, like a doctor or pharmacist?

Research: Since X (the established product) does not advertise, but depends on word-of-mouth, medical endorsement is what they think they have now. X follows a path in the marketplace that looks like an ethical drug. Users learned about the product from dominant others, in the same way they hear about "prescription drugs." New users of X *supply* the missing first term in the familiar formula of doctor-to-patient-to-friend with a similar problem. Nothing will top that kind of professional aegis. Even an *imaginary* MD outvotes a pharmacist, unfortunately. But you are right in supposing that women of this kind are responsive to personal advocacy.

Creative: But you can't really do a campaign that is geared to influence the sequence of word-of-mouth.

Research: I've never *seen* it done well, but that doesn't mean you can't do it. You know that these ladies want mothering, so your spokesperson should be a counselor, or should assume that kind of manner.

Creative: Could we have the friend or whoever tell the target lady that X is ripping her off by overpricing?

Research: Risky. These ladies won't take kindly to frontal attack. Anyway, it isn't necessary. Remember we said they were very suspicious types. They'll be more convinced if they figure out for themselves that if we price the product much lower, and we have a brand image they trust, plus advertising that the makers of X don't have, that we are being fairer to them. Of course X will respond by dropping prices, and if they're quick about it, they may get the defectors back. But maybe the consumer will recognize X as the heavy in the piece and stick with us. It is worth a shot.

With angry mutters, the creative faction returned to the drawing board and came up with a price-off campaign that tested well in a second wave of groups and won them industry awards, plus a first-year brand-share that exceeded the clients' wildest fantasies.[3]

There is no single standard outline of topics in a predisposition section. The section will have subheadings which correspond to the topics selected by the client as primary in client-researcher planning. It may also include topic coverage on unanticipated issues uncovered during the moderating of groups.

Casing the Panel

The first subsection of the predisposition findings, in all of the formal reports I write, is variously called "Interaction Climate," or "Group Character," or "Panel Interaction," or, once or twice when the findings were particularly dramatic, "Personnae." This section is something of a hybrid with one prosaic foot in the introductory "Sample" section. As such, it serves as a transition from the static introduction to the more involving present-tense discussion of the findings (thus coaxing busy or uppity client to read further).[4]

Although a heading of this sort always initiates the findings, no two of these sections are superimposable. The length and complexity of the section will depend on:

• The importance of interpersonal influence in a given product category.
• The interest which the client has shown in the active voice of his targeted consumer.
• Particularly striking or different group characteristics which may affect the topic agenda to follow, as when an evangelical religious teetotaler slipped past the recruiter and turned up in a project focused on beer. His solemn denunciations of "Satan's brew" were a jolt to the clubby warmth of the panel's grouping. And dismissing him, though discreetly done, was a further cold slap at group solidarity. The topic agenda presumed the fraternal solidarity which nearly always happens in beer panels. This was re-established, but slowly. A precautionary note was added in the report's interaction climate section, explaining why this one group was so tentative in answering early questions.

"Interaction Climate" always covers the way in which (and the extent *to* which) the individual panelists "group," or form a describable community, and the role assignments which the formed group recognizes. If the group is heterogeneous, the interactive climate section will make some reference to the fate of demographic or usage partitions, as an outcome of the grouping process. (A discussion of homogeneity vs heterogeneity may be found in Chapter 10.) The *timing* of interactive grouping may also be important to note. If the warm-up is light-hearted, but the group falls with a thud as soon as the product category is introduced, it might suggest that catchy jingles are not the way to go in creative execution. The reverse is true as well: solemnity and portentousness are probably not the ticket for extolling the joys of soft drinks, recreational vehicles, or vacation trips. Similarly, how the group handles embarrassing or upsetting material will depend on the depth and tenor of grouping and may also affect the grouping.

Finally, the constituency of the group particularizes the role of the moderator. Since much of the ensuing order (or pandemonium) is colored by the role assigned to the moderator (i.e., leader, member, parent, pupil, eavesdropper) it is important that the moderator, the viewers, and those who will read the report and/or attend the presentation understand which contract exactly has been negotiated between moderator and panelists.

Answering Predisposition Questions

Taking her cue from the role panel members have assigned to her, the moderator may adapt the way in which she offers the "General Lead-in." The moderator is not sure at all whether the panelists are going to cover the ground by the interstate highway of the guide or proceed, as fancy leads them, across the fields and back roads. Her role may consist of little more than holding up an occasional road sign.

The tone of the guide reflects the choices made by the group, by the moderator, or by both. But generally speaking, topic progression in the predispositions section of the report is roughly based on the sequence of the guide, with detour signs raised where panelists have made associative topic-shifts that the planners didn't think of.

In most panel discussions, the lead-in is a broad query that taps into the general areas of the purchase and use of the product/service, leaving the job of specific focusing to the panelists. A report on such a group will have as its first topic the immediate *context* in which panel members mention the product category to be discussed. The report typically moves on to detail when, how, where, and why they use it. In product categories that can be cast into a problem resolution format, the broad context is often a preliminary focus on the problem side.

There is a sense, of course, in which any product or service which is bought, enrolled in, or subscribed to, represents the solution of a "problem." That is, there is some kind of internal tension produced in the consumer by *not* buying, enrolling in, or subscribing to a product or service which is available to her or him. This tension is accentuated by brand advertising, so that the imbalance of "needing more . . ." becomes a need for more of a certain brand.

Understanding the need-tensions or the anticipated need-satisfactions which are appropriate to a product category—understanding them *exactly*—is critically important when competitive products or services are essentially at parity with the one for which the project is undertaken. As there are no unique virtues to extol, the purveyor can only hope to compete effectively by demonstrating that he understands more keenly his product's particular consumer.

A network news department requested qualitative research which would help them to retain their own loyal viewers and perhaps draw a few new viewers from the other networks. Six in-depth focus-groups among those who regularly watched network news programs were conducted. Approximately equal quotas were recruited for each group, among respondents who:

• watched "our" network's program.
• watched each of the two other network's programs.
• habitually switched, either from day to day or, during network news broadcasts, flipped from one network to another.

Since we already knew that husbands and wives tended to watch the news together, the panels were heterogeneous for gender as well. All of the differences between individual panel members produced an array of feelings and attitudes.

Certainly, in discussing what network news is and should be, the most salient finding is the conceptual and experiential disparity in the way network news is perceived and evaluated by individual panel members.

The one common element in the interviews is recognition of the unique impact of the time-slot. All of the respondents without exception allowed that this is a critical time in the day, a turning point of some kind.

• In some sense, all respondents were "down" at this point. This doesn't necessarily imply depression. For some it was just the cessation of outside bombardment. For some it was a pause between the day's activities and those of the evening (which often are gentler, more passive). For some it was the change from practical, rational, cooler activities to social, emotional, warmer ones. But for all, it represents the obverse of morning. ("In the morning . . . I get myself up to go out. . .and conquer the world. At night, when I come home, I let myself down and admit I didn't conquer anything.") One buckles on a public persona in the morning, and unbuckles it at the other end of the day.

• All respondents agreed that the network news with perhaps the local news—happening at or near homecoming time—fulfilled the function of a no-man's-land between the strenuous concerns of the day's work and the social-emotional-familial activities of the evening. Like the two equators in time, noon and midnight, the newshour is an exempt time, committed neither to what went before nor to what follows. In discussing the singularity of this time period in each of the groups, most of the respondents turned serious momentarily, as if giving a salute of thoughtfulness.

In these respects, the members of all the panels agree. The *ways* in which the temporal facts affect them differ. Since each is reaffirming his or her particularity during this time period, there are actually as many versions as there are panelists. But some of the differences are small, and I'll be guilty of only minor oversimplification if I say that there were two types of people in these groups, defined by two styles of response to the abrupt change from public to private self. Because they have to be called *something* (and also for other reasons which will become evident) I'm calling these two groups of respondents the "Sponges" and the "Butterflies."

Neatly, for our purposes, this grouping corresponds almost exactly to the split between dedicated viewers of our network news and those who regularly watch the two other networks. Almost all of our viewers are Butterflies and almost all of the others Sponges. The first group in each location was our loyal viewers, the second was drawn from the constituencies of the other two networks. There were a few "channel flippers" in all groups. There was also some leakage of commitment on behalf of a few viewers in our groups and a few viewers in the competitive panels.

Presenting the players strategically—assessing the opposition first—the two groups can be described as follows:

Sponges. Were more serious, more introspective, and more responsive—they understood the purpose of the interview and accepted responsibility for giving accurate information. They weighed their evaluations and documented their conclusions. They described the change of pace, direction, and focus at days' end in terms of interpersonal sensitivity. Specifically, they defined their attitude at early evening as a less defensive attitude: "You're home. You don't have to be so careful about what you say or how you appear. And you don't have to watch out for what somebody is going to say or do to you."

They also seemed more deliberate than the Butterflies. They left the workday behind as they began their evening's activities: "I think about the day and come to my conclusions about it while I'm riding home. I'm finishing that when I put the key in the door. Then when I get inside, I turn on the TV, if it's not on already. Or I switch it to my news station. And while I'm listening, I'm kind of opening-up to the evening, to being home with my family."

They listened to the network news, took it in, sorted it, graded it, and filed it away. And at the same time, they were also "opening up." This may alter the way they listen from the beginning of the program to its end. They feel an increase in *emotional* receptivity: "In the daytime, I *think.* It's my brain I use. In the evening I *feel* more, and I'm more likely to depend on intuition." They were for this reason apt to judge more quickly whether what they heard was the "truth." Since they were more open to feeling, they were also more aware of feeling resentful when their emotions told them that what was on the screen was a put-on: "I don't want to see a circus act. I want people who *know* something to tell me about the news. And all that phoney socializing doesn't warm my heart at all. They're having a party when they're supposed to be giving me the news. And it doesn't make me feel like I'm part of the group either. They're playing buddy-buddy. I'm feeding my cat."

The term Sponges suggests only part of the way these people watch the news. Besides being absorbent, they also willingly work at it, to meet news announcers halfway: "You try to fill in. You have to read between the lines—or the pictures. And you know they haven't got the time to do it in depth. So you look at it as a skim—as an index. Anything you are interested in knowing more about you will look for and read."

Butterflies. Were more likely to wisecrack, with everything that implies (uncooperative, self-referent, competitive, etc.). They sometimes gave accurate information, but were less willing to cooperate with requests to reveal their feelings. Perhaps they were less *able* to cooperate since they were not high on introspection. But the impression they gave was of *repression*, and there was definitely anxiety under the jokes.

They spoke quickly and much of the time didn't listen unless their mouths were open. Their experience of the day-to-night switch—which they described as being merely "tired" or "beat"—was probably closer to *depression* than that of the Sponges, though this was masked with gaiety. The Butterflies spent a lot of time talking about how confident, powerful or sexual they were, but their hearts weren't in it. When they were "down" they felt more *vulnerable* than open.

They listened to network news to be part of the crowd, to have a gloss of currency, and to protect themselves:

"Why? Well I guess because it's the thing to do. Everybody does. My folks did. My friends do—it's just the thing to do."

"You feel stupid if something important happens and you didn't know about it."

"Just to make sure they're not blowing up New York, or something like that. You have to keep an eye on things if you want to stay alive."

Although these were our viewers, they tended to see the network in much the same way the Sponges did. They just didn't *mind*.

"I know they're just actors, not newsmen. But I get a kick out of 'em. Nobody takes them seriously anyway. If it's something important, I'll turn on another network."

These Butterflies say that they watch and listen without concentration.

"I like a voice when I'm eating dinner or getting ready to go out. I don't really listen. I just let it come in. Usually, if it's something important coming up, I catch that and tune in."

The report went on to discuss differences in network commitment (according to frequency, contingency, and vehemence), and finally made strategic recommendations about retaining and consolidating present viewers, securing channel flippers and (less likely) recruiting from the Sponges.

The importance of understanding personal-motivational *context* is also crucial when a new product or service is introduced in a familiar category with mature and established competitors.

A publishing group was planning to introduce a new magazine targeted to the "serious and upscale" golfer. Focus-group interviews were held in three locations. A pivotal theme in the report appeared in the "predispositions" section titled "Golf and Limerence: Romancing the Game."

In the end, what the panelists did was not so much to offer reasons for loving golf as to elaborate on the theme of loving golf: they declared that a state exists in their minds (or "hearts" if you will) which is neither as superficial as "infatuation" nor as morbid as "obsession," but partakes of both.

Half a dozen years ago, a psychologist involved in studying the phenomena of love coined the word "limerence" to denote that romantic form of love most often celebrated in opera, theater, and TV series. Limerence is often—but not necessarily—sexual in nature. It is passionate, and perpetually haunts the mind. It is never wholly satisfied, and thrives on frustration. Suffering and sacrifice in the name of devotion are positively welcomed and enjoyed. Limerent feelings are idealized in moments of fantasized rapture.

These remarks of the panelists need no comment:

" . . . It's a sort of spiritual experience. You take a cool morning when the sun is shining and there's a breeze, and you are feeling pretty good . . . you haven't hit a bad shot yet, and you hit a good drive, and you know you're going to tear them up. It's the fact that it can happen that keeps you coming back. That you might get that rush."

"It's hard for non-golfers to understand that we would just as soon be looking at a golf course as a pretty girl. I find just as much joy and excitement when I see where they've laid out a hole, how they've challenged us, where they've placed the traps. . . ."

"Some of us took a golf trip to Cannes, and we never went to the beach, even once—and you know what is on the beach in Cannes. We spent all the time on the course. . . ."

If you're not convinced that this is indeed limerence, try substituting a human love object for the course, etc., in the following quote:

"In Cleveland for 12 years . . . I belonged to a course where I could have played that course for the rest of my life and never played another golf course. . . . The Des Moines course, after awhile, could have bored me. But this one in Cleveland. . . ."

You might concede such remarks are interesting and amusing, in their way, but wonder what on earth they have to do with publishing a magazine. The answer is that they re-define strategic issues. Although I am not free to discuss all of these, consider the marketing innovations that might result from envisioning the magazines as love letters (which is indeed the way these golfers treat them). Consider too the impact of golfing tips: how some limerent golfers might regard them as useful clues to taming a course or a game, where others would regard them in the way a man deep in romantic love might look at a crude porn film: as blasphemy (and this happens too).

Some form of subjective rapport—of "what it feels like to be our target"—is usually offered, if not first, then early in the report. In products for which point-of-purchase display is a prominent consideration— things that are "shopped for" such as dinnerware, home furnishings, stereo equipment, televisions, and so on—the *act of selecting* may be the part of the report dissected for accompanying feelings. Sometimes, as in media studies, the feelings appropriate to goods and services consumed at established times of day (like media programming), or in describable physical settings (like fast food) may be what the reader is invited to share.

Almost always, the report, like the discussion guide, moves from how the consumer feels to what he thinks. The reason for this is the same in both cases. Feelings generally are suspect, and are shoved into the background because they are "illogical." Since both rational and emotional factors are working all the time and in everyone, clients and panelists alike, both factors must be included in the report as in the interview. Once feelings are on the table, they are available for discussion in the interview and for comprehension in the report. This discourages cagey readers and cagey panelists from buttoning-up their logical overcoats as the report (or discussion) progresses.

Another sequencing consideration serves similar purposes in both the writing of the report and in the shifting of topics in an interview. In both cases, discussion of advertising and of other promotional communications comes late in the predisposition section. The formal rationale for this placement is simple and obvious: since both the interview and the report move from predisposition considerations to reactions to presented materials (concepts, ads, commercials, or anything else which impacts on existing dispositions), the positioning of reactions to current and past promotional efforts permits a neat segue into speaking of possible *new* ideas for advertising. The report, like the interview, flows better if presentation of materials immediately follows "Predispositions." The juxtaposition is useful too in the interpretation process. It provides the rapporteur with a kind of touchstone for evaluating responses to presented materials. "A lot more convincing than . . ." is easier to interpret than "very good."

REACTIONS TO PRESENTED MATERIALS

Talk of "running (something) up the flagpole to see if anyone salutes" can still really be heard in the corridors of client companies and advertising agencies, and not just in the funny papers. The longevity of the phrase, in an industry which chews and spits out catchy phrases every fortnight, is probably attributable to the simplistic inputs required of consumers in many copytest procedures, which measure "recall" or other simple indices of endorsement. This is the *quid pro quo* of quantitative research in general: to get numbers, complexity is forfeited. Conversely, a focus-group project, in common with other qualitative techniques, forfeits the tallying of numbers to gain complexity. It may be necessary for a rapporteur to remind herself of this implicit contract in writing the "Reactions to Presented Materials" section of a report.

To be sure, the written and verbal data provided by the panel offer more than "salutes," but this section is typically more mechanical than "Predispositions." It is altogether too easy to be lulled into simplistic statements like "Most of the panelists express some enthusiasm for concept A, but a handful take exception. On the other hand, responses to B are largely negative." After all, what the client wants is answers. If clients are offered the full motivational picture of reactions to each item shown, they get restive.

Both judgments are true. Clients *don't* like to sit through the sifting of "On the one hand . . . but on the other hand . . .", and they do want answers. This makes fulfillment of the rapporteur's contract more difficult but it doesn't alter the terms of the contract. Focus group investigations do not generate numbers because they can't. They do offer insight into the processes underlying the panelists' reactions. The task of the report writer is to explain enough of the motivational underpinnings of the panelists' *enthusiasm* or *negativity* to get the client to understand why either response happened, without driving him up the wall with impatience or boredom. This suggests that a rapporteur should not include in her report each deliberation she makes about the meaning of motivational statements. It does *not* suggest that she shouldn't deliberate. Clients may not know, or may not care, that *motivation* is not a commodity which is simply present or absent. A rapporteur hip-high in transcripts and charts is aware of at least four discernible motivational operations:

1. The *anatomy* of motivation: the division of the attitude or response into the part which a panelist clearly perceives as being his own and the part which he can accept but was not aware of initially; and by inference the roots and corollaries of the motivation of which he is not (often cannot be) conscious.

2. The *dynamics* of motivation: the climates and expressions of social influence and of advertising persuasion which dislodge or reinforce existing attitudes and feelings.

3. The motivational *hierarchy*: when more than one predisposing attitude is invoked by creative materials or by discussion (and complexity is far more typical than simplicity of motive) it is possible to observe the shift and relative power of the several competing feelings, both those the respondent recognizes and those he does not.

4. The motivational *glossary:* the idiom of the respondents, the living cross-section of consumer language. In the course of the discussion, language can be analyzed to reveal the feelings, attitudes, and covert influences which produce it and which in the long term shape purchase behavior as well.

The rapporteur's report will not include all of these aspects of respondents' motivations of course. What she writes will be what she is left with when the data have been passed through the filters. The result may reflect less what the client has heard, while the panel was being interviewed, than the rapporteur's refined judgment of the panelists' intentions. That is, the report may be dynamic rather than static, and more

predictive than reflective. To the extent that it resembles marketplace behavior, it will be the marketplace of six months in the future rather than
on the day the groups were convened.

THE SUMMARY, IMPLICATIONS, AND RECOMMENDATIONS

If time permits, the rest of the report should be left to marinate before
undertaking the final section of the report. It is a precipitous climb from
the detail-by-detail account of what happened and what it probably
means to the high overlook necessary to the perspective of a "Summary," "Implications," or "Recommendations" section. The rapporteur
must be able to distinguish more salient aspects of the detailed findings
from those which carry less weight, must bring together the disparate
material—private written reactions, interactive discussion, nonverbal behavior, biographical data, projective creations—into an articulated set of
premises and speculations. The title of the final section, whether "Summary" or "Summary and Implications" or "Implications and Recommendations" is partly arbitrary. But not entirely: setting apart a whole section as a "Summary", or designating the first two pages in the section as
"Summary and Implications" is a signal that the summary of the
material is not readily apparent from the detailed findings. Perhaps the
interviews were many and ran long, or the data highly conflicted, or the
project had more than two goals.

For one reason or another, the rapporteur fears that readers of the
report may be unable to find a path through the density of the findings,
and wants therefore to restate those findings from which the *implications* are drawn or on which the *recommendations* are based, as the
"Summary" or gist of the findings. If the major findings are crystal clear
but their actionable significance for the client is less so, an "Implications" section is called for. Finally, if the writer is confident about the
strategic significance of what she's written, she may dignify her hunches
as "Recommendations."

The Numbers Game

In marketing research circles, eyebrows go up if numbers are mentioned
in a focus-group presentation. The use of hard-edged numerical pronoun-

cements is prohibited by a convention whose power lies somewhere between the Hippocratic Oath and the Boy Scout Pledge. The crime is most heinous if numbers appear in the implications (indeed many in marketing research blanch at the idea of implications of any kind being drawn from focus-group interviews). The offense is less dire, but still pretty bad if numbers get into the "reactions to materials," (including all reckonings of votes, or of winners and losers). Tallies of any sort that appear in "predispositions" will provoke at least a wince, and numbers in the sample description are regarded as merely gauche or indiscreet.

It is *de rigeur* to preface a written report with a disclaimer of numerical representation and a warning against action based on the report's content. Even better, the preface should note that findings must be checked quantitatively. And marketing researchers might find more trustworthy a focus-group rapporteur who repeats these caveats before the summary and/or implications.

Within the body of the report there are, instead of numbers, quite explicit translations:

- "A couple" = one or two in each panel.
- "A handful" or "several" or "a small minority" = at least three in each panel, but less than one-third of the panel.
- "Some" = at least one-fourth but not much more than one-third of the panel.
- "A fair number" = at least one-third but less than one-half of the panel.
- "Evenly divided" = one-half of the panel.
- "Many" = more than one-half, but less than two-thirds of the panel.
- "A preponderance" = more than two-thirds but less than three-fourths of the panel.
- "Most" = at least three-fourths but less than 90 percent of the panel.
- "Almost" or "virtually" all = at least 90 percent, but less than 100 percent of the panel.

I'm evenly divided on this one. I keep all the number breakdowns on my charts. Most clients know the conventions listed above quite as well as I do, so they've got the information. If a client wants my worksheets, I deliver the charts with the report. I trust any client from whom I accept work not to do something stupid like making major decisions based on 24 women in Kansas City.[5]

On the other hand, the use of these conventional measures is a constant reminder that the panelists are not systematic samples of everyone, and that, had I gotten another set of individuals by the same screener and recruiter, the results might have been different. This is less alarming if groups are replicated within each locale, and gets still less so as regional replication is done.

When we get to real volume, like 12 groups or more (replicating every panel within a region and including at least three regions), we're getting into pretty respectable numbers. And I would rather have 36 groups in six locations as a basis for marketing strategy than two or three times as many individuals polled in the same six locations.

Long ago, I dropped the introductory disclaimer. It had become a ritual like the penances in a prayer book ("I have done those things which I ought not to have done, and I have left undone those things which I ought to have done"). I use the conventional quantity notation, at least in all projects with less than 12 groups. But I do not sprinkle the text with caveats. In the introduction to the "Implications," I state my views about the relative dangers of alpha and beta errors, (discussed in Chapter 7) and let the client decide how to use any recommendations made.

NOTES

[1]Farley, Jane C. "The Role of Voice in Interpersonal Communication." Unpublished M.A. thesis. University of Chicago Committee on Human Development, 1956.

[2]In my experience, adamant bias is more common among "creatives" than any other group. They tend to hurry through the "doubletalk" of the predispositions. But if the research findings contradict their hunches, they search the predispositions for soft spots and can rise to Aristotelian heights to explain why they are right and the researcher is wrong.

[3]You have to take my word for this one too. These projects took place more than a decade ago, but the client will not authorize a release of more particulars.

[4]In my reports, everything after the introduction is in the present tense.

[5]Like every rapporteur I know, I have, in a pinch, helped a client devise a campaign or launch a product on the basis of two groups, but if it weren't a pinch, we'd have known better.

Chapter 9

The Functional Tool

It would be difficult to name a marketing problem for which focus groups have not been used or seriously suggested. And marketing these days is as much a pattern of thought as it is the business of exchanging goods for dollars. Focus groups have been used in the marketing of paper-towels and presidents. Interpretive reports have been written on everything from astrological services to zweiback. There are few areas of life into which the focus group technique has not cast an eye. And you can safely bet the family car on it that the person(s) in whose interests the interviews were undertaken received intelligence from the enterprise which was in some degree new and useful.

It would be just to say that focus group interviews have endured as long as they have, and flourished as salubriously as they have, in part because of the information they provide. But that is a partial truth. Today, much of the popularity of focus groups stems from their supreme qualities as a spectator sport:

• As a work-assignment, watching focus groups easily beats internal meetings, sales calls, or even assimilating what is in the newspapers and periodicals in executive in-baskets. It is relatively undemanding, if one chooses to play it that way. The eats are good, and trips on expense-accounts are relaxing.

• The data drawn from the groups is apparently accessible. Each of a dozen concealed viewers can feel sure he knows exactly what the panelists said. Depending on how selectively he listens and watches, each can also feel reassured that the panelists supported his beliefs and strategies. In fact, because there is disagreement among respondents, each of the twelve viewers may feel equally confident even though the beliefs they perceive the panel as endorsing are poles apart.

• The peculiar role assumed by the viewers in the backroom has a glamour of its own. It bonds them in complicity. There is something delightful and faintly illicit about observing a group of people who are seen but cannot see. Moreover, the act of observing the panel and over-hearing their conversations with each other and the moderator, coupled with the obvious sincerity of most respondents, gives the whole transaction a high degree of believability.

• With videotape cameras available for use in most focus group facilities (and rentable everywhere), the whole many-splendored pageant can be employed to convince almost anybody of almost anything. Care-fully edited videotapes of focus groups are used as a matter of course by agencies in new-business presentations. They are also used widely by clients in intramural briefings attended by the sales staff, distributors, and anyone else whom it would have been too costly to bring to the groups. The magic bonding of complicity and the intoxicating power of eavesdropping carry over very well into videotape presentation.

It isn't particularly surprising that the broad constituency of marketing research takes a pretty dim view of the infatuation of marketers with focus group interviews. There is no doubt either that the lack of en-thusiasm in quantitative quarters rests in part on sound, supportable reason. The old objection to non-projectability of focus group findings is as true as it is familiar. And no one can quarrel with the claim that focus-groups are too frequently used for purposes that are beside the point of furthering understanding. But it's probably true, too, that some of the quantitative contingent's disdain comes from the relatively greater commercial allure of the focus group instrument. Few clients fall in love with the clatter of a computer, or with printouts of multiple regression analysis.

Less expectable is the fact that serious-minded, right-thinking focus group researchers recognize and deplore the over-use as well. But this is a hard line to walk. First of all, the blandishments of over-appreciation are almost irresistible. But even if this temptation is resisted and the report studded with caveats, the eventual use of the data is outside of the rapporteur's control. Data that are bought and paid for belong to the con-tractor, to be used as he likes. And the protest that "I don't think focus groups are the ideal procedure at this point" can be parried with "If you can't do them, I guess I'll have to find someone else." It is tempting—

and may even be true—to justify accepting the project with "If I don't do it, someone less scrupulous may."

The rules of focus group applicability are not set down, but must be created as needed on an individual case basis. Moreover, at some point the rules of interpreting projectability change. Given two demographic groups who are responsible for 75 percent of product purchase, with a schedule of 4 groups in each of 5 locations (a total of 200-240 individuals), I would feel more comfortable in trusting the data from these 20 panels than repose my confidence in a survey of 450, or perhaps even 1000 individuals. Neither qualitative nor quantitative researchers can afford to talk to everyone, and neither group can be sure that the questions addressed by those they *can* talk to will provide wholly valid answers to all of the relevant questions. We all agree that some approximation will have to do. Quantitative research presumes standard meanings for key terms (". . . 67 percent of female HOHs say *quality* is the most important factor . . ."). Focus groups trade breadth for deeper delving ("What do you mean by 'quality'? Do you always mean the same thing? How would you recognize quality in toilet paper?").

FOCUS GROUPS AS TOOLS OF EXPLORATION

The one aspect of focus groups that is universally smiled on is their employment as a reconnaissance operation. Very early in the course of a research program there is really no question about whether to use focus groups or something else. It's generally agreed that the focus group technique is applicable long before anyone has enough of a handle on the problem to figure out what in heaven's name to t-test. When the problem is as yet unformulated but the urge to do *something* is strong, it is always respectable to do some groups and tread water.

Respectable, maybe, but it is no longer the bagatelle it once was to mount a focus group project. The decision to schedule a few focus group interviews was a more casual one in the days when the panels assembled in somebody's dining room, nobody viewed them and the audio tapes were recorded on the moderator's reel-to-reel tape recorder, which was the approximate size and weight of a medium-size collie.

Recruiters then didn't know the meaning of the words "field experience," but improvised the job and the fee (asking perhaps $45.00 to recruit a panel of twelve qualified respondents). The panelists were paid

$10 (top dollar), and the hostess in whose home the interview took place thought herself lucky if she got $20 for the dining room table and coffee all 'round. For $25, she'd provide danish and take her phone off the hook. If the moderator was on salary anyway, the whole enchilada could cost an agency no more than $200 per group.

Those days created an *idee fixe* in the minds of agencies and advertisers who quickly learned that anytime an idea was slow in coming was the right time to try focus groups because they were "quick and cheap." Today, with souped-up facilities at $300 to $400 a pop, respondents who expect to be paid anywhere from $25 to ten times that amount, recruiters who estimate $40 to $60 for each qualified panelist and expert, professional moderator/rapporteurs, a 12 person focus group probably costs the client a minimum of $3,500 including a full report and presentation. This is still less expensive than commissioning 12 one-on-one in-depth interviews (with report), and is considerably less costly than an average survey. But that's *one interview:* interviewing in groups the same number of people polled in a survey would entail prohibitive costs. Today, focus groups must stand on their own merits, not on how little money is at risk.

The other part of the quick and cheap myth that haunts us still is that in those feckless early days there was no perceived need to clarify the goals set for a focus group project. That was one of the advantages: no need for clear statement of what you wanted. Since it wasn't possible to predict in advance where a group might take you, the report made by the moderator obviously would start by stating the goals, and then discuss what the panel had to say about them. Thought, besides being painful and tedious, eats up a lot of time. That was time saved up-front. No great amount of the moderator's time was tied up in a focus group project either. The assignment for the person who moderated and reported the groups was to "get them talking and see what happens." If nothing much came of it, no big deal. Now, it's a much bigger deal. Nobody can afford a fruitless group.

The need for clearly specified goals is most burdensome in the very stage of problem-solution for which focus groups are most often useful: when the client needs help formulating the specific question areas to be probed. Here, especially, the researcher must participate. When all that a client knows is that he wants to involve the purchaser in his thinking and that focus groups are a good way to do this, the moderator can help by offering him some of the more common formats for focus group explorations and seeing which fits best.

Understanding the *reasons* a client needs fresh input will help the rapporteur put herself in his place. Often, exploratory group interviews are needed because *something new* has been (or is being) introduced into the situation:

New people may enter the marketing team. The newcomers may be on the client side or may be a new agency team. Whether from an agency switch, creative reshuffling, or the client playing musical chairs with product groups, the need to become informed is the same. New people will be briefed as a matter of course about anything having to do with the *vendor side* of the purchase equation. They will have read marketing plans, survey sweep results and sales statistics, for openers. But on the *consumer* side they may be uninformed, or at least may lack direct information about how the individuals who buy (ask for, subscribe to) what they are trying to sell think and feel and talk about it.

New products or services may be freshly launched or about to be launched in the marketplace. (The use of focus groups in new product-generation is experimental and will be discussed in the "Afterword.") In either case, they will have established as yet no place in the lives of consumers and no accustomed vocabulary with which marketers must become familiar. But it is no less important to explore how prospective buyers anticipate using, feeling, and talking about what the client has just introduced or is about to introduce. If nothing else, the results of exploratory research provide a benchmark for later studies which allow the marketing team to understand how and why the product or service being sold has exceeded buyers' hopes or how and why it has disappointed them.

New positioning of an existing product, however successful the original positioning has been, is a recurring problem. The central themes or metaphors used previously have variable life-spans—some "wear" better than others—but they are never immortal. The relationship between positioning of products and services and the motivational seasons of consumers' lives is both responsive and causative. Changing composition of the target consumer group, and the changing life-styles and values of the same consumer group, both influence and are influenced by a product's positioning. A new remedial claim (for instance milk drinking as protection against osteoporosis) is at once responsive to a change in concerns, creates a new target group or groups (geriatric women and young adults), generates new product development (high-calcium milk), changes attitudes toward other dairy products, provides possible positioning for cold cereal and/or cookies, and so on.

A new sponsor for a product can also alter the way the product (service) is experienced. Increasingly today, knowledge of and feelings about the corporate entity offering goods or services affects buyers' confidence in what they are buying. A scare incident connected to one brand in a competitive field opens the category for a different or a fervently renewed, brand commitment. The outcome of such a shake-up will depend on how the crisis is handled by the implicated brand and by each competitor.

In less dramatic circumstances it is difficult for purchasers to uncover and identify the reasons for and the implications of this influence. But it is worth digging for. Sometimes a benign, warm, familiar corporate image supporting a new product can represent the security which purchasers need to make a voluntary change in buying (and living) habits.

A new research effort on a large scale may be planned. Questionnaires will be sent into the field for administration. Before sending any document which large numbers of consumers must understand and answer, it is advisable to check the way the document is interpreted by individual members of the target group: both the exact meanings and the range thereof, since the field staff has neither the time nor the familiarity with the category to translate.

Getting Acquainted

Introducing the target consumer to newcomers on the marketing team is probably the easiest assignment for focus groups. The client doesn't really need an interpretive report. What he *does* need is a moderator who is experienced in the category—preferably one experienced with particular buyers of the brand—and who can flush out underlying feelings when they are instructive. A post-mortem after each interview to field questions from new arrivals on the team, and a verbatim transcript by any careful typist with good listening skills, are all that is necessary.

The form and climate for this kind of interview is very close to the textbook prescription for focus groups: ". . . The researcher proceeds without a fixed plan . . . using a checklist or guide . . . to follow each clue or idea as far as seems profitable. . . ."[1]

A moderator experienced in the category and with the brand knows which stones to move because she knows what is probably under them. In this context, bias is for once a plus. But bias always has some negative fall-out. The moderator will have to invent the excitement of discovery in order to keep the panel sufficiently motivated as they reveal what she already knew was there.

The same form and content is useful in *casting* interviews, when the client and/or the agency opts for a "real" spokesperson rather than an actor. The pattern for casting interviews is that panelists convene as for any other focus group interview, and are guided to discuss the particular product claims or usage habits which will be utilized in the advertisement or commercial. The interview has a hidden agenda (casting choices will be made). Secrecy is necessary because real-life "performers" are apt to behave self-consciously if they know they're on camera. These are easy interviews to do from the point of view of content, since content is not the clients' primary interest. The moderator is often free to set and to follow her own line of questioning. But, on the interpersonal level, casting interviews are more complex. Only one or two panelists will be chosen, and the moderator is responsible for preserving the egos of the "losers." To accomplish this, and to preserve as well any substantive contributions the group has to offer, selected panelists should not be summoned by clients during the interviews. Clients should notify the hostess—or someone else on the field staff—who will then stop the finalists, inconspicuously, as they leave.

To put all the *new product* assignments focus groups are used for under one umbrella would be like trying to gift-wrap a giraffe. The scenario will vary according to

- *what* is being introduced;
- *when* the introduction took—or will take— place;
- *who* commissioned the groups and who sees the report;

• *how* the new product (/service) was or will be introduced in the marketplace;
• *why* the client thinks focus groups will be useful.

But there are a few cautions that all prudent focus-group researchers should keep in mind when carrying out any project which directly examines the impact of a new product introduction:

• The introduction of anything new is always *exciting* to panelists, even in cases in which the product category normally is not. Panelists seem to become energized when they're called upon to judge what will happen to a newborn product. Perhaps the excitement is bound up with the idea of the birth metaphor, or perhaps they really pick up (or imagine that they do) the thrill of heightened concentration moderators bring to bear on the product being introduced. It could be even less direct. The moderator knows that the client is excited about the new offspring (who isn't?), catches some of this excitement, and then transmits it to the panel. For one or all of these reasons the excitement is there, and even the most sincere respondents can mislead through the effort to please or through honest enthusiasm which they feel during the interview, but which may diminish afterward.
• There is always error introduced by the circumstances of the interview itself, when conscious and narrow attention—and also intent self-examination—are invoked to scrutinize an event (for instance, buying a new mouthwash) which in real life is probably determined by attention which is preconscious at best, and behavior which is largely reflex. This is evident in discussions of newly introduced products or services, but is particularly true of advertising concepts and executions. When the product introduction is imminent, we are not really discussing a new product at all but rather the *promise* of a new product—an advertising concept. Looking at products and services which are about to be offered is particularly tricky, because if the moderator does not have her wits about her, the whole interview could be viewed as a two-hour commercial for the product. On top of which is the occult delight of knowing something in the future, by the special privilege of being summoned to the interview.

At the data-collecting stage (the interview itself), the moderator can do a few things to reduce the artificial excitement of the situation. It is especially important in a new-product interview, to permit and encourage panelists to *bring up the new product themselves*. She may start with the *problem* which the product helps to solve:

"Which do you hate worst: cleaning the oven, going to the dentist, changing diapers, or dull cocktail parties?"

If "going to the dentist" doesn't win this one, that's okay. It can always be parried with something like:

"Really! I expected everybody to name the dentist. How do you account for it? Either you never have dental problems [which, by the way, the recruiting should have precluded], or you have marvelous dental hygienic habits . . . or of course you have the hots for your dentist. Which is it?"

One way or another the moderator gets into dental hygiene. She then asks panelists: "Write down any products you can think of—everything—that is available now for helping you take care of your teeth and your mouth . . . whether or not you use it, whether or not you believe it could help." They then check the items they use and circle any brands they intend to try. This list serves as a springboard for discussing what has led them in the past to try new products, how they audition these products, what they would like to have, and so on.

Soft pedaling the incidental excitement of newness does not mean inducing torpor. The moderator's introduction, as long as it doesn't overplay the product's inauguration, can be as exciting as need be (rule of thumb: the duller the category, the more exciting the intro and lead-in). This is *not* the occasion for a time-efficient thrust like, "This afternoon we're going to be talking about a new product which . . .". Nor is it the right time to zip through predisposition questions and hone in on associations and suggestions pertaining to the many advantages and fine points of the new product. But the need to give the panelists the time it takes them to get to product issues often requires that the moderator prepare clients and other viewers for the delay. (This kind of briefing is discussed in Chapter 11.) Otherwise, those troops behind the mirror may leap *through* it, in the belief that the moderator has slipped a sprocket. The backroom contingent is, of course, frantic to hear what the panelists think of their blessed event. But reactions to a new product are only comprehensible when presented against the background of previous behavior with the category:

• *The extent and nature of previous product-use in the category.* Most new products belong to an existing product category, and most panelists have a history of usage for that category of product. It is necessary to find out how and why related products have been used in order to gauge the importance of products like this, the problems which users feel are solved or bettered by existing products, and the areas in which the brands they now know about are deficient.

• *Brand-history* of existing products. If panelists can remember with confidence the brand first chosen in the category and the reasons for choice, it is helpful information to have. Brand history also includes any switches in the particular brand usage and the reasons for previous switching.

• Finally, some *estimate of brand commitment* to the present brand can usually be made—if not by the panelists, then by the rapporteur. It is necessary to bear in mind that panel members can provide more dependable information on matters of behavioral record than about their present or past feelings and wishes concerning a new entry in the marketplace.

Once the topic of the product is broached, the moderator should ask the respondents: "Who makes it?" But she should probably ask those who know (or guess) the name of the company to write it down and hold their tongues, in order to ask those who *don't* know, "Who *should* be bringing you this product, and why?"—a question that delivers some bonus information on both the client's and his competitors' corporate images.

When the panelists have extolled the virtues of the product, the moderator must be sure to probe the dark side: "Even though I gather that you welcome it overall, what's the worst thing about the product?" Comments by members of the panel on the moderator's caution ("Hey, do you want to sell this thing or what?") should not, on either side of the mirror, be taken as a rebuke. If the moderator has done her work conscientiously, the respondents *should* be wondering this. If it happens on cue, it is a perfect opportunity for her to say something like:

"Good question. And I'll answer it. The answer is yes—and then again no. Yes we want to sell it, but only if someone is likely to buy it. We're in love with it, and we need to understand not only why you could fall in love with it too, but why those who couldn't, couldn't."

Then she presents the concepts which she has cajoled the clients into writing. Against the honest background of this two-sided statement of goals, she asks panelists to write and then discuss what's good about each concept, and what's bad.

If the panel still says they will clasp the new product to their collective bosom, the moderator should double-check by asking for details:

"I know you can't be sure yet exactly how and when you will use it, but please try to tell me again what you do now, and how this will change things. Will you simply add this to your routine, or will it replace one or more products you now use?"

In the interpretation and report, the rapporteur must still be wary about excitement expressed for the product. (She must also figure in the human "newness panic"—resistance to change—which a truly revolutionary product can evoke.) She should monitor her own contributions as well as those of panel members to detect any note of thrilling surprise to come. Finally, projective input (for me, figure drawings and stories) is especially useful when the reason for the groups is understanding new products.

EXPLORATORY PROBES IN PRODUCT REPOSITIONING

In the life of any product or service there are seasons, as there are in the lives of any organic being. And anytime after what is (somewhat arbitrarily) accepted as "product maturity," the individuals whose livelihoods depend on the product's attractiveness may decide that the product needs rejuvenation. This may be just a general repositioning. It may be rather more specific ("It's time to reformulate. We can add _____ and call it new and improved. Let's do some groups and see what the market might be for a premium-price deluxe positioning, with

new dispenser packaging and a sleeker label."). Or it may be an idea
with some specificity of goal (for instance, trying to attract a younger—
or older—age group, but without specific implementation).

Reasons for repositioning range from naked avarice ("How can we ignore a group with all that discretionary spending?") to altruism ("You
know, we just aren't reaching young mothers who really are the ones
that need the stuff for the kids and themselves"), or may simply register
the alarm-clock of attrition that says it's time to rejuvenate. The opportunities for repositioning may have been researched . . . or not.

A moderator in exploratory sessions for repositioning an established
product must be prepared to do the same kind of hidden-agenda interview as in new-product interviews, but when the purpose of the interviews has been revealed, she must swing her authority in the *opposite*
direction; that is, she must pull against cynicism, rather than temper enthusiasm.

Repositioning is more complex than new product positioning. In
motivational thrust, repositioning a mature product means forcing it
back to the birth canal for a second coming. Before the product can be
represented as a different entity, the original positioning must be broken.
This is a two-step process—unlearning followed by relearning. And careful motivational tracking by the moderator must represent both phases.
Before getting into the claims and benefits stated or implied by new
positioning, she must guide panelists to focus, at least briefly, on the
original positioning of the product, what they felt to be true or untrue of
it, what unique benefits and weaknesses they ascribed to it, what
measures they could suggest to repair weaknesses without weakening
benefits, and so on.

As with new products, new positions are most usefully presented in the
form of rough concepts. Once responses have been elicited, additional
concept statements should be solicited from panelists, and these added
to the concepts given to subsequent groups.

Interpretation, like moderating, should be tuned to probe beneath immediate and superficial reactions. In these sophisticated days, repositioning is seen as a scam to which the intelligent consumer's response is disbelief. Rapporteurs should listen for contradictions. ("My thought is,
'Who d'you think you're kidding?' But I guess I'll go on buying the
stuff, even if it costs a little more. I don't believe that 'new ingredient'
story, but it probably won't hurt it. It's a good product. I wouldn't

bother to try something else, for the few cents extra.") Here again, projective data can enrich and translate inconsistencies in discussion and between written and spoken comments.

WHAT'S IN A NAME?: THE QUESTION OF AEGIS

The bonding of brand name and manufacturer is variable. For some, the company name is part of the brand signature (Hershey, Kellogg, Pillsbury, Colgate, and Campbell's, to name a few). Others carry proper names that are no indication of the manufacturer (Betty Crocker, Schick shaving products, Bayer aspirin, and so on). Others market products with some part of the corporate calling card (Kraft, Westinghouse, and so on). It is difficult for consumers to recognize corporate parentage, let alone forge strong feelings of loyalty. Efforts at building corporate image to the point of including the corporate name among consumers' reasons to buy are relatively infrequent. But they seem to be on the increase. Since the Sixties, young consumers in particular have mistrusted big business generally. And in the Eighties it has become progressively harder to know the players without doing library research.

Commitment and loyalty are personal phenomena. Without some sense of connection between manufacturer and purchaser, buying patterns lose coherence and predictability. This is particularly evident for brand categories in which competition is high, among products which for all practical purposes are at parity. A moderator who has logged a lot of focus groups in such a category can discern brand-personalities within a panel.

But research *centered* on corporate image is still infrequent. Increasingly, corporate perception is included as one line of questioning to pursue if time allows in panel discussions which are really focused on something else (such as product introduction, product change, update studies of usage or advertising probes). In some cases a moderator will stumble over strong brand identification in one direction or the other.

In a focus-group project investigating the viability and introductory positioning for a new product in a field dominated by another brand, the moderator could not fathom the reason for the respondents' readiness to accept the upstart product. Probing product claims had revealed nothing strong enough to account for it. As a last resort, she blocked out with a sheet of paper various parts of the prototype introductory announcement, asking: "If we leave this out, does it help or hurt the product?" When she reached the bottom, nothing was left but the company name. When this was blocked out, the group suddenly responded with an "Aha!" They became aware of the importance of the product aegis: "I never realized this before, but we've always used _____ products in our house, since I was a child. And I just carried it over as a matter of course. That name is just like mother to me.";"We used them too, and since I've grown up I notice the things the _____ company does in the community: like supporting hospitals and funding the arts. Things I would do if I had the company." Nobody had a bad word for the company, and all but two panelists had definite and positive things to say. This was duly noted in the report. And the recommendation section advised that the company's name be featured in advertising and packaging of the new product, with a coda to that section suggesting that upcoming package and label testing include at least one set of designs in which corporate identification was prominent.

A corporation's image may also have indirect effects on the purchase of its products. Since consumers rarely buy directly from the maker, the effect of image at any point down the line can promote or diminish the likelihood of purchase. I have heard people declare that they blacklisted products because of a company's unfair labor policies, toxic waste irresponsibility, foreign trade connections, etc. Nobody says focus groups are representative. But what one person can do, so can others. It's a topic that needs more coverage.

A major drug manufacturer recognized that pharmacists were becoming more important in the chain of influence (replacing the warmth and accessibility of the primary care physician, as medicine fragmented into specialization). Focus groups with pharmacists were scheduled to discover, if possible, the ways in which and the degree to which pharmacists were willing and able to express their feelings about particular drug companies.

Reticence to discuss company favoritism or resentment was what we expected. We got something else. The pharmacists felt strongly and said so. The basic reason for their attitudes was an appropriate display of respect for their profession, or a lack of it. This, they said, was expressed in many ways by the company itself and by the sales force. They measured the esteem the companies showed them against their treatment of physicians: "They invite medical school graduates over to look at the plant, and they give them gifts, like briefcases. You don't see them treating pharmacy school graduates that way."

When the moderator asked whether the relations of drug companies with pharmacists was exactly parallel to the same companies' relationships with physicians, the panelists' reactions became very heated and pharmacists drew a very different picture of the interaction of the three principals than the commonly held view: "The patient goes in to see the doctor, and the doctor diagnoses him as having an ulcer. Then what does he do? He steps out of the consulting room and goes to the telephone and calls one of us. And what does he say? He says: 'Hey Lou, what's the best thing for ulcers now?' And I tell him, and he goes back inside to the patient and writes the prescription!"

Asked what would make them happy, they said sardonically that what they wanted was impossible. They wanted recognition from both drug companies and the medical profession: "We're the ones who decide which product the patient will buy." "Yes, and we're the one's who cover the doctor's a—when he prescribes without checking. *We're* the ones who watch the patients' prescription record!" When the moderator asked why they thought this was "impossible," they revised the statement and said that it was "very unlikely," but that what *was* impossible was their *knowing* they had the appreciation of both parties.

At the end of each interview, the panelists were asked to rate, top to bottom, the same list of drug companies. Although each group and all the participants in each group had a different specific history of grievances and satisfactions, the lists were startlingly similar.

The report emphasized the importance of more equal professional perks for physicians and pharmacists. Almost as an afterthought, it also suggested that advertising in AMA journals express *to the physicians* the importance of the pharmacist, figuring that pharmacists were also reading these journals, as it were, over the physicians' shoulders. Apparently they were. Follow-up interviews found the pharmacists, if not exactly dancing in the streets, at least happier than they had been.

TRANSLATING SURVEY QUESTIONS INTO TARGET-ESE

The agreement between focus-group findings and those uncovered by surveys are, at best, iffy. When the focus groups are few and the survey broad, tradition says the focus groups must be wrong. Maybe. Certainly, if the only two options were that focus group respondents were the flaky minority or that the populace at large lied to the field interviewers, we'd have to accept the flake theory.

But there is another possibility: that respondents don't talk like test constructors and therefore the results of the two kinds of interview only *seem* to be contradictory. Close collaboration between researchers who conduct qualitative explorations and the designers of survey questionnaires is obviously a useful procedure, if often a difficult one. Difficult possibly because they are different kinds of people. Difficult certainly because they have different approaches to knowledge and different work habits. The combination will never win a sack-race. Qualitative timeframes are erratic, and need long intervals for mulling; however, if the questionnaire people can provide the focus group folks with a draft of the questionnaire, qualitative input is frequently worth the time it takes.

An HBA company was introducing a toothpaste which could boast important hygienic advantages. A broad survey was planned. Focus groups were also requested. These were done, by coincidence, two weeks before and in nearly the same geographic location as the first leg of the survey. The focus group report and the first survey results arrived together. And they seemed to point in opposite directions. The survey was budgeted to include an advisory board of dentists to ensure the proper use of dental terms in framing the questions.

In analyzing the differences in results of quantitative and qualitative instruments, it suddenly became clear that the women in the panels had a quite different perspective on dental hygiene than the dentally correct understanding assumed in the survey questionnaire. Even when panelists were given a paragraph of professional information to read, most of them reverted to their own simpler systems of belief when asked to comment on positionings for the new toothpaste.

The positioning chosen by the client, to conform to professional facts, was aimed straight at parental conscientiousness. Even though the toothpaste would do little to help adults with their own dental problems, they were urged to buy it for their children. The initial survey results were equivocal. Panel members in the focus group interviews also found the positioning underwhelming. But they had the option in the discussions to reveal their wishes for a toothpaste that was not limited to children in its efficacy. They knew—but preferred not to know—that it was unlikely to help them. ("But look, it wouldn't *hurt* an adult's teeth, would it? And if you think it's helping, you might brush more often, so . . ."). They didn't ask for false promises, just freedom to believe what they wanted.

Survey questions were reworded, and the option of "good for me" included in the list of benefits.

Not all discrepancies are so easily resolved. But the freedom of focus group moderators to ask: "What exactly do you mean by that?" is a potential asset to everybody. It gives focus groups more power and scope, deepens the subjective usefulness of quantitative assays, and serves the client better.

USING FOCUS GROUPS FOR SHOW

One kind of exploratory research rarely mentioned in marketing texts probably never existed before the golden age of focus groups: the theatrical use of the interview itself, or the documentary use of the focus group report, for the purpose of selling. The two instances most common (so far) are:

• The use of edited videotapes in agency presentations to prospective clients.
• The use of focus group reports to obtain venture capital (or other kinds of financing) for a new product or service.

Other than declining the assignment, there is little the researcher can do to assure herself that the order or content of the interview(s) filmed and edited will not be distorted in the agency presentation. Everybody understands agency presentations to be dog and pony shows exploiting showmanship and cleverness. There is no peg to hang scruples on. A sop to conscience is: "If I don't do it, somebody else will." Or even more fatuously: "If I don't do it, somebody less honest—and richer—will." Not that no scruples should constrain the performance. Creating reactions in panelists with offstage stimuli is beyond the pale, for instance. But the end result is more a matter of style than of content. If the moderator learns something new about the product--and the agency gets the account—that's gravy. But it's more to the point to get a provocative moderator who puts on a good show.

The use of reports to attract funding is another ballgame, and a very complex one, with scruples right and left. The two parties to be addressed by the report come to it with predictably different mental orientation. The first client (the one with the product or service) is more optimistic than is probably justified by the findings, and *his* client (the one with the money) is apt to be more pessimistic. The choices open to the rapporteur are several. Assuming that the interviews are skillful (and as many as the first client can afford), and the interpretations true and sensitive, she now writes a report which:

1. Is straight down the middle. Avoids expressing intuitive feelings of either optimism or pessimism unless clearly documentable.

2. Minimizes the possibility of reinforcing the funder's pessimism by getting maximum mileage out of all the hopeful signs.

3. Minimizes the possibility of encouraging the direct client in his jaunty obliviousness to risk by making sure all caution signs are lit.

4. Has two report-endings: one for the client, in which the voice of caution prevails and thus balances his unrealistic dreams; the other for *his* client, in which every avenue of hope is explored so that his skeptical bias is not allowed to operate unchecked.

Not very big differences, you understand, and only in the "Implications" section. The findings will stand where they stand. Both clients will be free to moderate the written implications.

I have tried all three of these options and I can't make a decision that is right for all cases. The rapporteur must use all of the data available. Not just the interview data but also what she knows about the risks her client can afford, about whether he is a born gambler or plays it very safe. Also about the source of the funding: who wins or who loses. Then she spits on her finger and holds it into the wind.

THE USE OF FOCUS-GROUPS IN STUDYING CREATIVE CONCEPTS AND EXECUTIONS

There is probably no research function over which researchers and those who create advertising fall out of bed more often than the infamous "Copy Test", A number of research houses offer standardized copy tests, usually based on *recall* and/or liking and capable of generating numbers which distribute around a mean or average score. Some advertising creative departments have learned how to construct advertisements and commercials which will score well by these methods, because if their creations *don't* score well and a client is sold on the test, the ad or commercial is killed before it is born.

Possibly because of the rigidity of go/no-go decisions, from which there is no petitioning, most creative teams mistrust focus groups *less* than syndicated copy tests. This is not meant to suggest an actual love affair—just less loathing. The argument *against* using focus group interviews to examine advertising executions at various stages of completion is three-fold:

1. The numbers (of respondents) are inadequate.

2. The situation of scrutiny is unlike the real-life viewing experience.

3. Panelists become copy-critics and are perverted by this power, making different kinds of decisions than they would make as normal consumers.

All of these points are well taken. That is *not* to say that creative material shouldn't be shown to focus group panels. And it certainly doesn't mean that panelists' reactions should be ignored. It does mean that a small sample of respondents with no creative expertise and imperfect introspective sensitivity should not be given the power to reject or to endorse decisively the best insights of a professional team possessing considerable expertise, and presumably having more highly developed sensitivity for interpretive nuances on this particular topic than these or any other respondents. As most focus group researchers believe this, we should be pretty harmless. Our reports only rarely (and should never) attempt to provide yes or no answers, or even win, place, and show rankings for creative executions. But focus groups are dangerous to client creatives because a panelist's expression of approval or disapproval has backroom clout. It is lifelike and plausible.

The moderator will have this anxiety in mind and will demand of the panel members that they make their responses two-sided: "Regardless of whether you like or dislike this concept, what's the *best* thing about it? What's the *worst* thing about it?" The rapporteur interpreting and writing up the project will treat each of the items presented in the same way, noting first what respondents found to praise and then their objections. Written, vocal, and behavioral material will be figured into the format as well, and before it is committed to written form she will also examine the projective material for any additional insights or reverberations.

I recall an eleventh-hour, fast-and-dirty copy test of materials due for client presentation "on Friday." The responses in written notation differed from what was said in the discussion. The copy was both new and bold, and needed more digestion time than the two-hour interview could provide. But in analyzing the figure drawings and stories I discovered that an average of eight panelists out of every eleven or twelve had given a perfectly recognizable spin-off of one of the copy-concepts as the reason his "user" figure would buy the product. The stories spelled out the persuasiveness of the copy, and the client agreed to go along.

The use of the two-sided response, which requires panelists to find something to *approve* even in material which they may basically reject and to discover *weaknesses* even in something they basically want to praise, has more going for it than mere ego-support for the material's creators. The necessity of examining each item closely enough to find both positive and negative points produces more thoughtful responses overall.

Another safeguard against misleading panelist responses is the use of a
ringer-concept. I ask the creators of the concepts or illustrations to include in the materials to be presented one or two ideas that nobody
likes, that everybody connected with the project thinks is way off target.
This gives panel members something to hate; and most people interviewed seem to feel they are not being selective enough if there's *nothing* they don't like. On the other hand, panelists who like the moderator
and don't want to hurt her feelings really are *not* being selective. A real
dud of a promotional piece will smoke them out, so that the moderator
can say "Do you mean to sit there and tell me you *like* this one?," and
perhaps get more useful—anyway more honest—responses from them.

QUALITATIVE RESEARCH REIFIED

If focus groups are so valuable at the start of a research program, and if
they are also uniquely useful (with some qualifications) to check
progress in media res, then might they also be useful at the end of the research plan as a final check? Might focus groups also be a less complicated way of determining the truth of the final hypotheses drawn from
all of the preceding research? Might focus groups thus serve as a basis
for creative or marketing decisions? Oh, I hope not. But would anybody
choose to use them that way? Sad to say, yes.

Every focus group professional who has been at it for more than a few
years has in her memory, if not in her portfolio, some such projects. We
all can bring to mind those desperate gambles when there was no time
or money for anything else, and concepts hatched in a couple of groups
on Saturday went into production Monday morning. They make great
yarn-swapping on a slow news day. But they also send chills up our collective spine. They were close calls that shouldn't have worked.

Because the strange thing is, they all did. However carefully I sift
through my anecdotes, and those of other researchers I know and trust, I
can't uncover a single disaster. Maybe we are all rewriting history, or
maybe we've all been phenomenally lucky. Maybe. But I have to think
it is something more than that; not the majic of the technique, and not
the wizardry of the person wielding it either. Focus groups are ex-
panders of possibility, not limiters. And verifying a causal theory is the
ultimate in closure. What I think I think happens is that someone connected with the problem—on the client side, or on mine if I've been in-

volved with the problem for a while *almost* knows for certain before the panelists walk into the room what the true answer is. The interviews or their interpretation then do what focus groups always do: they set possibilities ringing. And one of those new possibilities resonates with this almost-certain idea in the mind of whoever-it-was. And we're home!

But I don't want to press my luck. May heaven never send me another one of those.

NOTES

[1]Tull & Hawkins, op. cit.

Chapter 10

Choosing Panelists

In the early days of focus-group interviews, as I remember, researchers who had started to do them were terribly caught up in the method. It was a kind of confederated narcissism. The light which broke upon us from the assembling and querying of respondents, illuminating aspects of a problem, was never quite bright enough to block out entirely a more primitive exultation: "Just look what *I'm doing!*" Recruiting interviewees was a pretty primitive process too, but who knew? If the people in the groups (the fancier name "panel" came later) were all friends or neighbors, or went to the same church or the same beautician, nobody squawked. The important thing was to get enough of them in the same room to do a focus-group interview. After all, did Pasteur prescreen his sheep before he vaccinated half of them? He did not. Without deciding whether they "qualified," he took the first ones that came, catch as catch can, called them "experimental," and fired away. And so did we.

That is we viewed the respondents not so much as persons, but as *people.* Ironic that at the very time we were most infatuated with the new method of doing qualitative marketing research, our perspectives were the most similar to our quantitative forbears, who ". . . never measure people, but only the . . . characteristic of being present."[1]

Moderators did, in fact, make decisions about who and how many people to recruit for the interview. We just didn't know that they were "decisions" until we came across other moderators who had made *their* decisions differently. For example, those of us who had relatively longer or more intensive experience with group dynamics were more relaxed about being able to handle sizable numbers of respondents. We knew, from working with other groups, that the group ethos could be relied upon to exert some control over any members who got too far out of line, without our disciplinary intervention. And moderators who felt comfortable with groups the size of the Last Supper also saw real advantages in interviewing large numbers of people at one sitting.

First off, there is the implicit pragmatic dictum of giving the client/employer his money's worth. Even in the days when a single group cost approximately $200-$250 a sample size of 100 respondents, interviewed in 6-member panels, was a great deal costlier in time and money than processing the same individuals in panels of 10 or 12. But there were additional dividends in validity:

Depth. The multiplicity of viewpoints and reactions necessarily expressed in a gathering of ten or more people makes each individual member of the group more aware of the singularity of his or her own repertoire of assumptions and responses. The moderator, too, sees each individual more clearly, as she reacts to a fuller range of other panelists' responses.

Anonymity. Conversely, greater numbers of participants offer one another more camouflage and anonymity, so that the risks of deviating from particular perceptions and values expressed by others in the group are lessened.

Representation. While it may be true that large panels offer only negligible gains in the representativeness of individual ideas, practices, and intentions (simply by increase in the total headcount), a large panel is apt to offer a much truer picture of the influences and modifications introduced in marketplace behavior as word-of-mouth.

Discovery. Every group represents idea generation to some extent. The convergence and building of ideas from 10 or more motivated (and tacitly competitive) people vastly improves the odds for getting truly "great" ideas, or truly elegant solutions to problems.

Decisions about how many people to interview are simpler to make than decisions of composition—how many of *whom*. The alternatives "larger"/"smaller" are polarities which may always generate partisan disputes. But questions of *composition* are not so neatly framed.

For moderators who came to focus groups fresh from other kinds of people-handling where participation was more likely to be on a volunteer basis, the question of whom to recruit was even more arbitrary than how many. Presumably those first few researchers who jumped the tracks from quantitative marketing research were more adept at defining user-categories and did so. The social scientists (sociologists, psychologists, anthropologists) who came to the job as mercenaries, or because of the research possibilities, were less familiar with this kind of categorization and thus less systematic. We, the new recruits to marketing research, simply tried to think of all the kinds of people who might find relevance in the topic targeted for a focus-group project. And then we asked the recruiter to try to find about a dozen of them who could show up at the same time.

As the social scientists began to learn more about targeting and segmentation, and the defectors from more quantitative enterprise began to feel more at home with group dynamics, our paths started to converge. There are still no single answers to the questions "How many?" and "Who?" that will satisfy everyone. The answers given in particular instances today seem to be based on idiosyncratic preference and on the unique functions of the particular project. It is not possible to be definitive in answering these questions without first specifying answers to three other questions on which these issues are contingent:

1. Who is to decide the size and composition of the panels?

2. Who is to moderate the interviews?

3. What is the purpose of the project?

Who Decides on the Focus Group Specifications?

Historically, panel size was as likely to be determined by the size of diningroom tables as by moderator preference or usage quotas. It is doubtful whether early recruiters bothered with anything more elaborate than scribbled notes of time, place, and respondent availability. As interview sites shifted from respondents' homes to the central locations of research facilities, the whole process became more standardized. Most of the first formal screeners were written by field suppliers who were used to writing screeners, rather than by the moderators who mostly weren't. The moderator or the client got the ball rolling by telephoning the field facility—or the increasingly professional recruiter—who then wrote up telephone notes on the conversation, and translated them into a screener.

I suspect that the task of producing screeners passed to the researcher after one too many complaints that some of the panel members were unqualified. Today, either the moderator or the client research staff may actually transmit formal requirements of panel size and composition in the form of a questionnaire given to the recruiters. The recruiters read the questions to prospective respondents and, on the basis of their answers, dismiss them or question them further, up to determining available interview times.

In the adventure of planning a project, specifying panel size and composition is low on the scale of excitement, so that clients may shrug it off as an accessory of planning. When this happens, the moderator must make explicit every inference she has made about what the client wants in these respects and must formalize her surmises in detail in the screener. Clients who have been "too busy" to confer on such questions can generally be counted on to read the document before initialing approval. Once it has been ratified and sent into the field, the screener does not reappear until just before the interview, duplicated for each respondent, with his or her responses recorded.

When planning focus groups, the decisions made and communicated regarding panel size and composition are analogous to choosing the best size and fabric specifications when ordering garments from a mail-order catalog. It is necessary to take into account the personal style of the person who will be wearing the garment (i.e., working with the panel), the comfort it offers, and the possible restrictions on movement. It is also prudent to consider, in both cases, the probability of shrinkage. This is obvious in the case of mail-order clothing, less so in the case of panels recruited from a distant supplier. But every experienced moderator knows that those in attendance at the interview—those panelists who survive wind, weather, acts of God, and human frailty—are rarely identical to those recruited, and may fall short in number of those confirmed for attendance. Making certain that the panel of record, after the attrition of probable cancellations, is of a size that is comfortable for the particular interviewer to moderate and the client personnel to view, always involves guesswork. The field staff of the facility which will handle each interview are the people best equipped to estimate shrinkage of recruited panels in their geographical location, for panelists of the particular specifications desired, and at the time specified. But the usual over-recruiting allowance is about 20 percent: recruiting 14 respondents to guarantee 11 or 12. If all 14 somehow manage to materialize, the client or moderator must decide who stays and who is paid off and sent home.

Since payoffs to nonparticipants in a 12 panel project can add appreciably to the cost of the project ($750 or more), clients with tight budgets may elect to recruit only the number of panelists to be interviewed, and risk a low turn-out. Heterogeneous panels with quotas for each category carry the added risk of unbalanced participation. If the principal target for a product is men between the ages of 27 and 39, with incomes of $40,000 or higher, and half of each panel (six men) is to represent this group and the other half represents younger and older panelists in lower income groups, over-recruiting will replicate panelists in the targeted age and economic bracket. This would be done not only because they are believed to be central to the project but also because they can be assumed to be the busiest (and therefore most likely to cancel) segment. Without over-recruiting, the eight or nine men finally attending might contain only two or three from the prime-target group.

The principal risks in over-recruiting are "unnecessary" expenditures, in both recruiting costs and gratuities, for respondents not interviewed, or—if such waste is unendurable—seating of an unwieldy number of panelists. Failing to over-recruit can result in a panel that is too small and/or unbalanced for the goals of the particular project.

But what is too small or too large for one moderator is just right for another moderator. Professional moderators with impeccable credentials argue cogently in favor of mini-groups, and just as many of equal eminence cast lucid votes for the maxi-groups.

Mob Scene or Small Screen: The Mini/Maxi Dispute.

The numbers being disputed are actually quite small. A minimalist will set eight panelists as the absolute upper limit; a maximalist will set nine as the absolute lowest. Moreover, though the two factions are didactic and occasionally passionate in expressing their arguments, the advantages they cite are remarkably similar:

Freedom of Speech. Moderators who argue in favor of minigroups of four to six panelists say that, in a two-hour interview with time-outs for moderator participation and presented materials, each of twelve panelists can only be "on" for less than ten minutes, and each respondent in an eight person panel for less than fifteen while six panelists can each talk nearly twenty minutes. However, in the broken-field speaking of a focus-group interview, responses may average ten seconds, and a one-minute "speech" is distinctly a rarity. Ten minute, fifteen minute and twenty minute allotments are relevant mainly to formats in which individual panel members are interviewed consecutively, one-on-one—and this is not a group-interview. In any case, if one multiplies the spoken content of a 60 second commercial by 10 (a way to imagine ten minutes worth of talk), it adds up as a lot of words.

Greater Depth. This is an advantage claimed for *both* panel sizes, by their respective advocates. Those favoring mini-groups reason that the depth of expression and understanding depends on rapport, and that large groups do not foster the development of rapport.

Those who prefer larger numbers of respondents in a panel point out that the only opportunity for rapport which is reduced in large focus groups is that between each panelist and the *moderator*. And this argument leaves plenty of room for several different viewpoints. In the first place (say big-panel advocates), the moderator is some kind of authority in the respondent group, and respondents seeking rapport may be more interested in impressing her than in delivering honest remarks. Actually, larger numbers of people could be seen as *multiplying* opportunities for rapport rather than curtailing them. Furthermore, even if it is conceded that rapport with the moderator is the best facilitator of depth, the difference between one interviewee and four, in moderator availability, is greater than that between eight and twelve. Finally, the maxi-contingent claim is that greater numbers of participants yield greater depth because more facets of each individual come into play.

The question of *depth* is complicated by the infrequency with which depth—and the evidence that depth has been plumbed—is defined. Small-group advocates often equate depth with willingness to discuss "deeply personal" topics. Who could argue with that? But when this "too personal" material turns out to be the use of products coyly described as "intimate health care items," we reach an impasse. Defenders of maxi-groups contend that it would be difficult to imagine greater willingness for such discussions than the quick responsiveness they regularly encounter in large groups.

The twin of depth of expression is honesty (or accuracy). And again both factions claim superiority. Those in the mini-group camp insist that the rejection-proof support which individuals need in order to undertake introspective journeys, and to report what they find inside themselves, can only be found in the rapport between moderators and small panels of interviewees. Maxi-group devotees just as firmly assert that deeper concern with the moderator—who is a temporary stand-in for all the authority figures whose esteem has ever been courted by a panelist— will invite similar courting and impression management and discourage honest confidences. A larger panel can increase the number of scorekeeping participants, who can catch a self-serving participant in a contradiction, and thereby keep everybody honest.

Order and Ease. Small focus groups, according to their adherents, are slower paced, less contentious and easier to track. Both moderator and viewers can be more certain of what has happened, and have time to think out how to proceed. In a word, they are more *controllable.* Few large-panel enthusiasts would question the assertion. The question is whether manageability is in fact closer to the real life experiences which the moderator is trying to evoke, the opposing contention being that muddle is closer to the truth of most people's lives most of the time. This is especially true of the real-life phenomena of buying decisions, which generally belong to unconscious process: a notoriously muddled realm. If it is more difficult to moderate, to watch, and to interpret a large, often noisy interview, layered with cross-talk; if it is, as charged, harder to keep track of who said what—so be it. In complexity lies rich-ness, energy, and innovation. In any case, "harder" is not "impossible." The moderator must bring to the task a high level of concentration, and the back-room viewers may need to be instructed and motivated to work harder, but effort of this kind pays off on both sides of the mirror. (More about this in Chapter 11.)

Although I am unable to free myself from bias in the matter of panel size, and would vote the ticket with the large-panel party, in the end I feel that the number of participants chosen is probably determined basi-cally by the personality of the moderator/rapporteur. Similar arguments have arisen in the professional debate between therapists who favor group-therapy and those who believe the therapeutic dyad to be the one true path. These arguments, it has often seemed to me, have revealed themselves to be based on temperament and the therapist's personal comfort with a technique. So too in the controversy on panel size in focus-group interviewing.

Researchers who choose excitement over manageability and predictability, and who are comfortable with controversy welcome the interactive complexity of larger numbers of respondents. Other equally competent researchers who find a slower, less energetic and more manageable group climate more congenial do not. The choice has something to do, too, with the way a moderator views panelists. Those who believe that the panel members are fragile and need ease, uninterrupted conviviality and shelter are more likely to prefer small panels, in which the emotional thermostat is always within the moderator's control. Other interviewers, who are persuaded that respondents are resilient, adventurous, and quite capable of closing their doors on any exploration which is too dangerous for them to pursue, will probably choose the more emotionally arduous climate of the larger panel.

The line is not as hard and fast as the controversy makes it appear. Moderators do not always have the final say about panel size, and decisions against the grain need not affect the usefulness of a project. A good moderator is capable of conducting satisfactory interviews with groups of three or of thirteen respondents. But her sense of security with the group is undermined if the number of panelists is far from the number she thinks ideal.

A MIXED BAG OR A MATCHED SET: THE HOMOGENEOUS/HETEROGENEOUS ISSUE

Early in the planning of a focus-group project, client and researcher will have to decide on the *composition* of each group of respondents. And the first decision addressed should probably be whether the group is basically heterogeneous or homogeneous. No absolute heterogeneity or homogeneity exists in groups. Wholly heterogeneous panels would have nothing to talk about, wholly homogeneous ones would have no need to talk. So too with intermediate cases. In the case of a group of respondents selected as heterogeneous, the potential energy of curiosity exists in the panelists waiting to be realized, and the outcome to be hoped for is discovery. But the danger in heterogeneity is that the interests, beliefs, and behaviors of a particular participant will be so foreign to those of every other individual in the group that discussion will stall, unable to bridge the gap. In a more homogeneous group, responses to questions and to presented materials may be limited to monologues with choral murmurs of assent.

Moderator responsibilities in the two cases are quite different. In a panel of unlike participants, she, as a participant, must act the role of the cautious interpreter. ("Does everyone understand what he just said? Does *anyone* understand it? Would you rephrase it in your own words? . . . Okay, was that it? No? Well if I said _____ would that be close to your meaning?") As the mood-setter for the group she must infect every member with her "intense but respectful curiosity," until everyone present becomes a moderator and the climate is active and egalitarian. ("What a fascinating viewpoint. I don't believe I've ever heard it put just that way. Have any of the rest of you? What in your experience do you think caused you to see things that way? . . .")

In a group of similar participants the moderator herself must represent the alien positions. ("Do you all feel the way she does? Could anyone make a case—even if you don't feel it—for another point of view? Well then, let me play devil's advocate: If I took issue with you and said _____ how would you answer me?") She has a more active and managerial role in homogeneous panel discussions, and runs the risk of circumscribing the alternative viewpoints by confining exploration to those with which she is familiar. Furthermore, homogeneous discussions are draining for a conscientious moderator, since the energy of curiosity does not catch fire among the panelists. It is all taken from her reserves.

When the project aims to explore new-product opportunities or to investigate the probable impact of new-product introduction, the question of mixing or matching of buyers/nonbuyers isn't raised in planning, because it can't be raised. Making that distinction is the goal of the study. In interviews for new and as yet unborn products, the only homogeneous/heterogeneous decisions to be made concern those screenable items of panelists' status (demographic, vocational, political, medical, and so on) in which the client is interested (for example, a magazine that will appeal to high school seniors, an over-the-counter analgesic for use by *headache sufferers*, or a breakfast product positioned for use by a particular *life-style* group). When the client has no such limiting agenda, the name of the game is demographic spread.

But where the product has an established history, the question of like-ness/unlikeness is further complicated by the split between users and nonusers. The options are now multiplied. Should panelists be dissimilar in all respects (both users and nonusers, from a wide range of sociological categories)? Should they be dissimilar in usage, but otherwise matched? Should there be both all-user and all nonuser groups, with respondents who are diverse in other respects? Or should the population be split into four watertight groupings (users under 35, users over 35, nonusers under 35, nonusers over 35), each to be interviewed in separate panels?

Obviously, the questions of panel size and of the degree of homogeneity/heterogeneity are not independent. Panels of four to six respondents, each representing four or more classifications, would place an unjustifiable weight of representation on each individual panelist—not to mention the recruiters' difficulty in guaranteeing quotas. Very small panels, almost by definition, are homogeneous panels, or are assumed to be so. Large panels can accommodate variation, with some degree of quota specification: twelve panelists: half homemakers and half working women, with a few working homemakers; ages 21-69, but heaviest in the 31-45 age group; with demographic range overall, is a difficult but far from impossible assignment.

Heterogeneity in product usage—user/nonuser groups, half and half—is commonly suggested by moderators because such groups are more fertile in generating reasons why and why not to purchase. If the client trusts the rapporteur to keep straight in her head during the interview and in the interpretive period as well which responses were made by users and which by non-users, he will probably accept the suggestion, for at least some panels. But clients are more readily persuaded that users and nonusers are different kinds of people than interviewers are. This may reflect nothing more than the clients' assumption that their products are vitally important to consumers' lives, so much so that the clients believe that by purchasing them consumers somehow distinguish themselves from the crowd. And sometimes they are right:

A manufacturer of cosmetics and treatment products developed a shampoo for temporary coloring of grey hair. When the product had been on the market for almost a year, the client requested focus groups to check reasons for buying and not buying among women fifty years of age and older. The client acceded—reluctantly—to the recommendation that users and nonusers be interviewed together. In each of the six split-panel groups, the nonusers of the product were angry, quite personally, at the company and reported switching away from that company's other products. The women felt that their attractiveness—even their acceptability—had been called into question by the company's advertising of the product, which ". . . just assumes that anybody who cares how she looks will want to cover her grey hair. . . ." Participants with untouched grey hair were shown a before/after commercial message (a dowdy, grey-haired, haggard woman passed over by an attractive man of similar age, in favor of a coiffed nymphet/followed by a color application/followed by the same middle-aged woman--now auburn haired—with a good night's sleep, a few surgical nips, sleekly-fitting clothes, and a flattering camera angle. She is now appreciated by the same middle-aged male, in full sexual display, while the rejected pouting nymphet looks on . . .). They responded with hurt, with affront, with amused pique, or with indignation.

Although the moderator sensed that she was walking on glass, she probed the hurt and angry women, who eventually lined up in two sub-clusters: women who felt the commercial was all too true, but sensed that accepting the need for artificial hair coloring was simply opening the door to a series of makeover efforts which would finally end in failure. ("So I color my hair, and I buy some designer clothes. Isn't it more of a shock . . . when I turn around? . . . The rest of me won't match.") And the women for whom gray hair is a banner of selfhood and equal rights ("Look at him! He's at least the same age. It doesn't just say that *I* am chopped liver. He is a mess *inside* too. . . . I wouldn't color my hair. I'd . . . empty the salad on his head.")

Trying to turn the lemons into lemonade, the moderator asked if there was anything realistic that a shampoo company could do to help them. There were two answers. One was oriented to product improvement. ("My hair is not just gray. It's *different.* The texture is not the same, and I can't manage it. Give me a shampoo that changes the texture, and maybe a setting-gel that will hold the set better. . . .") The other was directed to the advertising message. ("Show a woman with gorgeous gray hair and a little self-confidence, and say something about gray hair, well-groomed gray hair, being a signal that an interesting, sort of spunky woman has it.")

The user panelists (those now coloring their hair), who were the pre-interview targets for the product, saw the commercial as derivative and the product as "just another temporary-coloring shampoo" which "I might try if I get bored." But some of the women who now color felt that they might stop, if "the right kind of commercial" was aired for "a really good line of products for keeping gray hair shiny and manageable."

In this case, the client was right about the importance of use/nonuse of the coloring products in the lives of these women, but wrong in supposing that separate user/nonuser groups was the best way to proceed. Subsequent nonuser panels, with nothing to mobilize their outrage, were less vocal in embracing a proudly-gray line of products. Perhaps they were more sparing of painful feelings in themselves and others. Perhaps advertising in a vacuum was less true to life than advertising against the background of commercial noise, which is loud and redundant in the women's shampoo category. But subsequent history suggests that the first mixed panels were closer to the purchase-truth in this consumer age-group and category.

When the budget is not a problem, and focus groups are considered to be important steps in solving a marketing problem (and not just amusing games or excuses for retreat), the most useful plan is probably a two-step exploratory program in which groups as heterogeneous as possible are interviewed, with the objective of identifying relevant segments of the population. Once the information gained in these explorations has been interpreted and transmitted, a second series of planning meetings should decide whether the next step is to be homogeneous groups, groups which are dichotomous for usage, but restricted demographically, or some other screenable variation.

Another expression of homogeneity is increasingly requested by clients. It is the proscriptive order for "only articulate respondents." Clearly, this directive is not intended categorically. It doesn't take much discrimination on a recruiter's part to excuse those who are incapable of expressing themselves for whatever reasons. What this request calls for is animated, communicatively proficient speakers. And on the face of it, why not? Certainly they are more interesting to interview and to listen to on the audio hook-up in the back room. Also, there is no danger of moderator-directiveness, in an interview in which responses are bubbling and ready, as opposed to an interview in which the moderator feels she must forcibly extract responses from the groups. (See Chapter 12.)

The problem is that these wordsmiths are not everybody. They are not even most folks. Indeed, they probably represent a minority of consumers. More importantly, they are more likely than a random sample population to represent a distinct sub-group whose exclusive participation might mislead. For instance:

Salesmen. As a group, salesmen are wonderful . . . as long as you know that's what you've got. But they are naturally attuned and carefully indoctrinated to win approval from anyone toward whom they are oriented—probably, in this instance, the moderator. And most of them are good at it. They can't help being less interested in what she is trying to learn than in getting the response they want. They read every shift in position or expression to gauge how well they are coming across. Not every salesman, and probably not *any* salesman one has known for 20 years. But in two hours, the best anyone can hope to be is a prospect.

Teachers. Since a focus group is a strange situation, and people in strange situations open with the roles they know best, a teacher is apt to lecture (what else?) to the rest of the panel. When she also knows a little something about the product or category, she is dangerously equipped to be an "in-group moderator" (see "Problem Groups," Chapter 12), competing for the chair and the constituency.

Vocational Monologuists. Those people who are used to captive audiences—dentists, cabdrivers, barbers and hairdressers—have adjusted their communication accordingly. Speaking has become routine for them.

Psychopaths. Just as recruiting instructions to trawl for "articulate panelists" would be likely to rule out *depressed* people (the most common complaint), so would it rule *in* psychopathic or sociopathic people, who by definition act out and speak out against the societal grain.

And, after all, "articulate" is a subjective judgment. The recruiter is unlikely to have participated in the planning sessions and thus cannot appreciate the fine balance of participants so carefully determined during this operation. It is foolhardy to entrust someone marginally involved in the project with the responsibility of selecting the panelists.

A panel which is chockful of "articulate" members is a distinctly unusual event, but there is another reason (than nonrepresentativeness, as noted above) that my heart sinks if a new field supervisor says to me: "You'll love them. They're all talkers." One of the most important assets of the focus-group interview, as a tool of exploration, is the window it affords on the world of word-of-mouth. In a two- or three-hour session which covers predispositions, brand behavior, and reactions to new ideas, *some* of the new ideas to which panelists respond are presented by other panelists rather than by the formal presentations of the moderator. Watchful eyes and ears on both sides of the mirror can see and hear inclination, resistance, persuasion, and tentative purchase interest in the product, in response to both client blandishments offered by the moderator and the assertions of other participants. Some of this byplay is arguably a microscopic look, *in vivo*, at the "two-step diffusion" process. This scenario identifies the *influential innovator* (I.I.), who is typically in the vanguard of purchasers of new products. Having tried the product, the innovator disseminates her influence among her more timid imitators. The process bears strong resemblance to the act of selling with the I.I. as a sort of lay salesperson. Like the professional vendor, she may extol the product more enthusiastically than she perceives it, in order to receive her pay-off of power. The I.I. is paid in full by being the instrumental first-user who creates a surge of buying interest. And she is not as candid as salespeople may be. She sincerely believes that altruism is her motive for pushing the product. What she is reacting to when products or advertising are shown is the *opportunity for powerful interaction*, not the message or the product itself.

Clearly, a packed panel of I.I.s can mislead. The enthusiasm which seems to run through such a group is likely, at best, to be shortlived (influencers are fickle, since they need newness to exert their influence). Consider the dynamics of such a panel. For I.I.s, the rewarding marketplace formation is triangular, with the I.I. at the apex. That is, the rewards depend on the relative rarity of the breed. A whole panel of I.I.s could not perform their vital function, and would be driven to a spiraling game of follow-the-leader. In rare pre-interview funks (having been promised a group of "all talkers"), I have been seized by the worst case-scenario fear that my twelve I.I.s would all end by diving out of the window like lemmings, in an excess of terminal frustration. I would infinitely prefer dealing with a few bashful or depressed respondents—even with a couple of chronic stutterers—to attempting to outflank twelve "talkers."

Assuming that the panels assembled in the field meet everybody's qualification standards, have all of the "Who" questions been answered? Have all the on-stage bodies been accounted for? Not quite, or not always.

WHO'S ON FIRST: THE QUESTION OF MULTIPLE INTERVIEWERS

There are projects in which more than one moderator or rapporteur is involved. In general, this situation arises when there are too many interviews to be done in too short a time for one person to accomplish without compromising quality. As a rough guide to the limits of what one moderator can do well, I would not advise—ever—scheduling a single interviewer for three two-hour (or longer) interviews in one day, or for more than six (two per day in each of three locations) in any ten-day period. Twenty interviews in a single month also approaches the upper limit.

When scheduling of this sort is *de rigeur*, moderators can split the chores in several ways. In *parallel projects*, multiple moderators do the interviewing, with one senior rapporteur attending all the groups and assuming responsibility for the interpretation and the report. Less commonly, contemporaneous interviews are entirely separate, with parallel interpretation and reporting. The exploration can, alternately, be divided into two or more projects, all of which are outlined with two or more researchers who are then assigned different components of the research package to moderate, interpret, and report. Then the several researchers collaborate on a summary report.

Occasionally, the presence in the same room of two designated moderators is called-for. This is a very delicate undertaking which requires a definite and frankly presented interaction between the moderators. Only three general types of situation have been formulated to date which justify this risky format:

1. The first is the *apprenticing* process, in which the learner is introduced to the panelists as a trainee (preferably by the junior herself). The apprentice's "presented self," should be discussed before any interviewing is done; opportunities for polarized interaction of the two moderators should be roughly charted; and behavioral signals for fielding other situations agreed on, ("There's something I'm dying to ask."; "Hold it a minute"/"Here's your chance.") The interpretive significance of responses to the comoderators individually should be discussed before interviewing starts.

2. Sometimes in projects focused on highly technical products (such as drugs) or services (such as investment banking), it is unwise for the moderator to attempt to carry the role of "expert" as well as moderating the group. Even if she is *able* to perform both functions, her relationship to panelists might change. If the interviewees are neophytes, a moderator-expert might evoke a response akin to religious awe, and respondents might become reticent from the fear of expressing "dumb"

ideas. Similarly, in cases of new-product invention or introduction, the practice of participation by a client representative can prevent the moderator from appearing to hawk the product. In both the high-tech situation and the new-product venture, the presence of a *participant-expert* can serve to sharpen the moderator's role and, at the same time, can discourage ingroup moderators. Also worth noting, in both cases: a mutually-understood signal for "That's enough," or "Button your lip" should be added to the basic signal telegraphy listed for apprenticeship.

3. Finally, to point up panelist-reactions to creative concepts or executions, it is sometimes useful to bring into the room at a planned moment during the interview a "devil's advocate" from the client side—not, however, from the creative department. The same signaling conventions apply in this case, with one additional indicator signifying "It's time for you to catch your plane."

NOTES

[1]Tull & Hawkins, quoted more fully in Chapter 4.

Chapter 11

How to Be the "Best Possible" Client and How to Be the "Best Possible" Researcher

In attempting to establish requirements for appointing clients and moderators to a "legion of honor," I realized that there would be severe skewing from moderator bias if the only source of data was my own experience and intuition. I did what any self-respecting qualitative researcher must do: I interviewed. The sample included not only my clients and not only rapporteurs of similar persuasion. I spoke also (on the client side) to advertisers about whom I knew only that they regularly spent a large chunk of their research budgets on focus groups and to agency research and creative heads who spend important money on qualitative exploration. On the supplier side, my informants were similarly varied. I tried to include, in both camps, people whose opinions promised to be varied and thoughtful.

All of the respondents were asked to discuss their judgments frame-by-frame, dividing the whole interchange into "as many divisions as you think there are." All agreed basically to the same 5 or 6 divisions.

1. *The interviewing or assignment stage:* the period between "Let's do some groups" and the acceptance of a proposal. Those clients who are firmly wedded to particular suppliers were asked either "How do you decide which of the researchers in your stable is to be assigned to a particular project?" or "If your regular moderator were honeymooning in Australia, and all your colleagues who know this terrific moderator were in traction after a whitewater vacation in Colorado, how would you decide on a researcher for a critical focus-group project?" Moderators were offered the same flexibility in defining segments of the research

process. With the exception of the few who derive most of their assignments from repeat, or other over-the-transom assignments, the moderators recognize this period as "the proposal stage."

2. *The planning and scheduling stage:* the period between the assignment of a project to a particular rapporteur and the first focus-group interview. Both clients and researchers agree that this is the second stage, even though two very different activities fill the time segment: the *planning* operation, which ends with an approved discussion guide, and the *placement and scheduling* operations, which commence with the selection of a field facility and the approval of the screener and end when airline and hotel reservations are confirmed and the recruiting is underway.

3. *The data-gathering stage:* the period which begins when all of the principals are in place (panelists scarfing up the refreshments and/or waiting in the reception area, client representatives in the darkened viewing room, and the moderator gearing up at the foot of the conference table), and ends when panelists have left the facility. The pre-interview stage may or may not include a backroom briefing, and the post-mortem. (More on this below.) But usually each interview day ends with a flurry of activity in which the moderator and clients carry out some social function such as arranging to dine, which returns them to the real world.

4. *The interpretation stage:* the period in which the moderator gathers her recollections of the group and creates a top-line report (rarely longer than one week), and the rapporteur listens to tapes, records verbatim quotes, analyzes these data into a full report, and readies a presentation (usually two or three weeks after the last interview) . . . while the client waits.

5. *The report-and-presentation stage:* the climactic period in which the rapporteur delivers the final report and an oral presentation in a joint meeting with the client. This customarily includes a question-and-answer interchange.

6. *The after the ball (or between dances) stage:* the period—recognized by all of the rapporteur/moderators—in which both parties retreat to

corners. Clients now implement recommendations from the report, and proceed with additional research, marketing or creative execution, and so on. The researcher goes on to other projects, and the collaboration is suspended.

Although the designated sequence and initiation/completion rituals are the same for clients and research suppliers, the significance of each stage in the project is often perceived differently by the two participants. The constitution of each division—its energy allotment, mood, emotional investment and return—may diverge so sharply that communication is most difficult at the very times when accurate communication is most needed.

WHAT AM I BID? GETTING TOGETHER

If the client consistently engages the same research supplier, the first step in the project is essentially omitted. Only occasional aggravations, like the client using another researcher or the rapporteur being booked by another client for the time requested, produce something like the tentative and uneasy interaction which is common in this period.

In the case of "regular" moderator-client interaction, the qualifications of the moderator and the acceptability of the client, which originally went into establishing the ongoing relationship, have been forgotten or taken for granted. They are no longer at the foreground of awareness. To sharpen this focus and make these qualifications salient again, representatives of both parties in my interviews were asked to place themselves in the situation of initiating a first meeting. Clients were requested to review the events that were instrumental in assigning a project to an unknown researcher and researchers were instructed to relive making or receiving a cold call to or from a strange client.

Barring intramural word-of-mouth, neither the clients nor the moderators were able to agree on information which would be useful in predicting either professional competence or a good match between moderator and client. Most clients felt that "experience in the job" was the most important—if not the only important—qualification for considering a prospective moderator: ". . . although of course someone could have a lot of bad experience: one assignment from each client and no repeat business. . . ." Surprisingly few mentioned academic achievement: "Of course, after you have met someone and liked them, it is comforting to know they have the Ph.D., and presumably know what they're doing . . . as long as it doesn't add too much to the bill. I don't want to *pay for* the education." Probed for this information, clients said that of course they expected "at least . . . a BA degree—completion of college. . . . " And most said that they would prefer—all other things being equal, an MA, or at least some graduate study in a related field (marketing or the human sciences). Ph.D.'s could be advantageous or distinctly not: "Fine, as a rule, but they can be too academic, or . . . too temperamental . . ."

Much more important, even this early and even over the telephone, was ". . . personal vibes." If the moderator initiated the call, the right degree of persistence was important. "They should ask for the business—let you know they really want it. They should call back if you don't set up an interview the first call. But they can't be too insistent either."

Moderators, too, picked up good and bad "chemistry" from clients, no matter who set the contact in motion: "You can tell the ones who really know how to use focus groups, and how to treat moderators. The ones who respect professionalism, and have the problem laid out for you." Skipping professional word-of-mouth, they learn as much as clients will tell them about the problem and what the client thinks focus groups will tell him: "If it is just a stalling technique, or if they are asking some little bitty thing like very specific wording in copy . . . "; or ". . . if I have some reason to think they want to prove a point and not just find the answer. . . ." Sometimes work is not pursued because of what a telephone conversation tells them: ". . . if the problem is not a proper focus-group problem, or if I feel he is not going to be satisfied with the results . . . I may say I am busy, or explain why I would hesitate to take the project. . . ."

To both parties the *interview* is the critical screening tool. In my small samples, the moderators are more definitive in listing the qualifications for a good interview than the clients.[1] *The ideal client,* at this stage of the game, researchers say, should:

• Call in for interviews only those prospective moderators to whom he seriously considers giving the assignment. If there is a "favorite moderator" whom he regularly uses, it may be easier—but is less respectful—to make his plans without saying anything to her, or to call her in and later tell her she "didn't make it" or that her "price was too high." It is harder and more respectful to call her and say frankly that he'd like another voice, and will use her again (if he means to).

• Interview only as many candidates as he needs to get a flavor of the available range of technical prowess, research philosophy, and individual style. Like all auditions, these interviews are more fun for the producer than for the talent: he needn't flex his political muscle at every candidate in town.

• When he raises the subject of money (and he should), he must say honestly and frankly what the budget will bear. Money is a perfectly respectable topic. In truth it is half of what the interviews are now about —maybe more than half. Of course frank and early disclosure will deprive him of the political advantage in this *pas de deux* ("How much would you charge?" marks him as a sharp operator; but "Here is what I am allowed for this project, can you fit it into your price scale?" marks him as a forthright, compassionate person.) It is true that he may bargain a few dollars off the total by keeping the budget close to his vest. But somebody has to *trust* somebody, and this is the researchers' turn.

• If he asks for a proposal more complicated than two paragraphs specifying overall problems to be addressed and probable cost, he should only ask this from as many prospective rapporteurs as he is prepared to pay a nominal sum for the effort and the long-distance phone bills that are involved in getting a field estimate. So far as my informants know, this is unheard of—"but you did say 'ideal', didn't you?"

• He should make his choice as speedily as possible, to avoid hanging-up the moderators' schedules, not to mention grilling them on a slow spit. And he should call both winner and losers himself, and answer candidly their questions about his choice.

Although the clients I talked to reported that they depend primarily on the interview for assessing prospective moderators, they were somewhat atmospheric in saying what criteria they use to size up candidates.[2] In the first meeting with moderators—the one that divides the hopefuls into "no" and "maybe"—there are three general qualifiers. Those candidates that become finalists are:

Presentable. She or he ". . . should look okay, dress appropriately and be pleasant to be with. You don't want Wanda the Witch or Billy Beast . . ." This includes, for most of the clients who were able to be more specific than "look good," the stipulation that they have "no . . . medical or other physical problems that . . . show, that could embarrass people. . . ." For some, it also includes *any* conspicuous physical trait that could arouse strong feelings in panelists (". . . not horrible or unkempt, but . . . a drop-dead beauty is almost as bad. . . .") For a few of the clients, this extends to "someone who resembles the target audience," either across the board, or "for especially sensitive topics." (See discussion of moderator/panelist resemblance below, "Through a Glass Darkly: Doing and Viewing".)

Intellectually and verbally adroit. A suitable person for focus-group moderating and interpreting, they say, ". . . shouldn't be a dope, and should have a general sense of what's going on in the world . . .; An animated conversationalist, who doesn't put herself at the center—who listens as well as she talks, and doesn't think she knows exactly what the respondents mean, if she *doesn't";* and ". . . a person who knows when people are finished talking about a topic, and can find an opening into some other topic, without making a visible effort . . . "; and "Some-one who . . . can keep things flowing, and can make a comment wittily, but . . . not a comic or performer."; and finally, "A moderator should have the confidence that she or he is in control of the interview . . . but nobody else should know it—should feel her controlling . . . except as a feeling of security. . . ."

Able to establish rapport with the client. As to the relationship of the client with the prospective researcher they should ". . . feel like friends. There should be good vibes, although 'seductive' would be the wrong thing."; "I should—would like to—feel as if I understood the person and he or she understood me. . . . But I wouldn't want anybody to whom I give a project to get so persuaded that we understand each other that he or she doesn't double check with me to make sure that is what I really meant. I'm not looking for a wife, after all."; "This may sound unimportant . . . but I'm going to see a lot of the person I hire, so it has to be someone I *like* and who likes me. I don't know how to break it down any more than that."

But no sycophants need apply: ". . . A moderator I choose should be self-respecting in dealings with me . . . and should be willing and able to debate a point with me and say just what (his or) her reasons are, but respect me and listen to my reasons too. . . . Not just 'I'm the expert and I want to keep the veto power. . . .' Say why you don't agree with me, and put it strongly if you think it's important, but in the end I'm the one who has the problem, so I have the veto power—about anything other than the actual moderating technique."; "Tact is something I look for in interviewing moderators. If she or he is tactful talking to me, the report will be tactful about killing anybody's pet idea or giving any bad news. I don't mean that anything should be left out of a report, but just that no toes should be fractured."

In practice, the contacting-interviewing-proposal-selection operations can be telescoped into two steps, or even one if time is tight and the client is choosing among several known moderators. But if he hits all the stops, there will be one more selection operation. After the interview and preliminary discussion of the project, he asks the few finalists to submit proposals. The additional information given in the proposal will cover in some detail the rapporteur's *understanding* of the problem; the way(s) in which the *focus-group format* will be utilized in addressing the problem; the *cost-projection;* and sometimes a statement of the degree of *responsibility/autonomy* expected by the rapporteur/moderator.

Clients say that they look to the proposal, hoping to find:

• A cogent restatement of the questions offered by the client as the substantive issues for discussion; a demonstration of her *understanding of the problem.* "If she can't listen to me and retain, she won't be listening in the focus groups either. . . ."

• A justification for the use of focus groups, which shows that the researcher *understands both the power and the limitations* of the method: (". . . she can put it in terms of depth versus breadth or exposition versus quantification, or any other way, but she has to know what this kind of project has going for it, as contrasted with alternative methods.").

• A cost-projection that commands respect without bleeding the wallet; the *lowest cost still appropriate to the hours* that will be put in: "I want to say the cheapest total cost is the best one, but if a highly qualified person costs herself out at $10 per hour, I wonder what's the matter. And if somebody I know and like asks for the same money as five years ago, my first reaction is 'whoopee,' but then I feel guilty, or worried anyway. Maybe the person is desperate. If it's too low, I wonder why she has no business. If a moderator is too grateful, she may not write the same report that a busy moderator would. She might try too hard in the groups. But on the other hand . . . if her costs are too high, I think she's got some nerve!"

• Something on which to base a judgment of *cool-headed responsibility:* the capacity for straightening out snarls, so that ". . . if the facility can't handle the job it signed on for, or the dates turn out to be impossible, she'll have a back-up plan, so that . . . if I can't be located in the time available, she will make the change to another facility, or change times and adjust schedules, travel arrangements, and whatever else is necessary. I want someone who'll. . . *make my life easier,* not harder. But she'd better make sure she tries to find me and get my approval. . . . I may want it easier, but it's still my life, and the problem is still my problem."

• *Communicative skill/writing skill:* "On a proposal, the moderator says what we've told her about our reasons, and says it in her own words. I look at that as a preview of the report. . . ."

Sometimes the client may ask for a sample report too, or if the rapporteur is extra cautious about breaching client confidentiality, for a list of previous clients to call for references. Most do not ask for tapes of interviews on other projects—less from delicacy about client confidentiality than "because it takes too long."

A STITCH IN TIME: PLANNING

Focus groups are sometimes praised in these words "If it doesn't actually *answer* the questions clients have, a focus group at least helps to *identify* the questions he should be asking." This comment has always seemed to me very faint praise indeed. Not that I undervalue the importance of identifying or formulating the question. Rather, I think this a wasteful and wrongheaded goal for focus-group projects which, in nine cases out of ten, could have taken this step as planning homework, before the panels were scheduled or the guide approved. But the plan-

ning period of the project is commonly fluffed off as one of social sniff-
ing around and getting acquainted, or as the time to arrange time, place,
and travel schedules.

Focus-group exploration is usually "preliminary to" something else,
doesn't generate reliable numbers (usually) and so has been treated as a
stepchild of the research effort—something it may be nice to have as a
luxury but which is not a serious or scientific exercise. For the unsure, a
focus-group project becomes something to do *instead of* thinking, because thought is difficult and focus groups are fun. Rapporteurs, too,
have fallen into the habit of regarding what they do as a kind of recess-
game, suitable as a way to *create* "focus" and not as a *product* of
"focused" thought. In such a climate, for a focus-group researcher to suggest serious time be spent on planning would be considered taking the
work too seriously or putting on unwarranted airs.

So it should not have been surprising that none of the clients whose
thoughts are recorded here, and none of the rapporteurs whose opinions
I solicited, had any specifications for "ideal" clients or researchers
which were applicable to this stage of the research. Planning is something which either happens or doesn't during the period of getting acquainted. It is eluded by hiring a moderator on the condition that she
"understand or be able to restate the client's presentation of the
problem." This squeezes planning out of a slot of its own and presses
the getting acquainted period right up against the borders of the moderating stage.

Most of the researchers I spoke to do put "planning" in their proposals
and their final bills. In the proposal cost projection, most will list an
item like: ". . . includes up to two full days planning . . .", as if they
were prepared to add to the bill for their services extra charges for any
planning beyond the two full days. But I've spoken to no one who did
attach such charges. One eloquent rapporteur says, "Frankly, I'm so
happy when a client does insist on joint planning sessions that I'd com-
mute for a week to do it. I rationalize it to myself by reminding myself
that it will make the interviews and the report easier, and I'll be surer of
giving the client information he can use."

Only one client alluded to more stringent qualifications for "understanding the problem" than simply the capacity to restate it. And he located this qualification not in the pre-interview planning stage, but at the
point of the report and presentation. "I know it's too much to ask," he

said, "so maybe it is literally a request from God, but I want a focus-group moderator who will give me the answers to the questions I need to have answered . . . not necessarily to the ones I asked." It *is* too much to ask for if the request is delayed until report-time. It's *not* if it is built into the planning period. This client serendipitously provided the only operational definition of adequate planning offered by anyone: a focus group is well or adequately planned when and only when the questions the client wants or needs answered are identical to those which both client and researcher are addressing in the project.

It is, I think, the responsibility of the researchers to diagnose and to treat any gap between what is spoken and what is wanted, because they are the only ones equipped to do so. Clients, like consumers, sometimes don't know their goals, and don't know that they don't know. Solving problems of this sort is a job which any good moderator packs in her lunch pail. Not to say that some formal group problem-solving techni-que must be employed in the planning of every project. The ac-complished rapporteur will *have* such techniques at her fingertips, if re-quired;[3] but this is a hard sale to make, and clients may regard the sug-gestion as pejorative. She can usually get sufficient mileage out of ques-tions like:

• What do you want to find out?
• What do you see as the possible alternatives?
• What would you accept as evidence that alternative "A" is true?
• [The same for each of the other alternatives.]
• What do you plan to do with the information? How would it affect what you are doing now?

Though none of my respondents said so, the ideal client, presented with these queries, would see them as a demonstration of both the re-searcher's interest in the problem, and her moderating skills; would do his best to answer, and would enjoy the intellectual exercise. At the same time, the moderator would think of such questions as being items on her most important discussion guide for her most important inter-view, and would practice the same patience, respectful curiosity, and good-humored perseverance which she employs in focus group panels.

THROUGH A GLASS DARKLY: DOING AND VIEWING GROUPS

The first requirements specified by clients as defining an ideal moderator have been noted above—they are the visible, physical aspects of the moderator's persona, some of which, in clients' eyes, qualify her for selection as a focus-group moderator, and some of which are felt to *dis*qualify her. When these articles of choice are presented to moderators, more often than not they are seen as legitimate requirements. But some are viewed to be arguable, and on at least one such restriction, clients are asked to make the exactly converse stipulation.

The particular physical attribute, among those often specified by clients, with which rapporteurs would be likeliest to disagree is that of *resemblance*—the notion that a panel would be best interviewed by a moderator who is physically similar to the respondents. In practice, this apparent kinship with the group is not only unnecessary, it can be a distinct handicap. A man, interviewing a group of men, cannot plausibly ask them: "What is so great about drinking beer?," or "What is so unpleasant about shaving?"—not without risking interpretations of the questions which might damage his usefulness as an interviewer, he can't. Similarly, a woman interviewer, dressed to resemble a housewife loose in the city (that is, too casually—or too fancily dressed—to suit a business setting) cannot usefully approach the topic of cake flour or oven cleaner, asking: "Could you tell me please how someone goes about making an honest-to-God scratch cake these days?" or "What three cleaning jobs in a house would you think of as the absolute pits?" Any panel of *actual* housewives loose in the city would be far too canny (polyester pantsuit or flowered hat notwithstanding) to believe in the authenticity of the questions for a second.

But a *woman* can ask men about any rewarding or punishing aspect of maleness or about the significance of such symbols of maleness as beer and shaving, and awaken nothing but friendliness and self-examination. And a *man* can ask homemakers about the philosophy or the minutiae of their lives, and be taken seriously. So, for that matter, can a "career woman" if properly set up: "I'm only 'domestic' in the sense in which I was born here. My vacuum cleaner barks at me and the kitchen is the place where I keep single-serving cans of soup and prescrambled eggs. . . ." The important thing to remember is that the moderator says to panelists, no matter what words she utters, "Please tell me what it is like to be you. I don't know, and I'd be fascinated to learn." A moderator who appears to be *unlike* the panelists has a jump on one who is visibly similar in most cases. Exceptions to this observation are cases in which the moderator presents herself as being in a loftier or more desirable category than the panelists. A group of overweight women, for instance, could turn on a lissome lovely who enquired about the comparative merits of Weight-Watchers' entrees and Stouffer's Lean Cuisine. If locked into such a spot, the moderator could try charm ("Heavens, I think I must have the wrong group. Could *you* be here to talk about *diet* products?"), but it's dicey. The approach might backfire, and the consequences would be ugly.

You have to know the valences of particular elements, just as in chemistry. Thin almost always rates higher than fat in this place and time. But health is not invariably superior to sickness, on panelists' scorecards. Sufferers from arthritis, headaches, and heartburn, to name only three, are way ahead of a healthy moderator. They may take their points in the domain of brave suffering, in sensitivity, in sensual adventurousness or any of a dozen other badges which their illnesses confer on them. The moderator can only marvel: "How you must suffer . . . " or "Does nobody in your family or among your friends understand how that kind of thing upsets you?" or "Boy, you really pay for a few moments of pleasure, don't you?" Until very recently, youth was always superior to age, no matter what the elder panel was there to talk about. But that balance is slowly swinging. Even now, seniors with raised consciousness can out rank everybody in sight.

There are a few cases in which it might be better if the moderator were presented as being like the panelists, but for the most part these are categories unlikely to be represented by anyone with the accompanying background and skills necessary for moderating focus groups. (This is touched on in more detail in Chapter 12.) The probability of resemblance between the moderator and the respondents is very close to zero. The moderator simply has to take her chances and run with what she's got.

Clients might be advised too to broaden their sights and reconsider the dictum that obvious physical and/or medical problems are an automatic write-off for focus-group moderators. Here, the impact of any such problem depends almost entirely on the moderator's own attitude toward her problem. There is something to be said for the shock of heightened awareness which group members must feel when confronted by a handicapped or obviously exceptional group interviewer. If the panel did not freeze out instantly, it would warm up in an instant. A high-risk strategy, and not for fainthearted clients, but it is worth noting that one of the best and most successful focus-group practitioners in the history of the technique had a residual hemiplegia which cost her the use of her right arm and visibly disturbed her gait. She had ceased to be disturbed by it, so nobody else was.

Physical factors have been treated so voluminously only because they are embarrassing and uncomfortable, and certain clients are apt to dismiss certain moderators as serious candidates on a categorical rather than a thoughtful basis. Actually, the physical apparatus with and through which a moderator conducts a focus-group discussion is of relatively minor concern to most of my respondents on both sides of the mirror. Both clients and colleagues agreed that the difference between a tolerable or mediocre moderator and the best possible moderator, at this stage in the game, is judged in terms of how well she performs in two simultaneous relationships: the manifest interview happening in the lighted conference room in front of the mirror and the covert compliance with the shadowy presences behind it. Moderators rank clients they have served along the same two axes: the diligence and sensitivity of their viewing and their support and respect for the interviewer.

Asked to define the skills a good moderator exhibits, moderators and clients both agree that the fundamental abilities are two:

1. *Evocation:* the ability to motivate panelists to examine their own attitudes and behaviors and to communicate them.

2. *Control:* the discipline exercised by the moderator in neatening up the discussion, guiding panelists into considering the issues most vital to the client, keeping cross-talk to a minimum, and generally making it easier for viewers to follow the order of what is said by whom.

The differences in evaluation of these skills is a matter of individual priorities. The moderators polled were in possession of one datum that some clients either did not know or had forgotten: that these two desirable qualities rarely appear together. They seem to be negative correlates, at least in part. Total control tends to impose important limitations on evocation, while giving full rein to exposing feelings has a similarly compromising effect on discipline. The consensus among these moderators is that an ideal moderator would exert as much control as is possible without sacrificing richness.

The clients, on the other hand, seemingly didn't know or had forgotten, that these two skills are at odds with each other—most asked for both. When reminded of the fact, they emphasized the *control* aspect of good interviewing more than did the moderators. A few might go nearly as far as to reverse the prescription: as much evocation as is possible without sacrificing control. The shift is a natural consequence of their relative functions. The importance of discipline is necessarily greater for those who must work at listening in the frustratingly passive ambience of the viewing room. To the client, the moderator is his extension, his voice, and his brain, operating on his behalf. To someone who must depend on another person as on a prosthesis, loss of control is acutely distressing. As one client says, "The ideal moderator . . . would probably be a proficient clone—me, trained as a moderator. . . ." He has approved the discussion guide. He trusts the moderator. But still . . .

Several of the clients in this sample recognized and treasured moderators' skill at evocation almost as warmly as moderators endorse it: "There is a truth in the collective mind of consumers. Our goal is probably to achieve perfect communication between the sender (the consumer) and the receiver (the client). The moderator is the middle term, and the group . . . is her instrument. She gets the information from them, non-directively, and the report should communicate this collective truth clearly enough for me to understand." Perhaps it is no accident that these are the same clients who give special attention to the planning stage, and who regard the information given in planning as reciprocal: ". . . making sure they understand what you are reaching for, and also *you* get information about the person who is doing the research. You get acquainted with the way she thinks and the way she operates . . . so that you . . . know what she is doing in the interview, and you don't set up a snowstorm of notes." Finally, these are the only clients who discuss, without prompting, the topic of "moderator-preparation" or "pre-interview-briefing."

Some of the moderators I queried brought up the "backroom warm up" as desirable but dangerous ("I'd really love to do some kind of preparation with clients before each group . . . but it is a touchy question. . . . They get huffy if you try to tell them how to listen—like 'I have been to many focus groups before and I know how to put it into perspective,' or else they just don't listen, but they think you're pushy."). One moderator, somewhat resignedly, said: "I don't want to get them mad before the group even starts. I type up a list of instructions, and whoever *wants* to looks at it, and whoever would be insulted doesn't have to look."

With new clients, the pre-game warmup is easier, less likely to produce defensiveness. Such a warmup can begin with something like: "We haven't worked together before, and I've noticed that some aspects of my interview technique can be puzzling the first time or two. For instance, I will sometimes give an interpretation that I know the respondent doesn't intend, to see how vigorously she corrects me;" or "I try to take into account all of the communication the respondents give me, and this means listening to the tone of voice and watching the gestures and postural changes of the speaker and all of the rest of the panel. You may find that this would be helpful to you too."

Preparation is different for different audiences and different problems. But the invitation to a client to broaden his focus by attending to the nonverbal communications of panelists is not merely useful in the promised way of enriching the experience of the group, but has other, more serendipitous benefits as well:

• It prevents (or helps to prevent) the client's seizing on a particularly fortuitous phrase, yanking it out of context, and taking it as the whole answer.

• It gives him something active to *do* other than inhaling enough *vin ordinaire*[4] or deli spare ribs to invite anesthesia at the time or heartburn at midnight.

• It leaves room for interpretation, averting the unpleasantness, when the report is presented, of a client insisting: "They never said that. I was there."

• It defines the interview as a joint undertaking in which those who watch can participate as equals, without pulling rank.

Finally, some minimal pre-group discussion is called for to arrange for incorporating backroom brainstorms into the front room discussion.

Even an ideally controlling moderator, following the guide explicitly, cannot represent ideas and questions which are prompted by what respondents say. There is a need for swift communication of such follow-up insights and probes. This is the reason some clients like the earphone system, in which the moderator wears an earphone steadily connected to the viewing room, through which a client may if he chooses transmit a two hour stream-of-consciousness into her ear. The obvious fact that such a device is very distracting for a moderator who is busy listening and responding to panelists, and that professional moderators are likely to balk at the suggestion, limits the popularity of instant-transmission devices.

But moderators are well-advised to make it clear the client's input is desired and have to make arrangements for some kind of communication, such as "I will come back to get any ideas you have had and any suggestions about what you would like probed more deeply. I will try to do this two or three times. If that is not enough or if you feel that the timing is right for a particular question, you can send me a telegraphic note—one that doesn't take ten minutes to read—by our hostess." This isn't an ideal system by any means. Topics cool in a great hurry, and by the time the client has formulated the question or topic area the group may have embarked in a new direction. But notes are probably the best compromise, as long as there are not so many of them they submerge the interviewer. Moderators do well to receive gladly a few such communications. Notes tell her that the client is watching, involved in the interview and *compos mentos*. They are also clues to topics which should be covered in the report, because the client is interested in them.

As mentioned earlier, conducting a post-mortem after each one or two groups is a distinctly mixed bag. However warm and trusting the relationship between moderator and client may be, the interview itself has called for different kinds of behavior, created different stressor-patterns in each: power/passivity, increased/decreased stimulation, and social expressiveness/silent assimilation are only three of the more obvious ones. The moods of the clients are sure to be frustrated, expulsive, active, and noisy. The moderator wants solitude and quiet in which to reflect on the happenings of the interview. They are completely out of sync. It is a poor idea to wind up a day or evening thus estranged. And interpretation is premature and thereby misleading and limiting.

One client suggests a compromise which comes close to pleasing all concerned: an *operational* post-mortem or "mid-course correction," which reviews technical procedure rather than content. It addresses questions of *inclusion* (". . . Should we try to create some rough concepts for tomorrow?"), *order* ("It's possible there is a sequence effect in the ideas we presented. How should we change the order to correct for that?'"), *timing* ("What would happen if we brought brand-consideration in earlier?"), and so on. It allows clients to express the ideas they have been sitting on and encourages the moderator to help clients express what they want to say, without infringing on the interpretive act. This kind of post-mortem can make every long, dark stretch of viewing easier to bear.

Since the bulk of the talking and the responsibility for its direction come from the just-released viewers, the moderator can now be passive and relaxed. She may take notes, injecting an occasional comment, and begin to wind down, because client viewers are not the only ones left tense at the end of a group interview. Most of my colleagues hoped for nothing better than a client who "will just leave me alone to go home (or to the hotel) and collapse. . . . " Because of a couple of clients I shall always cherish, my own "best possible" hopes are a little higher than that. (Clients in the "never-again or "worst possible" class are described in Chapter 12.) The best possible client, having cast his or her lot with the moderator, stays with her through the interview, and follows what is going on closely enough to understand her fatigue and appreciate her ingenuity and forbearance, even through an interview which is discouraging in its course from the client's own perspective. After a good session, the best clients will say: "That was terrific!," and after a bleak or turbulent one, "Boy, you sure get a purple heart for hanging in with that crew!" Then, during the walk to the bus-stop or the hotel, or over a quiet dinner, these excellent clients do not ask me what *I* got out of the interview but tell me *their* impressions, being careful to add that it will be "interesting to see what you get, after reviewing the tapes." This gives me a sense of client-bias at this stage, and some direction as to weighting against that bias if the data do not confirm it.

Net/net, the best possible moderator espouses the client's question or problem as her own, and devotes her skill and energies to solving it. She further understands the problems and frustrations of the viewing task, and solicits or accepts suggestions, incorporating them into the interview, so long as they do not seriously detract. The best possible client hires the researcher carefully, for better or for worse for the duration of the project, respects her skill and judgment, and does nothing to undermine the integrity of her performance of the assignment.

THE REPORT PREPARATION PERIOD

After the last group interview is over, the researcher takes all of the paper (screeners, panelist's notations, projective materials) and all the tapes back to the cave to chart, to listen to, to analyze, and to write-up. The period occupied by this travail is rarely less than two weeks, and generally (depending on the number of groups) averages out more like three. The work done by the rapporteur at this stage has been covered already in detail (in Chapter 8) and it doesn't bear repeating. But once again client and rapporteur are out of phase. The client hears the clock tick, but no sound at all from the researcher. The rapporteur is also aware of the clock, but it ticks faster for her, and gains thunder as her deadline approaches.

Oddly, the clients who have been most trusting thus far may fare the least well at waiting for the interpretive report. The reason is simple: the more trusting the client, the less likely he is to listen to tapes. He does not see that a two-hour tape takes four to six hours to listen to and transcribe, or pause to consider the time and motion connected with charting, if this is done. Even clients who understand this cannot easily appreciate the filling of the days. While the rapporteur is collecting excitement from the growing reinforcement of her hypotheses, the client is constructing despair from the long silence. By the time the report is presented the rapporteur is flying high, but the client has often lost touch with the interviews—sometimes with the purpose of the project.

There is probably no way to bridge this gap satisfactorily. The moderator must concentrate on compressing the time, and the client on building his endurance. The unbounded and intense curiosity which at the time of the interviews served as rich fuel for the moderator's energy should probably be switched for something of lower octane or more dilute. When *gathering* data, everything is interesting and significant, but the rapporteur interpreting and writing a report cannot be so prodigal. She must perceive selectively with the *client's* eyes, not her own. She is better off closing an avenue of thought that can't be helpful to him than taking an extra half-day fitting it in.

Contacts between client and rapporteur, prior to presentation, are as likely to hurt as to help. There is no such thing as "purely social" interactions during this interim, and if there were the client might reasonably begrudge them as time taken from the effort. If the researcher schedules a meeting with the client and offers preliminary information, it can make the client hungrier, not less so: "If [the researcher] calls and gives me a *little* of her findings," says one client, "it just makes me angry. I think she's teasing. If she . . . knows that much, maybe she knows it all, and is just playing it close to the vest, building suspense. . . ."

There is an exception to this. A regular client of mine schedules a "preliminary presentation" two weeks into the interpreting/writing period (on a six-interview project). No paper need be exchanged. The presentation is oral. Each time it happens I feel harassed, as I take down last minute notes in the plane or at the airport. But it has never happened yet that I am forced to change any of the findings given at these pre-report presentations in the final report, and it *has* happened that the central, organizing insight came earlier than usual, on the plane going back. Also it is certainly true that the writing was easier and less pressured. Early presentation does slice the top off the dramatic denouement of report-presentation, but this may be whipped cream anyway, fated to leave the rapporteur with a fat head. By report time, rapporteurs ruefully admit, it is not unheard of for the researcher to view herself as something of a Delphic Oracle. Clients may even flatter the rapporteur into that delusion. It is useful to remember that any oracle often preserves her infallibility at the price of intelligibility. They never say anything a pilgrim can understand, while speaking clearly is one of the terms of the researcher's contract.

Over and Out: The Report and Presentation

The report and presentation are not always simultaneous. Sometimes the client schedules a presentation a few days or a week after the report is delivered, to give all concerned a chance to read the report and plan questions. There are even instances when no presentation is written in, and individual clients take it on their own recognizance to query the researcher. But the mode seems to be an oral presentation with the finished, bound report as a leave-behind.

There are things to be said for each procedure. The *modal* format does require each client with an interest in the problem to show up. This means that all the interested parties have *some* acquaintance with the findings of the project. It also allows the moderator to make use of non-verbal cues that allow her to explain in some detail points that are difficult for her audience to grasp. And the dramatic satisfaction is amplified by a large audience. But in a large meeting, lower echelon clients are also onstage, and this format forces them to present their share of questions, which are sometimes nit-picking, or may be related only marginally to the report topic. The rapporteur may see herself as being the target, as well as the star.

The practice of delaying the presentation until participants have read the report scoops the presentation. Its contents are no longer the *news* they would be if delivered to virgin ears. Furthermore, those who will question particular findings have had time to organize their anti-personnel weapons, and will question intensively, not in a broad barrage. But on the plus side, clients will have had ad time to digest the report and are less likely to read only the summary. And questions may give the rapporteur a chance to present data she has reluctantly left out as peripheral, but is dying to offer.

The least satisfactory method is the report without the presentation. If the researcher has given a good report, she may have to be satisfied by her own closure. It is a rarely sensitive client who, on his own time, calls the rapporteur to say "Well done." And responses to individual questions leave her wondering whether anyone *else* is sitting on the same question, or how broadly her answer will be communicated. The enterprise has a strangely unfinished feeling, and the rapporteur has been denied her rightful reward of presenting exciting, stimulating, news. She has in effect sent a letter to her client, and has no feedback as to who read it or what the answer is.

There is no one usual pattern for a presentation. It is a stylistic choice. Reports may be anything from a simple walk-through to a complex production using an overhead projector and easel graphics. The former is more informal and flexible, less apt to derail if questions come up in the middle. The latter is formal and showy, less dependent on the meat of the findings, and contradicts the tone of the interviews themselves. My bias is clear. It has always appeared to me that a dog-and-pony show, with tables and projections, is:

• An imitation-quantitative presentation, apologizing for being what it is.

• Unsure of the value of what is being presented, and disguised to distract.

• Just a bit pompous.

For a walk-through presentation, rehearsal is minimal. Out of consideration for client time, the rehearsal should be timed. The presenter may extemporize or talk from outline notes or a highlighted copy of the report. At least half the allotted time should be set aside for questions. Verbatim quotes bring an academic point to life. If an audio tape can be accurately edited, the panelist' own voices are preferable, but this tactic loses its advantage if searching through tapes is necessary.

The "best possible" rapporteur presents information to match the issues raised in planning. She then opens up other issues raised during the project. She scores each finding, stating her degree of confidence in it, and makes recommendations, differentiating between supported findings and hunches. She recaps major findings and thanks the client for giving her the project.

The "best possible" client does his manicure before the presentation, and does not hum, answer the telephone, or go for coffee during it. When it is finished, he congratulates the rapporteur on anything in her implementation which he honestly admires. A really ideal client has a check in the right amount, which he hands her while he opens the door. There is no reason that clients cannot pay promptly. The company can forfeit interest payments a lot more easily than the researcher can.

AFTER THE BALL: BEST POSSIBLE RESEARCHERS AND CLIENTS BETWEEN ASSIGNMENTS

The relationship between a rapporteur and her client comes to a full stop when the job-contract ends. The client now moves on to action based on project findings, and the researcher moves on to new projects. There is no guarantee either that she will be called on for future work for this client or that she will accept further assignments if offered them. Other things being equal, the parting is harder for the rapporteur than for the client. For a time, she has been working within the shelter of money being earned. That shelter is now struck and folded for carrying.

The best possible client will declare his intention to use the moderator again, if he really intends to, and will invite her to keep in touch. The best possible researcher will agree to do so, regardless of her intentions, and thank him again.

Keeping a tickle file of clients or calling previous clients may be difficult or embarrassing, but memories are short. If a rapporteur has been invited to initiate contact, the call is easier. If she can legitimately ask "Whatever became of . . .," or report: "I see you used one of the strategies we talked about," it is easier still.

Best possible researchers do not assume they are out in the cold if the CEO doesn't answer their first call—or the fifth. They remind themselves that any decently courteous administrator will blame himself for rudeness if he has failed to return a call. Astutue researchers recognize this as an advantage—*he* now feels obligated to talk with her, and she also reminds herself that the world is full of clients. At no time is it safe to depend on a single client for a large proportion of work and/or income. If a new regime comes to power in one of "her" companies, other moderators and rapporteurs may come with them. So when it happens that one or two clients monopolize her calendar, a rapporteur is merely being circumspect if she asks for a retainer. And the best possible client will give her one.

NOTES

[1]It must be noted that the sample of canvassed moderators is not only tiny, but is also skewed in two dimensions:

• *Gender:* Most are female
• *Focus-Group Philosophy:* Most are of the "rapporteur" persuasion and most have graduate degrees in Psychology, Sociology, or Social Research.

[2]It must be noted that the sample of canvassed clients too, is not only tiny, but also skewed for gender. Most clients are men.

[3]My own group problem-solving approach draws on the Synectics technique of analogy-substitution, found in *Synectics,* W.J.J. Gordon, Collier Books 1961, or in George M. Prince, "The Practice of Creativity," Harper & Row 1970 and is spiced with Edward DeBono's "lateral thinking," as described in *New Think,* Basic Books, 1967.)

[4]I ask field staffs to discourage alcohol consumption in the backroom by making it available only on request, and by limiting the options to wine and beer. The client has invested time and money in the event and should be there—in all respects—when it happens.

Chapter 12

Coping with Problem Groups

There is a moment during the pre-interview waiting time when a moderator, whatever her previous successes, recognizes a chill of apprehension. The first few times before the mirror, this feeling, which may occupy most of the (ten minute) wait, is diffuse, unformed and totally self-centered. Put into words, it would probably be expressed: "Oh God, please don't let me screw up." Fledgling moderators do not clearly understand what it is exactly that they fear happening—only that, whatever it is, it will be their fault.

But by the time these same moderators have logged a few *hundred* interviews they know exactly what the fear is, though the nightmare groups are probably different for each veteran. With experience comes the awareness of how many separate people, each performing an integral function within a narrow range of tolerance, and of how many lucky meshings of function and fortuity go into a smoothly run focus group. Recruiting must be impeccable, planning thorough, communication between client and moderator as good as humanly possible and emotional commitment warm. On top of all that, the weather must be good enough not to stall flying schedules or present obstacles to panel members, but on the other hand, not so good that panel members will play hooky and go fishing, or that client sportsmen will be strongly tempted to try the golf course in the vicinity they've heard so much about. Finally, the respondents themselves must not know each other too well nor hate one another (or the moderator) on sight. If all of these factors are favorable the group should go well.

In short, moderators become more circumspect and slower to assign blame or fault. But, with still more experience, the moderator again accepts the *responsibility* for the usefulness and, in most cases, for the fluency and fervor of the interview. There are of course some convocations of respondents, clients, field personnel and providence that no amount of charm, or quick-wittedness or patient persistence could salvage from disaster, but they are few. And even the most unmitigated horrors can often be mined for surprisingly valuable ore. It is more often true than not true that the audio tape of the group (which a moderator winces to put into her machine to listen to) illuminates new aspects of respondents' attitudes toward product, promotion or corporate image.

I can remember groups blown totally away because of indignation about properties of products: ". . . everybody knows that if you have a corroded tool or fixture . . . just put it in a can with [a brand of soft drink] at night and in the morning it is clean . . . I wouldn't want it in my stomach . . . "; or purveyors of services: "I can't stand [a media personality]. If she likes it, I hate it. . . . I hear her voice or see her face, and the set goes off, or I switch channels . . . ." Panelists turn on moderators because they view them as advocates of advertising strategies: "Not only do I boycott their [product], but the way they show *me* and people like us, I boycott all their other products. . . . And I boycott you too. I'm not going to tell you anything that can help them." Today more than ever panelists are informed about the misdemeanors of corporations who pollute the environment, sell dangerous or defective goods, or victimize particular citizens, and resist talking about other "less important" issues. In cases like these the moderator is uncomfortable, the client is uncomfortable, the moderator worries about client discomfort, and the questions everyone hoped to have answered by the interview get short shrift. But they are valuable intelligence nonetheless, if client and moderator can regard them as such. They suggest spheres of implementation that take precedence over the issues discussed in the planning, and subsequent interviews can make room for them.

There are other uncomfortable, frustrating, difficult, or downright catastrophic interviews which are harder to make lemonade out of—more kinds, I'm sure, than I know about. But those which have been visited on me at one time or another, or have happened to moderators I know and whose perception I cannot doubt, are bad enough. Calamities tend to breed in captivity, and an interview which already has a cloud hanging over it often invites other bad augeries, which is another way of saying that any attempt to catalog "bad groups" runs into hybridization. An inadequately planned group can often flower into respondent behavior problems. Poor recruiting can produce bewildered, silent, or rowdy interaction in the panel or between moderator and client as well. But in their pure form, problem interviews are assignable to one (or more) of the following:

1. *Moderator/Client Error:* Generally bad planning, but occasionally poor chemistry.

2. *Errors in the Field:* Generally, bad recruiting is the likely problem, but other contretemps are recorded too.

3. *Inherent Natural Vice:* One participant of those involved in the interview—or more than one—is really impossible: incompetent, of bad character or simply intolerable.

4. *Acts of God:* Mainly, foibles of panel members, but include also weather, transportation glitches, accidents, disease, fatality, instrument failure, and so on.

"Problem" interviews need not ripen into "bad" interviews, though some do. The moderator is the only one who can save or steady them. The salvaging of a group that is headed for trouble calls for a few basic remedial actions plus a lot of luck.

COPING WITH MODERATOR/CLIENT HAZARDS

The first remedy is really a preventative. The moderator may sense that the seeds of a problem are being sown.[1] Or she may exercise her imagination to project the kinds of casualties that *might* befall this particular project, in a worst-possible-case scenario. She might then acquaint the client with these possible misfortunes and of how she would plan to correct them during the interview. Then, should misadventure occur, she need not be concerned about the client's misunderstanding her behavior. ("What *is* she doing in there?")

Even earlier, during the moderator-audition interviews, agreeing on what the major group-session problems are and how best to solve them is a good trial run for project-collaboration. Some potential problems are effectively cut off at the pass in this way:

Client or Moderator Bias: The client or moderator is convinced before interviewing begins that one of the problems to be discussed is the key issue and/or that he knows the answer to it. For the consumer panel to be heard and understood, it is important to recognize and evaluate the effect of bias: "I hear you saying that you are convinced even now that the heart of the problem is the promise of *safety.* You have pretty well convinced me of it too. But this means that neither of us may hear what the group is saying, or that we will surely interpret what we get from them to support that theory. To make sure we don't distort the information given to us, once I think the panelists have put on the record their first thoughts, I will do some probing for *other* possible product claims. Is that okay with you? Do you think you can sit still for digging in other directions without feeling I have betrayed you?" Or alternately: "From what you have told me, I have formed the judgment that the key benefit to be stressed is *speed.* I think I can balance this bias, but please keep an eye on me and send up a flare if you think I am leaning too much in that direction."

Particular Client Sensitivity to Potential Problems: "We all know that not all groups go swimmingly. Would you tell me which ones really make your teeth itch, and I'll dredge up my loathsome list? Then we can compare notes on what kinds of intervention seem to work best."

Client-Moderator Chemistry Is Seriously Flawed: Unfortunately, there is no very effective means for healing bad chemistry and salvaging the project. This is a diagnosis that can't be rushed—anyone can have a bad day. But if the feeling persists, and the client has said nothing about it, the moderator must: "I sense that we are far apart in approach. Do you feel that way too?" If the answer is negative, the moderator can express relief, but should push on: "I'm glad of that, but can anyone help me figure out why I feel that way?" If the feeling persists, moderators cannot exactly *fire* clients, but can manage a tactful resignation: "Feeling as I do, I'm afraid I couldn't do my best work for you at this time. I'd be worried that nothing I do will be good enough. Maybe I'm wrong, but I don't want to take the chance. I hope you will call me again, and that there won't be any apprehension the next time. But the problem is important, and I want you to have your best shot at solving it." If the client is still bullish, the moderator *may* have been wrong. But it's an important and hard-won truth that a bird in the hand can peck the bejesus out of you.

Group problems due to bad planning can happen to anybody and for a number of reasons: time constraints, nonparticipation of those on the client side who have investment in the project, failure to define terms, and so on. It is one kind of problem that happens even when researcher and client are well acquainted. In fact, one variety of problem ascribable to poor planning happens more often when a client knows the prospective moderator well and trusts her completely. The warm glow of good fellowship and mutual esteem is so heartening that preposterously complex goals sound feasible, and wildly diverse respondents meldable.

Such a project was outlined to me by a client of many years standing. A publisher of magazines representing a broad sampling of specialty areas, he wanted an overview of subscriber satisfaction with six of the journals in his empire. Having neither the time nor the research budget to commission six separate projects, he asked whether it would be possible to assemble, like Noah, pairs of subscribers to each of the six magazines, so that reactions to and suggestions for each of the six could be assessed and compared. At that moment, it sounded, if no piece of cake, at least quite feasible.

Looking at twelve panelists from six different vocational and interest spheres, I felt suddenly that I could not even explain to them what they were there to talk about, much less help them to frame a form of address. Fortunately, the publisher had been right in reporting that the caliber of his readership was exceptionally high; he'd said "The editorial content was written by experts, whom we've instructed not to write down." He was right also in believing that the magazines were "very important to the subscribers . . . really central to their job performance. . . ." If he had been mistaken in these pronouncements, there would have been a lot of blank tape.

I began by asking the six men and six women: "Judging by the questions you were asked when you were invited here, and by what you have just learned about each other [in the warm-up], make some guesses about what you are here to talk about." It took them less than five minutes to come to the conclusion that the topic must be specialty periodicals, and that they were there to talk about how they used them and how they felt about them.

So far so good. But how to make any comparisons between the satisfactory usefulness of a magazine on, for example, chemical engineering and another on restaurant management or sales promotion? I decided to share my task with them. "Yes, that is exactly what you are here to do. But something more as well. My job, after we have said good night, is to compare and contrast your use of your specialty magazines, and I need all the help I can get. I'd like you to talk freely about the functions your periodicals serve for you. But when you are not speaking about *your* magazine, I want you to listen very closely to what others are saying about *theirs,* asking questions when you don't understand. Then at the end, I'd like you to come up with some generalizations not just about how and how well your periodicals serve you, but how well others in the group are served by the ones they subscribe to. [Pause] Now will someone who believes he or she understands what I just said explain it to the others who are probably less sure?"

They did just that, and went on to talk, question and interpret. In the end it worked, but it shouldn't have. With each discussion of the ways in which a particular publication was seen and used, there were two—or four or six—discussants (some of the periodicals crossed vocational lines) and seven to eleven rapporteurs. Nobody dropped out, and the *official* rapporteur, feeling tired but lucky, bid the panel good night.

But luck is not always a thirteenth panelist. Undertakings as complex as that described above cannot reliably be accomplished. And the time to realize that is *before* the focus group, not *during* it.

CONFRONTING FALLIBILITY IN THE FIELD

By far the most common misfortune to be laid at the doorstep of the field facility is attributable to recruiting laxity, error or malfeasance. And the first line of defense consists of an explicit screener and a clear formulation of the moderator/client limits of tolerance. The most heinous recruiting crimes should be outlawed in frank terms:

Counterfeit Panelists: Easing a difficult recruiting assignment by introducing one or more shills is uncommon now, probably because all moderators abhor them. Before there were any conventions for recruiter deportment, such practices as instructing prospective respondents to pose as "users" of particular products or services, or giving phony addresses in groups with residential quotas, were fairly common. Not only were such practices lazy and larcenous, they were also stupid. No casually instructed misfit can make the lie stick in the self- revelatory climate of a focus group. Even if the moderator does not expose the dupe (avoiding panel discomfiture or client rebuke), she knows. The handling of this first-degree crime is simple: announce in advance that it will not be tolerated, that no charge will be accepted for the offending panelist, and that one such offense will be the last. No second chances on this one.

Professional Panelists: The articulate, gregarious respondent who "likes doing it" and makes a modest second income from filling quotas for the recruiter or facility is also less likely to turn up in a panel today. But it happens. The panelist may be quite innocent, unaware that her views no longer represent those of uninitiated consumers. She[2] may not even be aware of trying to second guess the moderator and give an "acceptable" answer to questions of preference or buying behavior. But she does it.

The recruiter, if naive, may be almost as well intentioned, feeling that such a delightful respondent, who knows the ropes, will be a welcome addition and will add to group elan. A harried, overbooked field supervisor may be happy—and only a little self-reproachful—to leave decisions like this up to an efficient and productive recruiter. But again, the moderator is bound to know. Professionals are too glib, too ready to follow the moderator's lead. If this is a facility used often, the ubiquitous panelist may even be recognized from recent participation.

This too is an easy practice to discourage: by noncompensation for the respondent's participation, and by the warning that the supplier is on notice to cease and desist.

No moderator is ever too busy for one interim call, to make sure the recruiting is on schedule.

Unfortunately, long and happy experiences with field facilities lead, as do moderator/client relations of the same kind, to over-estimation of the scope of the staff and to some form of telepathy by which the field director can know the moderator's unspoken thoughts. A call to a facility may go something like: "I have a project and I'd like to use you. My client knows _____ facility and is inclined to use them. Please give me some comparative reasons why we should use you." If the field director says: "_____ only recruits from that particular suburb, while we get a mix of respondents from inner city and several suburbs," and the price is comparable, the deal is struck. But the moderator cannot *assume* that the instructions to recruiters will be to "get respondents from the inner city and several suburbs," even though it would be wise to make that specification. If the field staff does not follow through, the moderator winds up with egg on her face . . . and deserves to. The rule is: *Nothing that isn't said is presumed to be communicated.*

• *No-Shows:* Nearly as bad as a field service that brings in the wrong people, is a field service that brings in too few people, and does it too often. Client and moderator agree on the number of panelists required, and the field supervisor estimates a no-show factor on the basis of which she over-recruits, to guarantee the quota requested. When the moderator routinely seats substantially fewer respondents than the target number, the field director is mistaken in her estimate of necessary over-calls. Either she must revise estimates of "confirmed panelist" margins, or she must tone up her confirmations. Some suppliers duck respon-sibility for no-shows. But it's a frequent observation that in two facilities only blocks apart, one supplier frequently disappoints while the other almost never does.

Recruiter "persuasiveness" may be constitutional or learned. But however gifted a recruiter may be in this respect, persuasiveness alone is not always effective in getting panelists to take telephone confirma-tions seriously. In addition, two of the facilities on my "regular" list have suggested a couple of procedures added on to the *je ne sais pas* of efficient coaxing. One of these suppliers uses civic and church groups heavily (one member per group), and panelists give all or part of their gratuities to the sponsoring organization. My adroit supplier calls the membership committees, if too many of their respondents skip the inter-view, and says: "I'm afraid we can't use you any more, if your people don't keep their dates with us. . . ."

Another field group will not take "No" for an answer. If "I can't get a baby sitter" is the excuse, someone at the facility has a teenager who is happy for the job. If it's "I can't get there," someone jumps in a car. A panelist once reported: "I had a cold, but I was afraid to say so. They'd 've sent an ambulance."

(The problem of "Best Friends in the Panel" may be due to recruiter slippage, but giving the recruiter the benefit of the doubt, maybe cataloged as an act of God; see below.)

The Hostess Function: Every facility I know of includes on its bill some fee for a "hostess" for each panel. Some are worth it, some are not. It's not an empty expenditure, but every project and every moderator is different. No matter how pleasant the hostess is, ESP is not included in her qualifications. It's incumbent on the moderator to make it known to her how she can best help: listening for panelists who say, "The coffeepot is empty," tuning in at intervals to make sure the temperature has not gotten too high or too low, turning the tape over promptly and quickly, so nothing is lost, ferrying in messages from the viewing room. All of these are part of her function if the moderator asks them to be. After that, it's not unfair to complain about a hostess who spends the two hours in the bathroom or at the telephone.

Where It's At: The setting, beautiful or utilitarian, with or without a view, banquet style or mediocre, comes in last. It counts, at the bottom end. The room, lighting, chairs, and acoustics must be adequately large, workable, and comfortable; but more opulence is not an unmixed blessing. The beauty of the facility often goes hand-in-hand with recruiting flaws. Opulence breeds over-confidence. The tendency of suppliers to pander to a client's baser drives as a ploy for glossing over poor recruiting has been noted (in Chapter 6). It may take longer for a well-fed and over-quenched viewer (who has been given a set of luggage tags and a flocked map of the city) to recognize that the basic requirements are not being met. But maybe not so *much* longer.

GRAPPLING WITH ACTS OF GOD

Assuming that everything up to here is copasetic, there are accidents, unforeseeable snags that make hash out of the best laid plans. Some of them happen offstage, before or between interviews, to the principalplayers or the walkons. Moderators or clients get sick or get injured, relatives die, babies are born. Less serious, but equally paralyzing to the job at hand are weather, airplane schedules, delivery services, hotel reservations, and the like.

Each has his or her own priorities, of course, but I tend to the view that if the moderator can walk with assistance and is *compos mentis* and if all the materials got off the truck or the baggage ramp, the show must go on. A cyclone warning forcing panelists, client, moderator, and field staff to retreat to a storm cellar for an hour changes the format of the interview, but doesn't necessarily stop it if there's a portable tape recorder handy. The same in a brief blackout. In fact, respondents sometimes rise to the occasion and become more fully available to themselves for report. It is easier by far to adjust to *external* fortuities than to adjust to the surprises nobody can avert which erupt *inside* the conference room. Humans are infinitely malleable, and anything that is in the human repertoire can happen in any group. But there are a few slings and arrows that beset focus groups often enough to be noteworthy. These should be stuck firmly to the inner surface of the moderator's head and viewers too should be alerted to the more common forms of bad luck. In fact, it is a crackerjack idea for front room (moderator, hostess) and backroom (client, agency staffs) to have a head-to-head discussion a few minutes before she goes into the conference room for her final tune-up, to talk about possible group crises, what the moderator will try to do about them and when she would welcome some assistance from outside.

Working from the general to the particular, common problems afflicting panels are:

Energy Problems

Panel members may share few viewpoints and may be of different social backgrounds, but the contagion of energy extremes is very high. If even two members are afflicted, it is probable they all will be inside of fifteen minutes.

High energy groups are talkative, boisterous, and hard to rein in. A moderator working with such a panel feels like an animal trainer and looks like an orchestra conductor, using hands, arms, and whole-body movements to suggest restraint and indicate which is the principal speaker from moment to moment. She often needs to yell to make herself heard, and cries of "Hold it! I want to hear everything." or "Your turn in just a minute" slice through the air at short intervals. But for her and the panelists, this kind of mayhem is often not too troubling. High-energy panels are sort of fun to *interview*.

But they are no picnic for viewers. Exuberance doesn't leap the moat of the mirror very well. Client ears cannot tune as precisely to each separate voice, and isolate what it is saying as can a moderator working directly with the speakers. A moderator can leave the din of such an animated interview feeling excited herself, and pleased with what she has learned, only to find those in the viewing room angry and morose. A correction must happen somewhere, and moderators can rarely stay out of the interview room as long as it would take to reassure clients, without panelists becoming restive (or in this case, starting to demolish the bric-a-brac).

The most useful strategy I've found is for the moderator to come clean, i.e., to raise both hands, yell "Hold it" and say something like: "We're having fun here—anyway I am—and your enthusiasm is wonderful. But if there is anybody in the backroom trying to follow us, they're out of luck. I don't want to send out for vallium. Your enthusiasm is heartwarming . . . but for the coach, and for me later when I'm listening to the tape without you here to help, can we please keep it down to a roar, and try to focus attention on one person at a time? I promise to watch closely, and if you are forcing yourself to keep a comment back, I'll get to you, and you'll have your moment. . . ." If the moderator feels uneasy mentioning the viewers, she can settle for coming *partway* clean, and talk only about listening to the tapes.

Low energy is a horse of another color entirely; in many ways the reverse of the manic party described above. For one thing, clients tend to be happy with amiable low-energy groups, while the energy neces- sary to grouping a panel and extracting responses all comes from the moderator, who feels increasingly like a tired dentist. She can visit the backroom during or after a panel which displays approximately the vitality of a scab, to find the viewing client bright-eyed and beaming.

Aside from the wear and tear on interviewers, the low-energy group is important mainly because it points up a moderator-client imbalance. The client may be rightly content with what a taciturn panel tells him be- cause it is all that he can really use. The moderator, whose pre-interview revving-up urges her to go for "everything," may be digging for deeper insights and a more personal understanding than are really required, within the purview of the project. More understanding than she needs is a luxury she can enjoy, if it comes easily. But energy is her running fuel. She should spend what is required to get what she needs, then con- serve it for the groups to come.

Problems with Chemistry

After settling the chemistry issue with client and field staff, the moderator can put such concerns behind her, right? Wrong. From time to time it befalls a moderator that a group hates her—or loves her— from the time they walk in. Both are obstacles to productivity, if only because they can bias even the most conscientious respondent. Whether the reaction is positive or negative, the emotionally attuned respondent will endeavor to check out the reactions the moderator is hoping for, and give—or withhold—them. This would pose no obstacle to interpretation, if panelists were infallible. ("They hated me, and I was secretly backing Concept II, so I'll tip the scales a little, and upgrade their reaction to II," or "They adored me, and sensed that I prefer Concept II, so I'll counterweight their hosannas.")

But panelists are *not* infallible, and moderators are trained to be neutral. So it is best to defuse such emotions before they harden: "Either I remind all of you of someone you hate, or you are right in thinking that I am a thoroughly bad hat. Still, I'm here and you're here, and we have a job to do. There's no time to go for letters of reference from my friends. Try to stretch a point, or if you can't, at least don't let personal considerations affect your reactions to the concepts. I didn't write them." Or, "Thanks for your approval. I really treasure it. But we all have to keep in mind that we're here to do a job . . . and it isn't deciding how adorable I am. It's how you feel about ginger ale and how you feel about ideas we might use to promote ours. Please don't react the way you think will please me. You could be picking up the wrong signals, or I might be wrong in my preferences. If you want to talk after the interview, swell."

But this can only be said *once*. Too frequent send-ups to the hostile crowd look like begging. And too-frequent demurring sounds coy. If this kind of leveling doesn't work, you have to stiff it out.

Early in the 1970s, a client wanted to test a snack product that he planned to target for "the black market." I suggested that mixed groups might be best for evaluating differences, and were anyway closer to the real world. He held out for apartheid, and asked if I were afraid of interviewing all black panels. Since I'd done a number of them without problem, I gave in and scheduled a half-dozen groups in the New Jersey suburb specified. The first evening panel was composed of black homemakers, 35 to 49 years old. And I knew from word one that I was the enemy. After what should have been the introductory warm-up (during which they had virtually spit out their names, occupations, husbands' occupations and the ages of their children), I made my speech. It didn't work. I had not been cool. I had reacted to my own anxiety, and it backfired. They were out to get me. Round one came up quickly. I opened as usual with "What did you think you would be called on to talk about?" "Baby products," said a glowering panelist. "That's interesting" I said. "It's *not* the topic, but I wonder why you thought it was." "Because," said my implacable adversary, "We're black, so you think we have a lot of children." I parried that one: "Hey, look, we've just been around the table on that one. Five, seven, four, five . . . I *know* you have a lot of children. Next guess." (And score one for the home team.)

Another stony faced panelist announced, "Household products." "Not what *I* think of as household products," I said. "Why did you think that?" "Because you think we're all domestics." "I don't," I said, "But I can't prove it." (Weak. Point to the visitors.)

The hostess came to take orders for coffee or soft drinks. I asked for coffee and she went around the room while all respondents ordered soft drinks. This was close to the topic, so I asked: "Is this what you usually prefer at this hour in the evening?" I reached for the cream and sugar. "Most of the time, not just in the evening," said my original opponent. "Don't you know that coffee makes you blacker?" Steady on the cream, I looked at her squarely and replied: "Not if you put cream in it, it doesn't." She held my glance for less than 30 seconds before breaking out in a great whoop of laughter (may she be given a seat in the loges in Paradise), and we went on to a productive discussion.

Problems with Impression-Management

These come in all varieties. The target may be the moderator, the rest of the group, or it may be reflexive. The desired impression may be "sexy," "upscale," "knowledgeable," "sophisticated and cynical," "witty,"—all possible combinations. This kind of problem is the main reason for avoiding certain forms of heterogeneity, as noted earlier: gender mix, almost always; age-mix, sometimes; certain instances of extreme demographic spread; and invested experts—like doctors and nurses in over-the-counter pharmaceutical panels, or advertising folk—always). Almost everyone does a certain amount of face-saving or best footputting, so the point at which it becomes problematic is quantitative and atmospheric.

In itself impression-management is no huge factor, but it's a problem because there is little the moderator can do about it other than treating one or two "expert" impression-managers as advised for the "group leader," or "in-group moderator," see below. It is possible, but a longshot, to introduce the topic of impression management in general: "I can understand why you order Johnny Walker Black at a bar and choose to keep a bottle in the cupboard, but when it's a party—and you've *said* it's hard to like, and more expensive—why put it out? What does it announce?"—and hope that the afflicted panelist, across the table, will confess and trust the moderator and other respondents not to ridicule him. But that is *all* that the moderator compassionately can do. Excessive impression-management covers self-doubt, and covers it thinly. Uncovering such a case proves the moderator a bully, makes the group anxious, and spills blood on the table. Recognizing and correcting in the interpreting process is usually fairly easy, and the only fair recourse.

The Joker

A joker at a focus-group table is not the same thing as a wit. Nor is it the same as someone who says something funny once, or more than once, without disrupting the flow of expression or exchange of information about the interview topic. Nor is he or she very funny most times. Insensitive of what the group is up to, the joker scans anything said for hooks on which to hang a line—generally, a rehearsed line—which he hopes will pay off in laughter. If it doesn't, he may even try it again later, only louder, cruder and with gestures.

Because he is often coercive about laughter—will not let up until he gets it—he is often irritating to the rest of the panel. Because he tries to steer the discussion around to something with a hook, he almost invariably irritates the moderator. He's really harmless, and fairly easy to put away. The moderator says with as much kindness as she can muster: "Please, we really need your help, not your jokes. That's why we're here and that's why we have taken your time and paid you. We can stay and swap jokes if you want to, after everybody has given us what help they can, but try to stay with us, if you possibly can." This kind of direct account of his antics almost always drops him in his tracks. He apologizes and is usually a teddy bear the rest of the interview. Once in a great while, he sulks and elects to leave, but it doesn't cause the upset that dismissal would.

The principal residual effect of a joker is that the interview turns dreary. Neither the interviewer nor anyone else dares to permit levity— he might begin again.

Best Friends

An insidious problem—which shouldn't happen if recruiters are alert but sometimes falls between recruiters—is that of two or more than two panelists who are well acquainted. If humanly possible, and if the group will not shrink alarmingly, all but one of these should be stopped at the door, or even fished out of the group as soon as the revelation is made. They can play havoc with almost every aspect of the interview.

Best friends *discourage anonymity*. If someone knows someone in the room, nobody feels really safe saying the things she might say to a very compassionate taxi driver or a stranger on the same park bench, feeding the squirrels.

Best friends give each other *more than one vote*. If one utters an opinion or asserts information, the other(s) rush in to endorse it. If other panelists are uncertain, they may climb on the bandwagon too.

Best friends can *intimidate* shy group members if they gang up on them.

Best friends *impair group formation* by not joining. They are their own group.

Best friends often keep up a *continuous obliggato* of whispers and laughter which, at the wrong time, can appear to be ridicule. This is always disrespectful to the panelist(s) who holds the floor.

If the recruiter didn't or couldn't spot them, the hostess can often tell, as they wait to be admitted—and can ask, if she isn't sure. If one is a latecomer ("Hello, I'm sorry I'm late. Where should I . . . Iris *darling*."), the moderator must cope. Whether hostess or moderator, it's the same speech: "We find that close friends in a group tend to be disruptive. I'm afraid I'll have to ask the last one in to leave. Sorry."

The In-Group Moderator

This is the articulate, informed panelist who sits in the panel (usually across from the moderator) but acts like a (bad) moderator. She leaps in to answer every question first, and once she starts, hardly stops for breath. She is didactic, sure of the facts and frequently strident. She has feelings, and seems to think everyone should share them. She is the bane of all the viewers, and the thing mentioned first as a fault of moderators.

Most moderators do not find the group leader quite such a terrible calamity. For one thing, most of them have faced the alternative: a table full of blank faces revealing no discernible minds. The group leader at least gets the ball rolling, and pretty soon everyone else in attendance sees that talking seems to agree with *her*, and are willing to give it a try themselves. Or else some of the other participants think she's hogging the time and the moderator's attention, and decide to compete. It is often most illuminating to identify the issue on which other respondents decide they can no longer sit still.

The other valuable trait of group leaders is that they have very thick skin. A moderator's comment, "You've made your point. Now let's hear from somebody else," which might demolish others in the panel, barely stops her. Once she has warmed everybody up, the moderator can say: "Thank you. I'm really glad you showed up. Now I think other people may be ready to talk. I'm not shutting you up permanently, but let's see if the rest of the people have found their tongues." I have known group leaders to be laughing and unfazed after being asked to "please stuff a sock in your mouth."

This list of the problems is not exhaustive. (They are not even all-but-one. One other is discussed below.) But it offers a broad assortment of problem types, and if you've been with me you've noticed that the suggestions for coping—different as they are—have a common core: candor. The moderator must recognize what the problem really is—what difficulty she would like resolved. Then she must ask that it be resolved as tactfully or gently as need be. No elaborate rationalizations; just "This is the behavior of yours that I object to," or "This behavior is the reason you must go," and finally: "I'd really appreciate it if you would correct it." And I really think those guidelines—stating the problem and requesting it be redressed—are applicable in every case—except one.

The Flake

Real certifiable nutcases or psychopaths are fortunately uncommon. Add to them those who are temporarily freaked-out, and they still don't fall across a moderator's path every day. But when they do, they are extremely difficult to handle. Usually, the person most competent to spot them—the moderator—doesn't get a look at them until they come through the door with a group of other respondents whom the moderator is pledged to protect from major unpleasantness.

Even if spotted earlier, the hostess or field director may be too frightened to act. A strange panelist, a latecomer, once alerted me to his eccentricity. His over-casual costume, sidling gait, and avoidance of eye-contact were unsettling. I kept the panel in firm control. On leaving the room, I asked the hostess if she had "noticed anything." "Well yes," she said. "He exposed himself to the receptionist and we had to call a cab for her and send her home. I was wondering if I should tell you." The assertion that she must always tell the moderator at once, before admitting such a panelist, plus a comment to the facility manager that this hostess wasn't suited for the job, were all the preventive options open to me.

Once the flake is part of the group, the moderator must decide whether he or she will be more disturbed by dismissal than by behavioral guidance, and whether the rest of the panel will be more disturbed by one than the other of these courses. A pre-arranged signal to the client to "Get him/her out of here" and someone on the field staff who is capable of being something of a blunt instrument are definite advantages. But when the offender is too disturbed to be safe on the street, or might endanger others, another signal is necessary to "Get her/him out of here, and hold him/her for me to talk to." Even in this touchy situation, the best policy is candor: "I know you are uncomfortable. I think you are sick, and I think you know you are sick. Let us get you to someone who can help you."

Coping with Inherent Natural Vice

There should be a booby-prize for those few participants in the execution of a focus-group project whose behavior falls off the bottom of the scale: moderators who burst into tears or stamp out of the interview room in high dudgeon, leaving stunned panelists in distress; those field-personnel who accept a project, only to call two weeks before the scheduled panels and report that "we can't handle the job;" and clients who, having committed themselves to a moderator, spend the period behind the mirror in critical commentary, which no amount of appreciation of a report can erase.

They can't be—and they shouldn't be—coped with. Even candor can't fix what is unfixable. Here—in any of the situations described above and a hundred more like them—all a moderator can do is chalk the experience up to education. The bottom is part of the barrel too. Turn out the light and leave, and vow never, ever, to put yourself in that place again.

NOTES

[1]But she can't always stop them from growing. A colleague despairs: "I thought the groups were fine but I'm not sure about the client. The product is just like _____ (a competitive product). But demographics of the two purchaser groups are entirely different. I *asked* him to consider the possibility that it might be an *image* he should be selling. He insists on looking for product claims and they're just not there."

[2]For whatever reason—social facility, available time, chumship with the recruiter—most professional panelists seem to be women.

Afterword

About a dozen years ago, furniture I had acquired in graduate school gave out. Drawers stuck, upholstery went lumpy, springs burst, and it was no longer possible to ignore the ugly stain in the rug made by a friend's chihuahua who, I think, metabolized battery acid. Never having disposed of or replaced more than one piece at a time, I was at a loss over what to do first.

Outside help was clearly indicated, and it came in the form of a glossy magazine dedicated to making a showplace of one's apartment. (I forget which magazine—Kismet selected the one which was left in the incinerator room by a neighbor.) None of the pictorials was remotely applicable, but an editorial contribution caught my eye ("Look before you Buy," I think). The writer suggested that people get so used to living with roomfuls of furniture that they no longer look at them. The prescription, I still remember, was to "go out your front door. Then, with the door still closed, imagine that you are about to enter a strange apartment. Concentrate on the strangeness, on blanking your expectations. And when you have done this, open the door..."

The suggestion *worked*. For the first time, I saw the rooms filled with objects that had no relationship to one another beyond the sentimental unity of my own life: the chest of drawers bought secondhand, stripped, sanded and inexpertly finished on a month of Saturday afternoons; the uncomfortable couch inherited from another graduate student, worn thin and scarred; the desk from my first clinical office; the few "good" pieces from the prosperous year during which I was gainfully employed as an industrial psychologist (5 days a week), completing a paid clinical internship (3 evenings), and writing my dissertation on a USPHS Grant (the rest of the time); a family passdown or two; a reclining chair saved for in green stamps . . .

Having saluted the lot, I proceeded to discard what was unusable, salvage what was usable and add on where there were functional blanks.

I have just finished applying the same principle to my worklife. I hope it has worked as well. In many cases, no previously validated dogma informed my choices. Conventions of behavior and interpretation stayed because they served the immediate purpose. All of these I have tried to bring forward in thought to question, amend, and update. What remains is not the same mental furniture that everyone would have chosen. But it is what I have chosen, in careful review. If the reader has learned from it a quarter as much as I learned in the doing, that is a lot.

And what of focus-group interviews, in the new quarters of today's and tomorrow's marketing world? Judging by its endurance, the focus-group interview is neither a fad nor a blind alley. It will probably be available—as a tool and as a career—for the grandchildren of today's marketers and researchers. It may advance to the status of an elder science, with academic authenticity; or it may fall to the other end of the spectrum, existing only as a theatrical ornament to marketing research.

I believe that the upper limits of usefulness of the technique are those of the usefulness of human interchange. Its flexibility too is potentially determined by the flexibililty of interpersonal communication. But new uses are certainly possible. I have recently begun, in alliance with two marketing consultant partnerships, to move in new directions: new product generation and direct (-mail) marketing. There will surely be others.

The fate of focus-group interviewing ultimately depends on whether it is taken seriously by the marketing community, as a source of unique and valuable information, or whether it is viewed as a decorative adjunct to or substitute for "real" research. In the latter worst-case scenario, the effort will be made to return to the old "fast and cheap" days. This can be accomplished in several ways. The most obvious places to cut corners would be in field costs (primarily in recruiting and gratuities to respondents) and in the expertise of the rapporteur.

The costs of recruiting vary, depending on the panelist-specs, but are always considerable and may be astronomical. Minimal resourcefulness surely must suggest bringing computers (which never charge overtime) into the act—*per se*, not a bad idea. Computers are another aspect of the marketing landscape which are sure to be around, and "qualitative" research has to make friends with them. But they are awkward bed-fellows.

For example, it is not inconceivable that a field facility, located in a small town (as most are) might simply put all the inhabitants—or all the *articulate inhabitants*—on call, at short notice, simply by programming and cross-programming their salient characteristics, for example, female HOHs/over 45/family incomes between $25,000 - $60,000/headache sufferers. In effect, the residents would be packageable for any client's exacting requirements. By careful phrasing, it would be possible to sell them fairly often ("...no respondent who has been interviewed in your product category for six months..."), and keep many townspeople supplied with additional income. The problem would be not merely the nonrepresentative character of professional panelists, but also the fact that such pros would wish to ingratiate, so as to remain on the bounty list, and would need to "please" the interviewers. Such a nightmare possibility has a silver lining though—panels recruited this way would be splendid demo-panels for agency presentation. They could also provide soothing for ruffled clients, as long as the researchers involved were completely cynical about extracting truth.

As for shaving the budget allowances for expensive, qualified rapporteurs, I have already received two chilling letters from entrepreneurs offering to "take the hard work out of focus groups" for me by writing my reports (one "specializing in pre-teen children"). It is true that report writing, including the interpretive operations, are the most arduous and longest stage of a focus-group project. Thus they are the most costly...but *shouldn't they be*?

Another way to cut field costs is to assemble panels by telephone. Travel costs are eliminated, facility costs are eliminated to a degree, and panelists need not leave their homes. But also eliminated is the experience of a face-to-face encounter, with all of the data thus supplied to a qualified moderator. And solitary, at-home responses are probably different from those offered in neutral surroundings, where work is the expectation.

In another end-run around the field facility, focus-group interviewers have discovered intereviewing in the home! And now have facing them the awareness which the same setting provided to the pioneers—that in-home interviews color both the nature of the interview and the climate of the (real-life) home.

Finally, another worst-case way to reduce apparent costs is to add on occult and expensive sounding, if irrelevant, instrumentation. Panelists could be plethysmographed, EEGed, and eye-cameraed during, before, and/or after interviews, in the interests of "more accurate" information.

But forewarned is forearmed. A marketer who falls for any of these possible tricks probably deserves what he or she gets.

Appendix A: Six-Week Schedule For A Focus-Group Project

Check List for a Focus-Group Project (assuming at least six weeks)

What Needs Doing	*Who Does It*
1. First contact (telephone or face-to-face).	Client or researcher may initiate.
Client explains problem in general.	Researcher listens, and asks questions she needs answers for in order to write proposal.
2. Proposal	
Client requests proposal containing:	Researcher supplies:
Statement of problem.	Recap of problem.
Research methodology.	Reasons for using focus-groups.
Questions to be answered.	Question areas addressed.
Tentative schedule for moderating.	Schedule for moderating (including available dates of field facilities).
Tentative schedule for report.	Date report will be available, based on estimate of complexity of analysis, and on time at her disposal.
Cost estimate.	Costs (field estimates, + travel and moderating time + analysis + writing of report + estimated out-of-pocket expenses, $\pm$ 10%.

3. Proposal conference:

    Terms accepted.   Researcher confirms.

    Request for budget changes in   Researcher accedes or denies.
    time or cost.

4. Discussion guide:

    Client may supply outline or   Researcher reviews, amends.
    entire guide.

    Client requests guide.   Researcher supplies, guide covering:
                                    Introduction
                                      Predispositions (where relevant):
                                        (Brand behavior)
                                        (Usage)
                                        (Brand Personality)
                                      (Reasons for trying/discontinuing,
                                          etc.)
                                    Exposure of materials
                                    Wrap-up.

5. Screener:

    Client requests and supplies   Researcher supplies, after recheck of
    demographic and usage specs.   field facilities.

6. Guide and screener conference:

    Client may accept either or both   Researcher gives reasons for any
    or may make amendments in   disagreement with the client, but
    either or both.   makes requested changes, short of
                                  professional compromise.
    After amendment, client initials.

7. Travel arrangements:

    Client makes his own; may make Researcher makes arrangements,
    travel and hotel arrangements for compatible with those of client, but
    researcher as well.   may choose to arrive earlier, for last-
                                  minute glitches in the field.

8. Seven-day-advance-field-check.   Researcher confirms details of time,
                                    attendance.

MODERATING INTERVIEWS

9. Post-Interview: Researcher takes and checks audio
                                      (& video) tapes, sends duplicates to
   Tapes   client.

10. Interpretation

    Communication in pre-report   Researcher delivers oral report, if
    interval   that has been agreed.

11. Report   Report and Presentation are most
                                      customarily (and satisfactorily)
12. Presentation.   simultaneous.

Appendix B: Qualitative Research Proposal For *Sales & Marketing Management*

RESEARCH OBJECTIVES

To uncover the motivations for renewal/nonrenewal of subscriptions to *S&MM*.

- Who has input (formal or informal) in the decision?
- What are the overt considerations in deciding?
- What appear to be the underlying motivations?
- What do *renewers* "get" from *S&MM* (both by statement and by inference)?
- Do *nonrenewers* have different needs and/or different perceptions of *S&MM*?

To Gain Directional Guidance:

- What do *renewers* feel *S&MM* does best/least well?
- What do *nonrenewers* feel *S&MM* does best/least well?
- What changes would *both* groups like to see (and why)?
- What evidence would they accept that wanted changes are or will be taking place?
- What about "purely emotional" factors?
  —Does format "say" anything about content?
  —Do they see *S&MM* as fast-paced and contemporary/as conservative and cautious?
  —Do they see *S&MM* as having a "warm" or a "cool" tone?

—If the magazine were a person, would they want him or her as a friend or mentor? Why? How about identification: if the magazine were a person, would (s)he be like the panelists? Someone they would *like* to be like?

• How do panelists feel about communications from *S&MM*?
• How does it stack up with competitive periodicals? Which competitive periodicals?

METHOD

Qualitative research is indicated, because it provides a depth of understanding impossible in large scale "survey" research. Focus-group interviews would be the recommendation because, without sacrifice in depth, the interaction of panelists tends to expose impression management, which is presumed to be a danger in this high-achievement group.

QUALIFICATIONS FOR PANEL ELIGIBILITY

Recruiting would be done from your lists of marketing directors, sales managers, and sales & marketing directors in the areas where the groups are to be interviewed.

LOCATIONS AND NUMBER OF GROUPS

At least two locations are recommended, and three would be preferable. One should be midwestern, one eastern corridor, and perhaps one southwest. I would like to interview both "pure" renewer-panels and non-renewer panels, because we cannot be sure how clear the differences will be, and if they are subtle, they could get lost in a mixed panel. Since this is a list-recruit, it is less essential to replicate, and one panel each of renewers/nonrenewers would be sufficient.

Despite general reluctance to doing mixed gender groups, I would not recommend doubling the number of groups to accommodate this bias. Women who have titles like "marketing director" are secure enough or tough enough (or both) to hold their own in a mixed panel. The danger in mixed-gender panels is that impression-management can take over as the group focus, and the danger is there in any case, as noted above.

Four or six interviews are recommended for this exploratory step.

TIME AND CHARGES

January is a busy month for supplier-facilities. In the three general locations (midwest, east, and southwest), only one facility can accommodate the project in the remainder of the month. Chicago could house us on the 18th and 19th of the month. Things loosen up in February, and facilities in New York, Kansas City, and Dallas have open time by or before February 14th. In all cases, a 10-day recruiting period is requested. The facility would have to be reserved, and the lists of eligible panelists—plus a screener—would have to be in-house at the facility 10 days before the first group to be interviewed.

Time estimated for analysis and writing of the report would be two to three weeks after the completion of the last focus-group interview.

Cost estimates for Chicago and New York field facilities are roughly the same, and for Dallas and Kansas City, a bit lower. *All* are costing more than I expected. All field directors say that, even with list-recruiting, it is extremely hard to get people of this ilk to commit to an interview, and over-recruiting is necessary because of the probability of short-notice travel.

For six groups, the total cost would be $\_\_\_\_\_$. Four panels (renewers and nonrenewers, in Chicago and New York) would net a total cost of $\_\_\_\_\_$ (both estimates plus or minus 10 percent).

- Total costs include:
  —Planning.
  —Moderating the panels.
  —Interpretation and report.
  —Recruiting, rental of facility, audio tapes, food for the panelists (at least one group—generally both—in each location will require substantial food, replacing lunch or/and dinner), incentives (to secure

management-participants, suppliers estimate "incentive" payments of $50-$100).

- Cost estimates do not include:
  —Travel expenses
  —Food for viewers behind the one-way mirror (*S&MM* staff).

Appendix C: Sample Screening Device For Selecting Focus-Group Panelists— *Sales & Marketing Management*

TOPIC: <u>MEDIA</u>   DATE _____

PROJECT # _____   TIME _____

RESPONDENT _____   TELEPHONE _____

ADDRESS _____ CITY & STATE _____

DATE _____ GROUP _____ RECRUITER _____

Hello, my name is _____ from _____ , a local market research company. Today, I am recruiting a group of marketing and sales executives for a discussion of media. If you fit our quotas, I would like you to join the group. May I ask you a few questions about your job and your media habits?

1. How many employees are there in your entire corporation or firm—that is, the total number of employees, including all plants, divisions, branches, and subsidiaries?

Less than 25 ____	250 – 499 ____	2,500 – 4,999 ____
25 – 99 ____	500 – 999 ____	5,000 – 9,999 ____
100 – 249 ____	1,000 – 2,499 ____	10,000 or over ____

(A MIX OF BUSINESS SIZES IN BOTH GROUPS IS DESIRABLE)

2. What is the nature of your employer's business? Please be specific (e.g., steel manufacturing, wholesale food, retail textiles, engineering firm, etc.):

_____

(WE WOULD LIKE A MIX OF INDUSTRIAL, RETAIL/CONSUMER, AND SERVICE COMPANIES.)

3. What is your title or position? Please be specific (e.g. regional sales manager, national sales manager, marketing director, etc.).

(SALES TITLES PREDOMINATE IN THE LISTS, BUT WE WOULD LIKE A REPRESENTATION OF MARKETING TITLES AS WELL. IDEAL IS HALF/HALF, BUT NO LESS THAN 3 IN EACH GROUP.)

241

4. Gender: (MEN FAR EXCEED WOMEN IN THE LISTS, BUT WE WOULD
   LIKE AT LEAST 2 WOMEN IN EACH GROUP—PREFERRABLY 3 OR 4.)

5. Which of the following groups includes your age? (READ)
   25–34
   35–44
   45–54   (AS MUCH AGE SPREAD AS POSSIBLE)
   Over 55   (NO MORE THAN 2 OR 3 OVER 55)

6. Do you have direct authority over your company's sales force? _____
   (If yes:) Over how many sales force people?

1–19	____
20–49	____
50–74	____
75–99	____
100 or more	____

7. I subscribe to (Check those which apply):

8. I have read or looked through past 4 issues: Subscribe   Read
   (Check those which apply):

	Subscribe	Read
Advertising Age	____	____
Ad Week	____	____
Business Week	____	____
Fortune	____	____
Forbes	____	____
Inc.	____	____
Incentive Marketing	____	____
Industrial Marketing (name change recently to Business Marketing)	____	____
Marketing and Media Decisions	____	____
Marketing Communications	____	____
Marketing Times	____	____
Meeting News	____	____
Meetings & Conventions	____	____
Potentials in Marketing	____	____

(NO QUOTAS)

Premium/Incentive Business   ____   ____
Sales & Marketing Management   ____   ____
Successful Meetings   ____   ____
Training   ____   ____
Wall Street Journal   ____   ____

9. What is your marital status?

Married ____   Widowed ____

Single; never married ____   Separated or Divorced ____

10. What is the *highest* level of formal education you have attained, to date?

Graduated from high school ____

Attended college ____

Graduated from 4-yr college ____

Postgraduate Study ____

11. What is your total family income before taxes?

19,999–24,999 ____	50,000–59,999 ____
25,000–29,999 ____	60,000–74,999 ____
30,000–34,999 ____	75,000–99,999 ____
35,000–39,999 ____	100,000–199,999 ____
40,000–49,999 ____	200,000 or more ____

(SHOULD HAVE AS MUCH DEMOGRAPHIC SPREAD AS POSSIBLE)

On [Day/Date] at [Time] we will be conducting a market research discussion group in our offices, and I'd like to invite you to participate. The meeting will last 2–2½ hours, and *it will be necessary for you to stay for at least the full 2 hours.* You will be paid [Amount] for your participation. Will you join us for this meeting?

(RESIST GIVING ANY INFORMATION ABOUT THE GROUP, BEYOND "MEDIA". SAY THAT YOUR CLIENT IS A NEW YORK RESEARCH CONSULTANT, AND THAT YOU DO NOT KNOW WHO HER CLIENT IS.)

Appendix D: Discussion Guide For *Sales & Marketing Management*

I. *Warm-Up* (Introduction of participants, moderator, explanation of discussion protocol, etc.)

II. *Predispositions* (Direct questions to be avoided, but the following question areas to be explored):

- *General Lead-in* (Ask if anyone knows the topic. They should guess "media." Narrow the topic):

  —We're primarily interested in the print media—the papers and magazines you regularly use in your work . . . for information, for advertising, in general.

  Can you say *how* you use them? Do you approach the stack of periodicals in your in-basket as if it were an assignment—something you have to do? Or what (probe attitude, skimming versus depth reading, automatic versus deliberate attention, etc.)?

  —What's the lifespan of most of the things you read for business? If the short end is a quick skim and forget it, and the long end is that you have every issue you ever got in the library and regularly consult back issues, which—or where—is your pattern?

  —Is there regularly some intramural communication? Do you pass on particular items to others in your company? What kind of items?

- *Comparative Definition* (Ask them to write "off the top of your heads" the names of the magazines they find most valuable in their work lives: "The top few—up to a half-dozen," and a notation about what is "valuable" about each):

  — *Debrief:* Which ones did you say? Do you use the same rating system for each one, or are "valuable" for quite different reasons?

  —Are all of these publications quite specialized or more general? If you feel interested in a particular area or topic, do you know exactly which one to pick up? Or is it a reconnaissance operation every time?

  —How often do you tackle this kind of reading? As the spirit moves you? As they come across your desk? Or do you set regular time aside in the day, the week, the month? How much?

  —Why do you spend part of a busy worklife on this kind of publication? What, exactly do you get out of them? What would you be missing if you didn't have them?

  —Do you decide on a target-for-today and just go right through one paper or magazine, pulling out and digesting all you are going to use, right then, and then pass it on or toss it (which do you do, by the way) when you are finished? Or do you keep it in your office for periodic browsing? Why? (If specific comparisons not made, probe all above.)

  —You've been very logical and articulate so far. Right now, I'd like you to turn off the logical part of your heads for a moment, and deal with some *illogical,* feeling-type distinctions. I'm going to pick some of the magazines and papers you singled out for mention, and ask you to imagine that each one is a *person,* whom you are trying to describe to somebody. Tell me about the (e.g., *Ad Age*) person. How old is he or she? Is it he or she? Married or single? What kind of a car does (s)he drive? Fat or thin? Conservative or vogue-y? How about politics? Serious and buttoned-up or more freewheeling? (etc—mention *S&MM* second.)

Now put the other head back on, and tell me how and how much this kind of consideration governs your subscription decisions, and the time you allot to the publications.

• *Selection Procedure:*

Who is the person in your company with the final yes/no on business subscriptions? If it's not you, how do you input your preferences?

Who decides about advertising media? If not you, how do you exercise your vote?

What decides how long the subscription list is (probe relative importance of time-budget/financial considerations/spectrum of publications)? How do you decide whether to subscribe to a particular magazine or another with similar scope? (Example)

III. *Focus Reveal* You were/were not able to give clear definitions of the "personalities" of some magazines. What experiences do you think contribute most to your idea of "who" the periodical is?

• We're going to narrow the focus again, from print media to a particular magazine: *Sales & Marketing Management.*

—You've all had some experience with the magazine, but you didn't wake up knowing about *S&MM*. How did you get acquainted? Did you inherit it when you moved into a job? Or did you initiate subscription? If you did, why did you (try to probe hearsay, contact from the subscription department/exposure to the magazine)?

—How instrumental has direct solicitation from *S&MM's* circulation department been in getting you to subscribe or renew? (Example?)

—Did any of you subscribe purely on the basis of correspondence from the magazine? Who? Can you say what about the communications led you to choose *S&MM* rather than a "similar" magazine? What *are* "similar" periodicals—or is it unique?

—Did any of you find communications from *S&MM* lacking—or even a turn-off? (Details)

—However you feel about the magazine, what is the very best thing about it?

—However you feel about the magazine, what is the very *worst* thing about it?

—Is all of the communication between you and *S&MM* one-way: them to you? Or do you express your approval or criticism? Have you ever asked for particular coverage? For any other amendments?

If you had the editors in your office, what improvements *would* you suggest?

—Figuring value for dollar, where does *S&MM* rank, in terms of the other periodicals you buy and read?

What do you mean by "value"? (Try to probe entertainment/enjoyment as well as utilitarian considerations.)

—What do you *always* read in *S&MM*? Where are you when you read it?

What do you never—or rarely—read?

—If someone who had never seen it asked you to say what is covered in *S&MM*, what would you say? (Probe general/special coverage.)

—Do you like the way the magazine is structured? What in particular do you like about it? How about the way it looks and handles?

—In the areas you know the most about, is *S&MM* up-to-date? Accurate? Provocative? (Details)

—What ideas from *S&MM* have you ever used, specifically?

—How often during the year do you hear from the magazine?

• *The Renewal Decision* (Even though answers may be given above.)

—The last time you had to decide whether to renew or not, could you say what things influenced you—in either direction? If you *did* renew, what were the alternate periodicals that would have covered the same areas? Why did you choose to resubscribe to *S&MM*?

—If you *didn't* renew, could you review your thinking pro or con? What was the competition? Why did they win?

What might have changed your decision?

• *Creative Materials Exposure:* (Sample alternate formats/ Tables of contents/ Any revisions on which panel input would be useful)

IV. *Wrap-up* (When somebody asks you what on earth you were doing here for the last two hours, how could you summarize what the group said?)

V. *Demographics and Figure Drawings*[*]

Following this page, you will find two sheets of blank paper. Please do the following:

1. On the first page, write the number "1" at the top.
2. Now, anywhere on the page, draw a full figure of a person who would subscribe to and read *Sales & Marketing Management.*

---
[*]Instruction sheet for Drawings follows.

3. Now, on the second sheet of paper, at the top, write the number "2."
4. Draw, on the second sheet of paper, a full figure of a person who *would not subscribe* to *Sales & Marketing Management*.

   (Somewhere, on this second sheet of paper, write down the name of the magazine that this person would subscribe to, *instead of S&MM.*)

5. Finally, go back to the first blank page, where you drew the first (subscriber) figure. Turn the sheet over, and *on the back of the sheet*, write a story about this first person. Pretend (s)he is a real person whom you are describing to someone else. What kind of a person is (s)he? What is (s)he interested in? What is his(/her) occupation? Personality? Moods? Values? etc. What is happening now, in the picture? How will it turn out? What will happen to him (/her)?
   Not a novel, you understand. Just a thumbnail word-picture of the person, the "situation" you imagined, and the outcome.

Appendix E: Sample Introduction To Focus-Group Panelists

(Transcript from an actual session)

INTRODUCTION (To Panelists)

Verbatim communication	Implied message
"...Hi. Please come in and seat yourself wherever you like. Did you all have time to eat? I think we should have the buffet brought in here. Even if you ate, I'm going to work you very hard, and I don't want anyone fainting from hunger...	WE ARE CONCERNED WITH YOUR COMFORT...BUT THIS IS A WORK SESSION.
Okay? Everyone fueled up? You will find a pad and pencil at your place, and even if you are still eating or drinking, free a hand, and would you write on the pad your name, your occupation...	AND YOU MAY BE ASKED TO WRITE, AS WELL AS TALK.
and if you are married, your spouse's occupation as well. And if you have children about the house, we'd like to know their ages...and who else, if anyone, lives with you. And finally—	(CHECK ON SCREENING SPECS)
for now—one more personal fact about you: When you're not doing what you *have* to do, what do you *like* to do? Can be anything. Can be as many things as you want. You've got the whole pad to work with...	IT IS YOU AS A UNIQUE INDIVIDUAL—NOT JUST AS A CONSUMER—THAT WE ARE INTERESTED IN.
While you're thinking about that, I'll go through a few ground rules that I think are useful to this kind of an interview. If you agree with them, we'll go with them, and if you don't, we'll negotiate...	I WILL CALL THE SHOTS HERE, BUT I'M REASONABLE, AND WILL TRY TO BEND TO YOUR NEEDS.

EXCEPT, there are two things that are non-negotiable. One is the microphones which you can see in the ceiling. Yes, you are being bugged. We record these sessions because my memory is less than perfect, and if I take notes while we're here, I'm *not* here.

NOTIFICATION: I'M CANDID, AND SO CAN YOU BE.

There are two things I want to tell you. First, I'd like you to forget about the tapes, as much as you can. We really need to know what you think and how you feel about the things we're going to be discussing, and I'd like you not to edit. It would be ideal, from my point of view, if everything that comes into your mind comes out of your mouth. Don't think about "wrong." There is no such word. And don't think "unimportant" either. Any reaction you have is right and important.

ANYTHING AND
EVERYTHING YOU ARE
THINKING IS IMPORTANT
AND INTERESTING. WHAT
YOU ARE DOING HERE IS
VERY IMPORTANT TO ME
AND MY CLIENT.
YOU CAN'T BE WRONG OR
UNIMPORTANT. YOU WON'T
BE EMBARRASSED FOR
WHAT YOU SAY.

But on the other hand, when I'm sitting and listening to tapes, it's very hard to disentangle two conversations at once. I'm sure you all have tape recorders, and you know that if two things are going on at once, it's a wipe for both of them. And I can't afford to lose one word. So if someone is talking, and you have something you're dying to say (and I hope that happens. It means that you're here, and you're involved), I will ask one of you to hold it a minute. If it's *you*, please don't forget what you were going to say. I won't forget that you were going to say something, and I'll get back to you.

A CERTAIN DISCIPLINE
MUST BE MAINTAINED, BUT
IT'S NOT ARBITRARY, AND
IT'S NOT BECAUSE YOU ARE
UNIMPORTANT. YOU'RE TOO
IMPORTANT FOR ME TO
LOSE A WORD.

AND DISCIPLINE IS ALWAYS
SECOND TO INVOLVEMENT.

The second non-negotiable item is the mirror [points]. It's exactly what you suppose it to be. It's a one-way mirror. I'm pretty sure I can promise you there is no one who will be sitting back there with nose pressed to the glass watching every move we make, but I can't promise you no one will ever be there. I'd like you to forget that too. I try to. Of course, that's easy for me to say—my back is to it. But try not to let it interfere with what we are talking about.

THERE IS A CLIENT BACK
THERE BUT HE IS SEPARATE
FROM US. I'M WITH YOU.
(AT A DEEPER LEVEL: "I'M
THE CLIENTS' MOUTH.")

Besides saying what comes into your mind, I want you to feel free about responding to whatever anyone else says. You don't have to agree. If somebody says something and you all sit there nodding and smiling, I'll assume that person is speaking for the group, and I depend on you not to let me go away misinformed. So if somebody says something, and they're *not* speaking for you, say so. Even if you think it's a little niggle. It may not be so little to us. If a fist-fight breaks out, I'll interrupt it, but anything short of that is controversy, and it's fine.

THIS IS NOT A COFFEE KLATCH. YOU ARE HERE TO WORK AND TO ENLIGHTEN, NOT (NECESSARILY) TO MAKE FRIENDS.

WE NEED YOUR "NO'S" AS MUCH AS YOUR "YES"ES.

I CAN HANDLE (CONTAIN) ANY ANGER THAT IS PROVOKED. WE CAN USE IT.

Now let's see. I asked you please not to edit, and I asked you to try not to talk all at once, and to disagree if you disagree...is there anything else?...Oh, for the two hours we're here, the world ends at that door...Now it *doesn't*. The bathroom, for one, is outside this room and to the left. You don't have to raise your hand. Just hurry back...But what I *mean* when I say the world ends there is that we're only concerned with you. Your feelings, your thoughts, how you behave. So if a question is raised, don't say what your best friend thinks, or your mother-in-law, or the "average person"—whoever *that* is. Just you.

REVIEW, PREPARATORY TO ENDORSEMENT OR "NEGOTIATION".

(BATHROOMS ARE NOT EMBARRASSING). I WANT YOU TO BE COMFORTABLE.

REPRISE: IT'S YOU AND ONLY YOU WE CARE ABOUT.

Is all of that okay? Can we go with it?...Great. Now let's find out who we all are. Would you start right here (immediate left of moderator) and *say* what you *wrote* on the pad. And then go on around the table...

DON'T BE NERVOUS ABOUT WHAT TO SAY. YOU MAY READ, IF YOU WANT.

[Moderator asks brief questions of clarification or makes brief comments to every respondent, and signals with eye-contact when it is the next panelist's "turn." Panelists can use whatever name-form they like.]

I CARE ABOUT AND RECOGNIZE YOU (SINGULAR). [ESTABLISHES EYE CONTACT AS MEANS OF ADDRESS].

Appendix F: How To Score The "Buzzword" List

Step 1. Read through the list of words and phrases in this booket, quickly and privately.

Step 2. Using the *black* pen, circle the numbers of those words or phrases that describe or suggest products or product qualitites that *you might be interested in buying.* Don't edit or debate with yourself about what the words or phrases *mean* (they mean whatever you think they mean), or whether the product described is "really good" or "really possible." Don't even *think* too long about it. Just react impulsively.

You may circle as many as you like, but there should be at least 20 or 25. You have 10 minutes. Go!

Read on only after you have completed Steps One and Two.

Step 3. We will trade your black pen for a green one. With the *green* pen, look at the 25 items you have already circled as appealing, and choose the *five* that, for any reason at all, are *most appealing to you, as something you might be interested in buying.* Now, circle these five items again, in *green.*

Finally: We will trade your green pen for a red one. This time, look only at the items you have *not* circled—the less appealing ones. Choose those that would not interest you at all: the real *losers*, and circle those in *red.* As many as you like.

LIST OF "BUZZWORDS"

1. Bare Face
2. Specialized formula
3. Color-Blended
4. Anti-grey base
5. Two-step facial
6. Color stabilizer
7. Works while you sleep
8. Lip conditioner
9. Works hardest where it's needed most
10. The mark of a successful woman
11. Made by a black woman for black women
12. Gess
13. Barrier lotion
14. Color-neutralization base
15. Fragrance free
16. Water based
17. Neutralized the acid in your skin so the color stays true
18. Timed-release translucent powder
19. Three cosmetic lines; outdoor/office/evening
20. Neutralizing barrier lotion
21. Color-fast pigment
22. Salon tested
23. Professionally color-blended
24. Zinc oxide base
25. Oil-absorbing foundation
26. Smoothes your natural skin tone
27. Attractive packaging
28. Good for your looks. Good for your skin
29. Fresh start
30. Face facts
31. Penny-savers
32. Eye shadow floats on
33. Refillable brush-duster
34. Show-time
35. Seals color onto the skin

36. Wrinkle-reducer
37. Physical fitness for the skin
38. Protein based
39. Repairs as it prepares
40. Pore-minimizing formula
41. Protects beautifully
42. Skin freshener
43. Helps maintain skin elasticity
44. Executive face
45. Clean look
46. Vitamin enriched
47. Tube
48. Barely there sunny scent
49. Custom-blended
50. Built-in oil controllers
51. Water activated
52. Skin massage
53. The educated face
54. Stick
55. Muscle toner
56. For the life of your skin
57. Quality products that are worth the extra price
58. Available only in department stores
59. Present perfect
60. Skin fit
61. A color tonic for the skin
62. A Natural glow
63. Oil-eaters
64. Seals out environmental pollutants
65. No checking; no patching
66. Lash thickener builds longer, thicker lashes
67. Available only at better drug stores
68. Show your true colors
69. Lipstick leaves lips dewy, not greasy
70. Toner refines pores
71. Social security all day
72. Mascara that's swim-proof, smudge-proof, sleep-proof
73. Brush-on color leaves no hard edges

74. Liquid cleanser that surrounds excess oil and carries it away
75. Color so real you'll believe it yourself
76. Once-a-day makeup takes your mind off your face
77. Daisy-face
78. Makeup with built-in oil eaters
79. Contains PABA
80. Hassle-free applicators in show-off casings
81. Foundation that softens "spots"
82. Light citrus fragrance
83. Liner stays neat and tight
84. 4-inch overnight case
85. Mood-coordinated
86. Triple-misted powder
87. Lipstick that skins in
88. Lena
89. Family jewels
90. With sunscreen, to prevent premature aging
91. Self-adjusting for combination skin
92. Smudge-proof
93. All Natural
94. Lipstick that stays color-true
95. Your best portfolio
96. 8-hour staying power
97. Waterproof
98. Cleanser that leaves an acid mantle
99. Makeup that's actually good for your skin
100. Lets you show through
101. Junior/senior formulas
102. May-morning fragrance
103. Limelight
104. Maintenance-free
105. Dream weaver
106. Breathe eas
107. Anti-irritant
108. Powder mattes without masking
109. Allergy-tested
110. Time-out
111. Foundation blends in melanin spots

112. Contains collagen
113. Soft color sticks
114. Fair and mild
115. Micro-blended foundation can't clog pores
116. Day face/night face
117. Non-greasy
118. Face cocktail
119. Clinically developed
120. Compact designed for jeans or black tie
121. Adjusts to day or office light
122. Specially made for black skin
123. Wash and wear skin
124. Vitamin-enriched
125. Products designed to work together synergistically
126. Natural healthy glow
127. Undercover
128. Beauty consultant for black skin
129. Cosmetics purchased through your beauty salon
130. Trade up
131. Dermatologist-tested
132. Makeup remover unlocks skin for cleansing
133. Puff-bottle powder leaves only a whisper
134. Custom-fitted cosmetics come to you
135. Special shades and textures for summer and winter

Appendix G: Short Report Exploration Of Consumer Responses To Introductory Concepts For Cocktail Mixers

Following is a report of all focus-group interviews conducted over the last 90 days for (Brand) Cocktail Mixers.

BACKGROUND AND PURPOSE

(Brand) is about to introduce a new line of non-alcoholic cocktail mixes. Preliminary guidance was requested preparatory to developing positioning, advertising strategy, and copy concepts. Specific question areas:

• How often and under what circumstances do respondents drink cocktails (rather than some other ˜orm of alcoholic drink) and how much?
• How/do these consumers . ise cocktail mixes? Where do mixes fit into their patterns of drinking alco₁,₀ic beverages?
• How do respondents feel about mixes?
—What do they perceive as the chief values of mixes?
—What do they think are the main drawbacks of mixes?
—Do they display the mixes they use in the same way they display liquor? Why or why not?
—How do they feel—as *hosts*—serving a drink made with a mix, vis-á-vis serving a drink made from scratch? How do they feel—as guests being served drinks made either way?

• Who makes the buying decisions on bar supplies in these consumers' homes (either does the actual buying, or instructs the purchaser)?

• What do respondents think is the best that could possibly be hoped for from a cocktail mix? How does this differ from the best possible cocktail?

• How close do the mixes they've used come to meeting this standard? How do their current mixes fail?

• How did they happen to try the brand of mix they use (or used last)?

• What makes them try a new one?

• What advertising—if any—do they recall for cocktail mixes? Why was this advertising persuasive—or why wasn't it?

METHOD AND PROCEDURES

Depth group interviews were chosen as the instrument for this because both drinking and conversation about drinking happen in a social context. This means that much of what any individual knows, or thinks, or does about alcoholic drinks is born or influenced by word-of-mouth exchange with others. Since we wish to watch an idea form from the information we offer, and to see whether it survives rebuttal, grows or changes with interaction, or wastes away from lack of interest, this kind of "forum" seemed the most natural way to proceed. The interview sequence was:

• Discussion of drinking habits and functions generally.
• Fitting cocktails (mixed drinks) into the array of alcoholic alternatives.
• Discussion of mixes: usage, brand-choice, advertising.
• Presentation of creative materials: description of illustrations and concept boards.

—The first two groups saw only a rendering of bottles of Daiquiri, Mai-Tai, Pina Colada and Marguerita mixes.

—Groups three and four saw: "Sip Into Something Different..." The same rendering of the five bottles shown to previous groups, but with rough conceptual headlines: (Brand) Perfects the Cocktail Experience. "Sip into Something Different Every Night" and a takeaway line "(Brand) For Drinks With Taste."

—Remaining groups all saw: "From The People Who Brought You The Perfect Gimlet..." A rendering of a (Brand) bottle, and three (Brand) mixes (Daiquiri, Whiskey Sour, Marguerita) emphasizing labels by exposing only the body of the bottles. Copy trades on the reputation and quality of (Brand), and promises "perfect" cocktails.

—Two groups saw: "...Serve As Proudly As Your Own." Bottles of the three mixes, and glasses filled and appropriately garnished, are shown on a silver tray. Copy is substantially identical to preceding copy, but the emphasis shifts from selling (Brand)'s reputation to selling the readers' pride in accomplishment as hosts.

—Two groups "officially" (and two more, as a postscript) saw: "...Better Cocktails Than Your Favorite Bartender..." Bottles of the three mixes plus filled glasses, garnishes, lined up as if on a bar with a bartender's knife shown, and miscellaneous bottles indicated in the background. Copy asserts (with research claims) that bartenders find (Brand) cocktails "better," appeals to the reader's desire to serve drinks of "professional" quality.

—Two groups saw: "...The End Of The Boring Cocktail Hour." The same three bottles and glasses, less stiffly lined up, are displayed. Copy picks up the glamour and variety of a variety of cocktails which were previously beyond the scope of the home bartender, and implies that the host(ess), as well as the drinks, will become more "interesting."

Copy on all of these boards is nearly identical. It expresses the care and effort put into the various drink recipes by (Brand), and the quest for the perfect (exotic, imported) ingredients. The ingredient story supports both painstaking attention to quality, and the glamour of far places, both of which are mentioned as important attributes of liquor, cocktails, and the "ideal cocktail mix." Copy also puts emphasis on "natural flavors," followed by a statement of six-months shelf-life. Both *naturalness* and *ease of storing* are also among the "most important" qualities in an "ideal" cocktail mix, in most groups.

• Presentation of Creative Materials: Procedure.

—Boards were shown (initially, also read) and tacked up for reference.

—Each respondent was given a black-and-white "stat" of the board, and instructed to: "Treat this as though it were an advertisement. Spend about as much time looking at it as you would spend if you ran across it. Read as much as you think you would read if you saw it somewhere else. Then turn it face down and write."

—Respondents then answered written questions about message and appeal of the concept.

—Finally, the copy was read (or reread) and the group was invited to discuss the board.

• Presentation of Product

—After the last board was discussed, respondents were asked to write down what they expected of the product, then to try it and make a written comparison of the first drink they mixed (some wrote about all three). Some discussion of the reactions to the mixes was done informally. (More discussion in some groups than in others. Also more informality.)

• Figure Drawings

—The last task given to the respondents was to draw two figures (the first person would use this product: the second would not) and to tell a story about the user-figure.

SAMPLE

Ten interviews were performed in (Place). Fifty-eight men and fifty-six women participated. All of the respondents had total family incomes above $25,000; all were college-educated suburban residents. In the first two groups panelists were between 35 and 49 years of age, but this was broadened to 25-49 in all the subsequent panels. The first two groups were also more restrictive in terms of usage, in that all respondents were required to be users or ex-users of both alcoholic and non-alcoholic mixes, and to drink regularly the specific cocktails pictured on the bottle-drawing. In the later groups, no specifications were made about mix-usage, and no specific cocktails were named, though all panel members drank *some* form of cocktail on a regular basis. In all of the female panels, at least one or two of the women worked outside the home (part or full-time).

SUMMARY OF FINDINGS

Predispositions

From *their* points-of-view, I think each of the panelists would describe the interactions in the group as positive and involving. That is to say, each panel, relative to their several capacities, "groups" well, and reaches a high level of interpersonal exchange, with (again relatively) considerable authenticity. From *our* point-of-view, the "grouping" in these panels is uneven, and the findings often inconsistent.

However, there are some matters-of-factual-report about which all of the groups agree:

• The man in a household purchases, or requests purchase of, liquor and his taste is also the principal consideration in the purchase of the various potables with which liquor is mixed. There are individual cases where the pattern of purchase decision is different, but this is certainly the norm.

—Men generally are the ones who physically make the purchase in liquor stores, and women generally make the actual purchase in supermarkets. Men may also make supermarket purchases, but women rarely do in liquor stores.

—The pattern of male decision-making is less clear in the case of packaged and bottled mixes than in the non-alcoholic mix*er* brands. This seems to be attributable to the fact that mixes have too tentative a place in these panelists' lives to have become habituated. Men still seem to be primary buyer-deciders, but the demarcation is not so sharp.

• Regardless of individuals' different personal preferences, when a mixed party is being given, cocktails are served, and some form of "sweet cocktails" must be available. These are evening parties. Women, entertaining women, may serve "sweet cocktails" in the afternoon, but among our male respondents, sweet cocktails are as rare as vampire bats in the daylight.

• None of our panelists mentions advertising as a reason for trying a cocktail mix. They do not mention it spontaneously and when asked about advertising for mixes, they draw a blank. Purchase is described as a point-of-purchase impulse ("I just saw it on the shelf"). They do—

some of them—play back to us and the group some advertising content which is recognizable, but which they seem unaware of having seen. This, combined with the tentative usage patterns, suggests that the people in these groups—most of whom do use mixes anywhere from occasionally to regularly—are having some conceptual or feeling problems with the category.

• Virtually all of the panelists list the same attributes of an "ideal" cocktail mix as (roughly in order of frequency/fervency):

—*"Fresh" taste:* resembling the natural fruit. This also implies a more *complex* taste than artificial or "canned" fruit, which has only one flavor note. (*Just* sweet or *just* sour, etc.)

—*Easy Storage,* and some choice of sizes.

—*Natural Ingredients,* no chemicals or additives

—*"Missing Something":* The mixes should be *nearly*, but not *totally* complete. It is important to most of our respondents that they supply *something* to transform the mix into a cocktail.

• We think it is for these reasons (missing something) that *most of the men and women in the groups prefer non-alcoholic mixes to alcoholic ones.* They give "practical", "sensible" reasons like the fact that the bottler would economize on the hard stuff, but they really mean that they feel the need to perform some ritual act of completion before serving the drink to anyone.

• By far, the majority of respondents think most currently-available mixes are less than fully satisfying.

The rest of the "Predisposition" section of the interviews differs sharply from group to group. Happily, the distinctions between attitudes and viewpoints expressed by the panels do not seem to be arbitrary. Both in terms of *interpersonal style* (energy, aggressiveness, confidentiality, impression management, "up-frontness," etc.) and in terms of *content* (feelings about cocktail drinking, personal investment in mixing/dispensing, responsiveness to creative material, etc.) what we think we are looking at is *three major categories of potential users:*

• *Women* (who, despite their individual differences, reach something like consensus on the whole cocktail ambience, and are largely consistent in their responses to copy-concepts).

• *"Visceral" Men: men who drink sweet cocktails* (who—whether en-masse or islanded in a group of "buttoned" men—are remarkably consistent in their attitudes and preferences).

• *"Buttoned" Men: men who drink sweet cocktails only occasionally* (who, on the whole, drink more than either of the other two groups and have more idiosyncratic investment in what they drink; but their reactions to creative materials have at least some "cluster" consistency).

To flesh the bones a little: The *women* in our panels tend, more than either of the male drinker-types, to regard alcoholic drinks generally as a potent catalyst, transforming themselves and situations in ways closer to the heart's desire. For most of them "alcoholic drinks" *mean* "sweet cocktails", and they say that cocktails do the following things for them:

• If they are shy, a cocktail or two makes them more "outgoing."

• If they are lacking in self-assurance, a discreet tipple makes them feel surer, more attractive, more interesting.

• If they are "high-strung", drinking loosens, eases them: makes them more serene. Note that this is slightly different from the more localized "unwinding" men describe, in the shift from business to social pursuits. The women are talking about deeper, more temperamental transformations. They sound as if their fairy-godmothers travel with a backpack of banana daiquiris.

• Few of the women actually *say* (but many agree or imply) that alcoholic drinks dramatically lower their sexual resistance (especially sweet cocktails).

By way of corollary, the women say that in a *cocktail-drinking situation:*

• There is an enhanced atmosphere of festivity in a group of people (especially true with "exotic" cocktails).

• *Everybody* sparkles (they are not only more attractive themselves, but also find everybody else more lovable).

• Some of the women say that, over cocktails, men become more protective and solicitous of them.

• That's not *all* men become more of—cocktails can change a "date" or a pre-dinner meeting into a tryst.

The "visceral" men among our respondents do not see themselves as being changed much by alcoholic drinks. Despite some fraternal lip-service to "unwinding after a hard day", that is not especially where it's at for these men. They use the sweet mixed drinks they favor for basically two purposes:

• *Self-gratification, indulgence, comfort, etc.* ("It tastes so good.")
• *Expression of affection through nurturance.* ("I like to give my friends pleasure.")

This plays into situations in which:

• They *reward* themselves for accomplishment (or promise themselves reward when they have finished).
• They *console* themselves when things are bumpy.
• They *delight or/and surprise their guests* with something delectable, and "hover" to extract all the vicarious pleasure possible.

The "buttoned" men—who drink sweet cocktails infrequently—are inclined to think of alcoholic drinks as externally instrumental, rather than as doing something to or for themselves. Drinking plays an important and regular part in their lives, but in social contexts, it is used more deliberately, and more superficially:

• As a ritual kind of "punctuation" of their lifescape: a ceremony which marks the transition between the workworld of power and pressure and softer, more spontaneous social encounters.
• Manipulatively: as an aid and a measure in the power "game": drinking softens the edges of competitive deal-making; also, they can feel "one-up" if they hold the stuff better than their compatriots.
• The *least* superficial drinking of "buttoned" types tends to be solitary: the drink, as a companion in reverie. This is almost never a sweet cocktail for "buttoneds", and differs totally from the "Golly, it tastes good" of the solitary "visceral" indulgence.

By way of situations:

• The fraternal after-work day-swapping between peers.

• Manipulative drinking:
—In work power-plays (never a sweet cocktail).
—In seduction of women (almost always a sweet cocktail...for her at least).
—*As host.* (Where women are *excited,* and "visceral" men are flooding everybody in sight with the milk of human kindness and ice-cream brandy alexanders.) This man tends to start out highly concerned with impression management—how he comes off to his guests. Having done his star turn, however, he retires secure and lets everybody fend for themselves.

Reactions to creative materials fall into some kind of understandable perspective, if we differentiate the reactions of these three types.

REACTIONS TO CREATIVE MATERIALS

One useful function of early qualitative investigation is to allow consumer input to function as a kind of backboard, responding to the stimulation given, and coming back in new directions. Our rationale in this project is to begin as generally and ambiguously as possible, and move toward specificity and definiteness in creative positioning. Accordingly, the "creative materials" shown to the first two groups consist simply of the pictorial "announcement" of (Brand) cocktail mixes. The board shown to the second two groups adds only a simple positioning concept.

Pictorial Introduction

Instructions to the first two panels request them to comment on the "message" in this "ad," exactly as though copy were included. Remarkably, the groups seem to have no difficulty in receiving some "message." The women respond to the excitement—almost *adventure*—implicit in the variety of "exotic" cocktails which would now be available to them. The men (all, as we now know, "viscerals") respond both to the "tempting" array of options, and to the quality premise implicit in the (Brand) name.

Both of these premises lift the new cocktail mixes above currently available brands, which are seen by our respondents as producing generally inferior end products and as justifiable only by convenience. The men say that "With a really high-quality product...like you *know* (Brand) is quality... you would trust it enough to spend less time mixing drinks and more time with your friends." They also say that the mixes would allow them to "please everybody" by serving a wider range of cocktails.

They ask three questions about the mixes:

- Would they have natural ingredients?
- Does the person using the mix add the liquor?
- Will there be a choice of sizes?

Affirmative answers (which are what they have hoped for) are given, and the respondents are asked to comment. The women, more than the men, are turned on by the idea of "natural flavors," although this interests the men, too. The women find "naturalness" appealing mostly for rather diffuse nutritional reasons. Apparently the role of the homemaker as *nourisher* extends to everything that is served in her house. The men see "natural flavors" as a promise of more "life" (and more lifelike complexity) in the flavor of the finished drink.

Although the women, initially, are not as responsive to the "class" implied by the (Brand) name (indeed, they see (Brand) as a kind of hard-drinking Sara Lee), they suggest that there are some ingredients of "class" which could move them ("exotic" and "imported," to name two).

"...Sip Into Something Different..."

The women in our next round of panels like the "Sip Into Something Different" approach, and find it responsive to their desire for excitement in the "cocktail experience." They comment that the bottles are "different" and "mysterious." These ideas were not raised in response to the picture-only board, and may be attributable to the effect of the headline. Aside from one or two women who "get" the double entendre, and find it a touch too coy, the reactions of our second panel of women are enthusiastically positive. Even the two women who are mildly critical in discussion *write* positively about the concept.

The men are another color horse altogether. They are, in the first place, different *individuals*. Screened only for "cocktail" drinking, the recruiting roll of dice turns up a male panel in which none of the men drink *sweet* cocktails (by hindsight: "buttoneds" only). These men find the positioning irrelevant. They say that "Sip Into Something Different" is aimed at women; and "What's a cocktail experience? That's something you have in Jamaica." Excitement is not something they associate with drinking or serving cocktails as they ordinarily do.

In only two respects does this second panel of men ("buttoneds") find common ground with the first ("viscerals"):

• They are impressed by the quality image of (Brand) which, for them, has the endorsement of the highest authority they recognize. ("Well, you know it'll be quality. Walk in any bar, and what does the bartender use for gimlets and a lot of other stuff? He uses (Brand).")

• They, too, welcome the opportunity to come out of the kitchen and drop the apron. ("If it's really that good, I can actually *be* at the party, instead of being the bartender.")

"From The People Who Brought You..."

The first and second rounds of interviewing convince us that "class"— as *reputation*, as *meticulousness*, as *foreign-ness* (combining "imported" and "intrigue"), as ''professional endorsement'', etc.—was the clearest common denominator for all our panelists. Accordingly, our ''class'' board is used in all of the remaining sessions. Discussion responses to this board vary more than written responses (almost all of which are strong, and most of which are positive), but *everybody* understands what is being said. And everybody *reacts*; it is not a neutral concept.

The ones who like it best say that it is "dependable:" "...you wouldn't be ashamed to serve it...," "you could take the fling," "...it would show that you know how to do things." The ones who dislike it most react to the deliberate overclaim of ''perfection'' as an "arrogant" promise ("Who do they think they are?"). But even this kind of reaction does not sound as though such a ''class'' positioning is one that would be as invisible as cocktail mix advertising tends to be now.

As expected, the *kinds* of reaction differ according to the three target types:

• *Women* are intrigued by the inference that "knowing about (Brand)" is some kind of select fraternity. They are also occasionally outraged by the shut-out...but impressed, even so. They are also generally enthusiastic about the thrill of far places, and morally supported by the weasel-promise of "natural flavors."

• Some *"buttoned" men* voice a sophisticated cynicism about the "over-claim," but privately, most of these scoffers recant. Most of them affirm, even out loud, that they are impressed by the reputation of (Brand), and by the inference that it is the "pro's" way of mixing gimlets, and therefore might well become the bartender's friend for daiquiris, sours, and margueritas. ("You know, they have these empty bottles under there, and when they mix, they pour from those. You *know* they use (Brand), and what's to stop them from putting *these* into empty bottles?...")

• Many of the *"visceral" men* are closet self-doubters, who don't say much about this board in discussion ("Well, you know, (Brand) is just a staple thing, and you'd probably get to thinking these were too, pretty fast"...). In written responses, however, they are clearly buoyed by the promise of "perfect" cocktails. They also pick up the "select fraternity" seen by the women, and enjoy the idea of membership. The one negative feeling—never very definitively expressed—is that of being somehow superfluous: if (Brand) supplies what's necessary for perfect drinks, who needs *them,* the loving hosts?

"...Serve As Proudly As Your Own"

Another common denominator in the first groups is the importance of the mixed drink as an act of gracious affection. Since we also know that mixes now tend to be mainly party-conveniences for our panelists, a board aimed at just these two factors is an inescapable option. This board stirs a lot of positive conversation among both the women and the men (a mixed group, but mainly "buttoneds"). However, the content of the accolades tends to be as frothy as the heads on the drinks. They praise the picture, the labels, the "lifelike" drinks, but their hearts are not really in it, and the written reactions are lukewarm. The women seem to like this board better than either male type, but they don't get as involved in it as in the "From The People..." board. In fact, for many women stung by the exclusion implied by "From The People...," the warmth of the responses to "...Serve As Proudly..." appear to be little more than a bite of the thumb at the previous "chauvinistic" board. The "buttoned" men respond with faint praise, and the few "viscerals" in the group are even more forlorn about their superfluity after seeing this board.

"...Better Cocktails Than Your Favorite Bartender..."

The women find this as irrelevant a claim as "buttoned" men do the "Sip Into Something Different..." headline. They have no particular stake in being a bartender, good or bad. The "classy copy" (the same in all boards) is still intriguing, but comparison with a bartender ("What favorite bartender? I don't go to bars that often.") is at best divorced from their lives and goals, and, at worst, defeminizing:

• Bartending is man's work, they say.
• It makes them feel a little as if we're saying they are lushes...which is also man's work.

The "visceral" men respond in similar ways to women. Bartending is cold and commercial, and very far from the warm nipple *they* offer. "Buttoneds," on the other hand, are caught by the headline, and read the copy. They say they may not believe it, but it does snap them to attention. Some are annoyed and competitive, but for most of the "buttoned" men, the board is engaging and provocative.

"...The End Of The Boring Cocktail Hour..."

This board stimulates much conversation—some good, some bad, though the balance is on the positive side. What is most remarkable about the responses to this concept is that almost all of the written comments are positive, substantial, and enthusiastic. The social "rub," which prevents airing of much of their endorsements in discussion, seems to be that if you like this concept, you are admitting that your cocktail hours are now boring, which means:

• Nobody likes you, so you drink alone.
• Nobody like you *or* your drinks so they leave your parties early.
• You are just generally a kind of a dim bulb.

They see the board and read it. They privately like it, but there is the danger that early-users of a product advertised this way would be inviting stigma. On the other hand, "Halitosis" doesn't seem to have hurt Listerine.

IMPLICATIONS

We are as certain as one can be from qualitative small-group research that we know what the big motivational strings are that "(Brand) Cocktail Mixes" can pluck—and in some cases, *uniquely* pluck:

• Class and reputation
• Excitement
• Support for social occasions

We also are as certain (*etc.*) that we know that some, if not all, of these themes will be understood differently by the three targets who are showing up on our radar screens.

At this point, and subject to quantitative verifying, it appears we will have to choose *one* of these target groups and aim our strategy, hoping that there is enough positive fall-out of other kinds to engage—or anyway to avoid antagonizing—the rest of the world. And at this point, our recommendation is that the *"visceral" men* be the ones in our sights:

• Men are the decision-makers about liquor-related items.
• These are the men who drink the kinds of cocktails we are selling.
• They are not case-hardened against advertising claims, and they are interested in all products that proceed by way of mouth and pharynx into their stomachs.

It's true that there are likely to be more "buttoned" men in this country than "viscerals," but the recommendation stands. It's true too that this would tend to cast out positioning like "...Better Than Your Favorite Bartender...," which does very well with "buttoned" types. But the recommendation still stands.

If you decide to play our hunch, it seems to me the way to aim the product is halfway between Hallmark and Greyhound:

"Caring enough to send the very best" is important, especially if it comes across as a pair of tender hands doing the mixing, as in
• "Leave the driving to us."

The good news is that this approach wouldn't alienate anyone else, and that you could incorporate enough *class* emphasis to make the "buttoneds" sit up, and enough excitement to keep the ladies dreaming.

Appendix H: Full Report

The report which follows demonstrates the power of planning that is both creative and assiduous. Over a period of several months, four conferences were scheduled, each lasting several hours. Three of these meetings preceded the delivery of the Screener and Discussion Guide, and the last was an editing conference on these paperwork items.

As a result of these early discussions, the resulting group-interviews were exceedingly rich, and the report covers broader areas than is common in such reports. Even with the editing which was necessary to protect product strategy, breadth and depth of coverage is clear.

TABLE OF CONTENTS

INTRODUCTION
  Background and Purpose
  Methods and Procedures
  Sample

IMPLICATIONS AND RECOMMENDATIONS

SUMMARY OF FINDINGS
  Predispositions; Exploration of Lifestyles, Values
  Spontaneous Responses to Cold Cereals to (PRODUCT)
  Reactions to Creative Materials

APPENDIX
  "Scenarios" Volunteered by Panel Members
  Discussion Guide

BACKGROUND AND PURPOSE

This section has been withheld as being highly specific to the brand. What can be said is that the client is a prominent manufacturer of food products, and the brand for which the research was commissioned is a mature brand, targeted for breakfast use, and positioned as wholesome (i.e., not pandering to palates accustomed to high levels of sodium, sugar, and other flavor-enhancers). To avoid the expectation of low taste appeal which frequently accompanies "good for you" foods, it was hypothesized that linking consumption to a timely and much admired lifestyle could skirt the taste issue and rejuvenate the brand's image.

The lifestyle selected was taken from a popular "typology" system. The selection of this system and this particular lifestyle poses a second (minor) problem: to recruit panelists who fit the description, the system provides a very lengthy questionnaire, which makes it unwieldy for recruiters. Therefore, the client's research department has developed a short form which, if it checks out, could be used not only in this project, but in subsequent work with consumers in this target group.

The report now follows, with few deletions.

Qualitative exploration of this approach was requested, and four Matrix Group Interviews were conducted in San Francisco on April 28th and 29th, to explore in depth the *lifestyles* and values of *"Inner-Directed"* consumers.

SPECIFIC QUESTION AREAS

• Predispositions—Exploration of values and pursuits. Who *are* these "Inner-Directeds," in the privacy of their own heads (phenomenologically), and as viewed by the rest of the world? How can we portray them accurately?
—How do they feel/what do they do about *family*?
—How do they feel/what do they do about *work and accomplishment?*
—How do they feel/what do they do about the balance of work and play (recreation)?
—How do they feel/what do they do about the broader community?
—What is the balance (and relative intensity) of their needs for solitude and for social interaction? Which *activities* or *times* ...e pursued or spent alone vs. with others?
—Where do material things (including money) fit into their value-priorities?
—Where do they "locate" themselves in time and space? Are they *existential,* accepting the present 24 hours as the universe? Are they future-oriented? Past-oriented?
—What are their (stated or inferrable) moral codes?

• What is the meaning and importance to them of *food in general* (sensual delight? fuel for living? security measure? health maintenance? adventure?)
• What are their *breakfast* beliefs and practices?
• Specifically, what do they think/how do they feel/what do they do about *cold cereals? About (Brand) in particular? About (Brand) users?*
• What are their *reactions to Creative Materials?* What's good/bad about each selling-statement or rough copy/illustration? What alternative suggestions can they offer?

METHOD AND PROCEDURE

Matrix Group Interviews were chosen for this study as a way of facilitating expression of each individual panelist's needs and feelings, in some depth, without sacrificing emotional and social exchange among panel members. The general format of a Matrix Interview is a focus group in which:

• Some anonymity is fostered, to encourage openness.

• Disagreement is specifically encouraged, to "test the limits" of feelings, attitudes, and values.

• An attempt is made to disengage panel members from preset viewpoints or prepared responses, by "making the familiar strange."

• Focus topics are introduced, when possible, by respondent suggestions (rather than arbitrarily by the moderator) and arise out of the context of respondents' experiences.

• Several types of interpretive comments are offered during the interview:

—To elicit deeper introspection.

—To summarize before topic-shifts.

—To draw out tentative statements (or encourage clarification).

—To polarize dissenting points of view.

—To challenge, or test the strength of, opinons or feelings.

• All communicative channels are utilized. In addition to *group verbalization:*

—Panelists *write* usage information and reactions to creative materials, before discussion.

—*Body Language* is interpreted and acknowledged in the group discussion.

—*Vocal Indications* too are used in interpretation.

—At the end of the session, panelists are asked to complete *drawings* of "someone who would buy and use the product" and "someone who would not buy." These drawings are used projectively, in interpretation.

The *Procedure* was essentially the same for these four group interviews. To particularize the rather abstract information we were searching for (feelings, attitudes, values), a "fantasy situation" was imposed on the panels, which allowed them to talk concretely about dreams, wishes, and goals, and which ultimately ("...it's not thirty days or six months, but the rest of your life...") imposed a life-change which rotated their ingrained habit patterns and commitments enough to call values into question. Along the way, panelists were probed constantly about the relation of the fantasy to their actual lives, as now lived.

After this lengthy general "lifestyle" exploration, the focus of each panel was narrowed successively:

- To food
- To breakfast
- To cold cereal
- To (Brand)

In the first two groups, the (Brand) reveal occurred *after* the exposure of some creative "selling statements". In the last two groups, (Brand) was discussed *before* creative materials were exposed.

Creative Materials shows were:

- *Selling Statements:*
—"The Cereal that is the intelligent choice for people who give careful thought and demonstrate concern in everything they do eat." (The word "intelligent" was deleted after the first group.)
—"The Cereal for healthy, active people who get the most out of life."
—"The Cereal for people who are rediscovering simpler lifestyles and getting back to basic values."
- *Copy/Illustrations*
—*"Bank President" (Real People):* An executive opting for voluntary simplification, and including (Brand) as part of the prescription.
—*"Ice Fishing":* A spartan and unusual recreation given as an example of getting back to basics, offering (Brand) as another example.
—*"Our Town":* A slightly "limboed" setting for a community that is getting back to basic values (and earlier times?), and to (Brand).

Sample

Two panels (19 individuals) of men were interviewed, and two panels (22 individuals) of women. One male and one female group were screened to be (Brand) users, and one male and one female group were screened to be (Brand) non-users. In practice, there were a few user/non-user switches, in both directions, but this did not seem to be a problem, in terms of obscuring group distinctions. Demographic spread was good in all four groups, with ages pretty well spread from 20 to 50+. We had asked for education levels at or above "attended college", and excepting two of the women in group I, this criterion was met.

Twenty-six of the forty-one panelists were married. Seven were single. Nine were divorced. Occupational spread was broad. There was some upscale skew in income (24 had incomes of $30,000+), resulting partly from the two working spouses pattern, partly (inferrably) from higher educational status.

All panelists were screened to be "Inner-Directed," with an abbreviated form of the (lifestyles) questionnaire, developed by (the client).

IMPLICATIONS AND RECOMMENDATIONS

There are segments of the research community who would always think that a "Recommendations" section on a qualitative study of 41 individuals is presumptuous. Qualitative, small-sample research poses circular problems. The people interviewed are not the universe of possible consumers, and are not a dependable sample of that user-universe. They are, however, a *complete universe of the individuals interviewed:*

• Either we keep in the front of our minds the tinyness of the sample, and the subjectivity of the inferences which can be made.
• Or we take the whole thing very seriously indeed, treating the panelists as a total universe (of themselves) with yet-to-be seen implications for larger populations.

In the first case, the risk is that impressions, nuances, and useful interpretations may be glossed over as unimportant. In the second case, the risk is merely of being pretentious or silly.

Having made this salute to research methodology I'll now proceed to take these four groups very seriously indeed. I'll also assume that the screener "works," and that the people whose interviews are reported here are, as ordered, forty-one authentic "inner directed" men and women. The general questions to be addressed by this exploratory study are:

• Do these people have common characteristics, so that we can hope to appeal to them all—or to a lot of them—rather than reaching a few and alienating others?
• Do we have any clues to *how* they can be reached (and how they cannot)?
• Are there points in the "(Brand) story" that make productive contact with qualities or behavior patterns that are recognizably "true to them"?— i.e., are there particular reasons why a *cereal* would appeal to them? Are they likely to favor a "natural" cereal, a "whole grain" cereal? An "untrammeled" cereal, etc.?
• What are their reactions to the several conceptual alternatives presented? To the several executional strategies developed? Does their receptiveness seem to justify further work along the same lines?

The People

These people are indeed a recognizable cluster. They look similar from the outside, and appear to perceive themselves as similar. But the resemblance is complex. At heart, they are alike because they do not accept the partitioning that is standard social issue to everybody else (male/female, old/young, work/play, day/night, etc.). That is to say, they are alike in being unique, which is a hard tune to play in 30 seconds.

The Summary of Findings (below) spells out inferences about lifestyles and values in some detail, in terms of:

• *Immediate Impressions.* (Group climate: they are porous, accessible, adventurous, emotional.)
• *Attitudes Toward the Family.* (Fewer of these people live in socially conventional families. More are divorced or have not married than would be true in the usual demographically mixed sample of adult men and women. Family ties, however, tend to be unusually warm. Especially, there is more tender nurturance from fathers than is common. In general, there is a great deal of non-defensive gender roleswapping.)
• *Attitudes Vis-a-Vis the Community.* ("The community," to our respondents, is the number of people with whom emotional contact can be ade-

quately vascularized. "The world at large," or political bundles of people are not especially relevant to them. They are not particularly "do-gooders" at large.)

• *Time Frames.* (These people "locate," in geographical terms, very solidly, where the bulk of their life happens. Travel and "vacations" are typically unrelated episodes, and beside the "point" of their lives. But they are time gypsies, feeling bonds with both the past and the future. This is especially true of the men, who long to relive the early days of America and, equally, want to sail the skies in the next century).

• *Alone(ness)/Together(ness).* (Togetherness is very close and warm, and they are also conscientious about doing "their share" in relation-ships. But at the same time, they all need as much, or even more, to have time that is theirs alone. Many of them seem to be renegotiating their relational contracts, asking for shorter hours.)

• *Material Goods.* (Excess of money and things is not desirable. In-deed, the "changes" most of them are making or thinking of making have to do fairly centrally with shuffling off material possessions. Money is only important when you don't have it. Too much is "fat," and insulates them from experience.)

• *Work/Play.* (They are, in personnel terms, "vocationally unstable." Most of them have made at least one work-upheaval change. Some have made several. They are not looking for "advancement." They work for accomplishment, for love of work, to provide what they need, for dig-nity, for comradeship. But not for vice-presidencies. They *choose* to dis-engage from the accepted criteria for "making it." What they truly aim for is work that isn't work because they love it.)

• *Moral Values.* (In general, these people are not so much moralistic as *ethical*. The American tradition of fair play is mainly what moderates their "go and find and enjoy" intellectual hedonism. But in this area is the single major difference that emerges between (Brand) users and non-users: The (Brand)-users still feel morally committed to work, for work's sake. The organizational meat grinder has lost them, but the Protestant ethic still has its hooks in.)

The Summary also deals briefly with *Feelings and Behavior Related to Eating* (they're quirky, unclockable eaters), and in some greater detail with:

• *The Case for Cold Cereal.* (These are heavy cereal consumers, but not necessarily as "breakfast." Cold cereal, to them, is an almost invisible, non-distracting meal that is immediately answerable to impulse. Moreover, it is "light" and doesn't use up in digestion any of the energy it yields. It is efficient fuel. It also has ties with the past, with childhood.)

• *Perceptions of (Brand).* (Both users and non-users want the same things in cereals: *durable energy, lightness, compactness, wholesomeness/healthyness,* and *good mouth experience.* (Brand) users think this spells (Brand), natch. Non-users are happy enough with what they are using to have no pressing urge to switch. Where (Brand) is truly unique is *versatility.* Non-user women prick up their ears to learn more about making hot (Brand). Non-user men are intrigued with the uses of (Brand) in cooking.)

• *Perceptions of (Brand)-Users.* (These are generally continuous with previous exploration of consumer views of the (Brand)-user. The lacks, for these panelists, in the (Brand)-user--the things that would keep "him" from being a person to be identified with are: He is not *stimulating, fun or quick-witted, emotionally open, or socially warm.*)

Reaching Them

Athough there is no easy formula for reaching people like these (their tissues reject easy formulas), there are a couple of important precautions:

• These are individuals who have made unusual decisions, and do not automatically accept conventional measures of success, failure, or satisfaction. Since people who work in corporate life are apt to subscribe more nearly to conventional measures and yardsticks, it will be easy to judge these "inner-directeds" as "kooks" or "losers." And if we do this, they will know it. It is true of any product that it is nearly impossible to appeal to potential consumers if the appeal is rooted in something less than respect. It is especially true of these people, who are smart and sensitive.

• Their sense of what is *real* in life has a lot more to do with feelings and reasons-for than with simple behavioral descriptions. Incidents in execution need not be intensely dramatic (though they may be that), so long as they are motivated, and the people in them are believable.

• Incidents from daily life are probably more persuasive, other things being equal, than dramatic or intense episodes.

Reactions to Selling Statements and Copy Illustrations

Overall, the panelists in these groups, both (Brand)-users and non-users, respond very favorably to the ..."*rediscovering simpler lifestyles and getting back to basic values*" selling statement. It is attractive to them and they see themselves in it. The recommendation from this study is that creative next steps be taken in developing this copy platform.

One of the three copy illustrations (Bank President) seems to them potentially both exciting and true. This *kind* of story they see as becoming more true all the time. There are quibbles about absent motivation or exaggeration, which will, of course, be worked out in the detailed execution. The recommendation is to go ahead with this execution as well.

A second execution ("Our Town") get mixed reactions from panelists, but seems to have developable possibilities. Panelists also provide 19 (motley) scenarios of their own.

It would be ideal, for these people, to have a whole skyfull of different creative executions to fill in different aspects of this complex personality group. To decide which aspects are most critical to show would be the research next-step.

SUMMARY OF FINDINGS

Predispositions: Group Climate

Each of these panels, in a matter of minutes, knits itself into a microcommunity, with stability and differentiation. Panels sometimes reach this degree of mutual recognition halfway through, but this kind of instant-interlock is a first. It seems to proceed from their attitude toward strangers and toward an uncharted situation. Groups typically work from wariness into a synthetic and hectic friendliness, impersonal in its generality. Discrimination later comes, through contention, and cohesiveness begins then (if it ever does).

These people enter the discussion room like Margaret Mead landing on New Guinea. They are alert and porous, open to whatever the experience will be. They listen, rather than wait for a turn to talk. Even the initially silent ones—when talk is demanded of them—do not hang back or mumble. They address the opinions that have been expressed and endorse, elaborate, or amend them.

They treat each interview topic like a group task they must perform together, and they create the best form possible for this particular panel, to carry out the assignment. The particular forms are different. *Group I* (Women) is emotionally warm, but can be dispassionate in discussion. They organize like a daily paper, using the moderator as city desk. *Group II* (Men) is more like an art colony, collaborating on a mural. In this sense, they are both very conscious of their "product," the living document of what they have said. The two later groups, of whom a "product" is required ("write me a scenario") organizes somewhat more politically—like military task forces, with chains of command.

But in all four, the community they create has a real life, and modifies its members. There are, for example, eccentrics in each panel: people whose values or behavior falls outside the compromise positions accepted by most other members, for the privilege of membership. In one group, it is a "traditional housewife/mother" who is the oddball. In another, it is a seeming lightweight who accepts the polyester "equality" of Club Med as the real thing. In another, it is an aggressive black-militant feminist. In another, a man who talks like radar, keeping up a steady stream, not to communicate, but to get locating blips back. These people are not ostracized, but are used the way primitive societies use their deviants—as spice, and as a measure of the integrity of the rest.

Predispositions: Common Characteristics

The single most pervasive impression produced by these respondents is their particularity. They seemed to have passed through socialization with a particular kind of lubricant that has kept convention from sticking to them. I mean that most of them are not *un*conventional in the sense of flouting established practices, or even deciding soberly to renounce them. More they are *a*conventional, almost as if they don't *see* what it is that they are not living by.

We are not talking here about table manners or forms of greeting (most of them are polite enough), but about the basic file dividers out of which the average citizen constructs social order: age, gender, circadian rhythm, work, and purpose. Age distinctions, in these panels, are not communicative blocks to be broken through. They are distinctions as frank and unstatused as "left" vs. "right." The same is true of male/female roles, which these panelists crumble to powder. They are also fairly easily free-wheeling in time, alternating workshifts—or doing without scheduling altogether—with remarkably few bruises.

They work at many different occupations, for a number of reasons, so their adjustments are *different*, but they don't seem to recognize occupational hierarchies (jobs that are "better than"). Furthermore, though some grouse about surrendered freedom, not one is actively unhappy with the time spent at work. When they *were* unhappy at work, they left to find something else more pleasing. Most of these people have had a number of jobs. There are some men and women who talk about "unstimulating" work, but add (or imply) that they handle this by retaining the lively sovereignty of their heads, which are free to go where they will. The stimulation comes from inside.

Even the panelists who describe lifestyles that are closer to modal for the society got there by a back road. ("We have a good marriage, even though we're actually divorced for tax reasons. We live together, and do most things together."; "It took me so long to get the children here—and I hate being pregnant—that I'm going to get a lot back. I don't want to miss anything."; "Before I'd leave on my (30 day) trip, I'd make sure of servants to do the work. I don't want to have to deliberate about how much of the work I owe other people. It wastes too much time.", etc.)

Predispositions: Attitudes and Behaviors Toward the Family

Approximately two-thirds of these panelists are married, and a few more of the now-single sound as if they are heading toward marriage. In most of the marriages, both spouses are working, and this includes households with children. These are busy people. But their investment in the life of the family is striking. Even more striking is the *way* they invest. It is emphatically not according to normative roles.

The absence of role-conforming feelings and actions is more conspicuous in the men's groups than the women's. It has to be allowed that female non-marrieds outnumber male non-marrieds, and that the never-married and no longer-married women tend to be outspoken in their critiques of marriage. But I don't think that is all of it. Both men and women cross the gender/social border, in these groups, but the men do it more persistently, and with more easy acceptance.

There is no flexing of muscles, for instance, to counterbalance the admission by nearly half of our men that they "do most of the cooking at our house." Some also do the cleaning. Above all, the feelings and the behaviors they describe in dealing with children are most accurately described as "warmly nurturant." It is not so odd for some fathers to feel and do some of these things, but it is noteworthy when so many of a selected population do so. And it is positively riveting when so many men in a group will acknowledge such feelings and actions, without defenses like "...the wife works...", and without "macho" compensation. They just do not see the signs that say "for men only" and "for women only."

It isn't even the mellowing-out of fatherhood that does this to them. In the childless, dyadic relationships, these men and women talk as though the signs are not there. Again, we've become used to women taking sexual initiative and (at least in fantasy) "partying" with strangers. But it's less common for a man to discuss his "longing" for a wife, when he is away. There is also a point—after an unabashedly lyrical exchange on the beauties of the morning—when one man expresses simply a need for intimacy: "What I really want, though, is someone to share it with. Somebody I can say to "Look at that," and who will feel the way I feel about it." A few other panelists agree, and nobody laughs.

Predispositions: Attitudes and Behaviors Vis-á-Vis the Community

If these respondents are closely bonded to particular people—their relevant universe—they are not especially concerned about humanity at large. There is little sanctimonious bleating, in these panels, about "doing things for others." One woman in the first group, who begins to sound like this, is met with silence. It is not a hostile silence. The group just doesn't know what to do with her comment. There is a similar situation in one of the male panels, but the speaker catches himself and explains that do-gooding is not what he means. I think that what I am saying is that these people have a stable sense of the social "space" they can usefully occupy, and do not step beyond it. They can ''vascularize'' small groups of important people, but if the blood runs thin, they don't bother.

This may apply to geographic space as well. A number of panelists, offered the "30-days of anything," choose travel. But they don't choose travel for six months or for the rest of their lives. The exotic rambles are to be stored, like food, for later enjoyment. And it's the "later" that counts. The mainstream of their lives is where they most fully live. Picturing them in the Tyrol, or in a temple in Tibet, would be only *temporarily* true for them. Picturing them doing something characteristic in the course of a regular day would be more *permanently* true.

Predispositions: Time Frames

Many of these people travel or would like to travel. But it is my hunch that exotic places *per se* do not figure with great importance in their priorities. Time is another story. In the women's groups, and in particular in the men's groups, I have never interviewed so many people who invest in the whole stretch of time—past and future. The women talk about "studying" nature, and mean geological interests in Indian arrowheads and ancient trees: the artifacts of time. The men are more ambitious. In both groups are men who want to revisit old battlefields, to walk the Sierras, or to cross them on horseback or even by Conestoga wagons. They want to live "the way it was." They also reach into the future, and want to try space travel or "postpone the 30 days to the year when the old astronauts are supposed to return." They feel the connection with the past and the future and are fascinated by it.

It is possible that some of the general preoccupation of these panelists with nature and the out-of-doors has to do with the timelessness of nature. Certainly much of the interest in travel is historical. Destinations, in all four groups, are often chosen either "because my roots are there" or because civilization has left important footprints in particular places.

Despite the fact that they are not inclined to be political in any formal sense (politics is a "belongers'" game), it is likely that they would fight for ecological integrity, or for wilderness protection. My hunch is that the passion they feel for species survival and territorial preservation is rooted in a more basic will to deliver the past into the future to preserve history for their children.

Predispositions: Alone/Together

As noted earlier, conventional male-female distinctions are not merely blurred in these panels. In a number of ways, they are reversed. The need to come together and the need to stay apart both exist in everybody, but it is a cultural expectancy that men and women differ in this respect. More particularly, we expect women to need more together-time, and men to need more alone-time. At first glance, our respondents seem to fly against the wind. More of the men speak of sharing the "30 Days" with their families, and more of them express tenderness for wives and children than in the women's groups. This may be a fluke, because more of the women are ex-marrieds, but certainly suggests that— if these men and women are at all representative, we should look for, and perhaps mirror, men who are more accessible and open to tenderness, women who tolerate longer leashes or none at all.

In the same breath, most of these people—men and women—seem to need relatively large amounts of alone-time. Some of the most intense experiences recounted, some of the most urgent "fantasy" requests cen ter around time alone ("I love to start early in the morning. The world is so fresh. You've caught it off guard and it's yours. Nobody else is around."; "...the only way to go somewhere for the first time is alone.

Nobody's blocking your view."; "...I don't care where. Maybe I'd go nowhere, but I'd have more space, where people couldn't infringe."; "...just as long as there is somebody there to do the work, so I'm free. I'm not sure I'd take anybody, because I don't want to worry about...doing for them."; "...the car blew up on me. I left it and took the bus home. I never knew those things were there. ...If you have to watch the white line, you never see anything else.")

They sound as if they are renegotiating their relationship-contracts, and getting shorter hours. The men don't want to convert all of their energy into money, and lose their lives "watching the white line." The women want not to owe all of their time to others.

Predispositions: Material Goods

Astonishingly few of these people are greedy. Offered total subsidy for 30 days, only three people out of the forty-one get drunk on the luxe of it all. One woman amasses property, one goes on a shopping spree, and a man hits one country a day, "first cabin all the way." The others buy freedom, history, adventure, or "education." When the rules are changed to "all your life," there are no fantasy millionaires ("I'd like to not have to worry about things, but a lot of money—honest, I don't think I would take it. You have to think about it too much."; "...I think what I would miss is never being able to really want something and campaign to get it..."; "I think I really have that. I live on alimony, which I think I have earned. I'm not rich, but I can do what I need to do.").

For these people, money is important only if you have to worry about it. Affluence is too much of an insulation from experience to be desirable ("...people treat you different.")

Predispositions: Work (Accomplishment)/Play (Leisure)

Nobody in these panels hates the work (s)he does, but also nobody is, in the usual sense, ambitious. That is to say, nobody we heard is hacking his or her way up some corporate ladder. Some never got on. Some have dropped off ("I knew I was too lazy to be a really topflight chemist, and I didn't want to settle for less than that, so I left the whole thing and started raising horses."; "I made the mistake of going into business for myself. I felt so pressured I didn't enjoy looking at my tool chest anymore."). A lot have made numerous job changes. Any tidy personnel officer would reject them for "occupational instability," except that the personnel officer would probably be rejected first. The organizational motivators of carrots and threats are for the most part irrelevant to our panel-members.

They work for accomplishment, for love of it, for enough money to survive, for dignity, for comradeship. But they are not working for vice-presidencies. The point is important to understand, because this is an unconventional choice, and it would be possible for someone who has made a different kind of choice to see these people as "losers." If we think of them as being *unable* to "make it," rather than as *choosing* not to, it is possible for the attitude to color the way we address them. Most consumers, these days, are becoming astute at "reading into" advertising the assumptions on which it is based. These are unusually bright, perceptive people, who would be able to spot a drop of condescension in an ocean of copy.

The ideal work situation, for virtually all of these men and women, is "doing something you really enjoy." This suggests a finer line between work and recreation. Not 49 weeks at a desk or a lathe "knocking my lights out," and three weeks on a beach in the Caribbean, recovering. When work is enjoyable, there is energy left for more work-like play ("I know a couple that's building their own house. Everything. Digging the cellar, putting up the foundation. They're learning a lot and they really feel as if it's theirs.").

Predispositions: Moral Values

Moral values make their appearance, as planned, when panelists are asked to "fantasize" *lifetime* subsidy. After the first joyous whoop ("Is that okay?" "Okay? Are you kidding? It's marvelous."), the next sound is the squeal of mental brakes.

When the smoke has cleared away, more of the panel members *don't* want the "lifetime tab" than *do* want it. The reasons given can be clustered under two general headings. Some respondents resist because accepting would be somehow *wrong* ("I haven't earned it. I get the money whether I do a good job or not."; "You're taking away responsibility!"; "I'd know I'm not entitled to it."). Others demur because they think their lives would be paradoxically impoverished by effortless riches ("I'd never be able to want something. I wouldn't *enjoy* time-off.").

This split would be beside-the-point, and hardly worth a footnote, except that for some reason or other, it is the *one major distinction*, in our panels, between what might be called the *"character" of the (Brand) users and the non-users*. Most of the (Brand) users refuse subsidy on moral grounds. They feel the need to work, to earn, to accomplish as a moral imperative. The organizational meat-grinder may have lost them, but the Protestant ethic has its hooks in. Though perfectly capable of seeing the existential consequences ("Well, and then too, I wouldn't enjoy things if they came too easy."), these are secondary.

Another at least quasi-moral distinction is that the two panels of men seem to be more concerned with the "oughts" of life than the women. For one thing, both groups of men are intensely caught up in the American Experience. Not just the thumping adventure of it, but the values too: respect for the land, fair and honest dealings with other people, courage and enterprise, strong ties of family and comradeship, and lack of affectation. The male (Brand)-user panel are practically pilgrim fathers. Whether or not these are things they have "redis-covered" (see discussion, next page), they seemed to have pitched their tents here and settled in.

The women in both groups are less parochial in their interests. But they share with the men a love and wonder for the natural world, are strongly bonded to their family and friends, and value straightforwardness in dealings with others.

Predispositions: The Case for Cold Cereals

In all the panels, the transition from values-to-eating-to-(Brand) is a bit dizzying. In the two non-user panels it is downright abrupt. With very few exceptions, not much has been said about food. They enjoy eating, but tend not to build their days around it. With the exception of the handful of women who function more or less traditionally as housewives, the panelists in these groups are irregular—even quirky—in their eating habits.

The housewives, like their mothers before them, hang their lives from the framework of meal-planning ("You may not have to make a bed today, but you have to cook dinner"). To the extent that there is pattern in mealtimes—and family living generally dictates *some* regularity—the meals have quite distinct characters.

Breakfast, for nearly everyone, is centrifugal. You need from breakfast enough revving up to get from bed to out-the-door. Breakfast focusses you and gives you energy—escape velocity.

Dinner is centripedal. The reverse of breakfast, it touches you down, expands the focus from solitary effort to social exchange. It is an achievement award for the day ("I really feel dinner is like a reward. I've earned it."). Where breakfast tends to have a fast count-down, dinner is stretched out.

Lunch, generally, is nowhere. More men than women in these groups eat lunch at all. It is, routinely, a *time-slot* more than a meal.

Our panelists do not respond on cue to "What is the most important meal of the day?" At least as many say "dinner" as say "breakfast", and some say "meal?". But most of these respondents will allow that breakfast is critical, and "sets the tone of the day."

"Energy" is the key word, and what makes the difference between a good and a not-so-good breakfast is not just the *amount* of energy but the *staying-power* ("You can tell. Some kids in my room are just off the wall at the start of the morning, and by eleven o'clock they are sitting on their neck and they don't hear you."; "I don't want to get that eleven o'clock slump."; "If you have a really good breakfast, you don't really have to eat again until supper, and you still feel powerful.").

Sugar is generally felt to be a flash in the pan, energy-wise. The penultimate gold standard of something that "stays with you" is eggs. The territory in between eggs and a candy-bar is less clear. Surprisingly, a number of these nutritionally hip panelists feel that toast, pancakes, and hot cereal are *good breakfasts,* and would "give you a full tank," where cold cereals cannot get above *"barely adequate breakfast."* As the discussion of cold cereal goes on, they recognize that the cold cereal breakfast is factually "much better than that. A good breakfast, really." But the *emotional* reaction is still "adequate."

They see the contradiction, and try to resolve it. Using the clue that "hot cereal *feels* like a better breakfast than cold cereal," they recognize that heat, and the act of preparing, both have some launching magic at breakfast time. This is especially dramatic in one female panel, when a (Brand)-user (who isn't supposed to be there) says that she makes hot (Brand) according to the package recipe, and "it's the best hot cereal I ever ate." The response is electric. The women are really excited by this idea.

Although almost nobody gives cold cereal blue ribbons as a breakfast, these are cereal eaters, and there are reasons why. For starters, *speed and convenience* ("If I had my choice, I'd be sitting in Modesto having Portuguese sausage for breakfast, and eggs, with a nice hot plate and hash-browns, and a waitress who laughs a lot. But I can't afford the time or the hassle, so in reality I may eat cold cereal 4-5 times a week."; "...If I'm in a hurry, I can get up and while I'm brushing my teeth, I can pour milk and cereal in the bowl and eat it while I'm putting on my coat."; "...and there's nothing to do afterward. It's neat. The most you have is a bowl and a spoon.").

Then there is "lightness" ("It's light. I don't feel I have to occupy myself with it."; "You're not lazy afterward...there's no need to sit down. You just get up and go. In the morning, you don't want something that puts you back in bed."; "You can visualize cereal in your stomach. There's milk and little pieces of cereal floating around. If you eat bacon and eggs, they're in a big hard clump with grease."; "I can eat cereal before I run, where I couldn't eat bacon and eggs.") Net/net, what they are saying about the "lightness" of cold cereal is that with a *heavy* meal, you do not have the use of the energy it gives you. Cold cereal fuels you in mid-air, without breaking stride.

The generic discussion of cold cereal gets diffused some, because:

• In these groups, many respondents eat *odd breakfasts* ("wine and salad"; "...Sometimes I'll want a hot dog...whatever's left over from dinner.") or *no breakfasts* ("I can't eat for hours after I get up.").

• Most of our panelists do not think of cold cereal as only—or even especially—a breakfast food. ("I'm more apt to eat it when I get home from work."; "I take salad and a little pouch of cereal in a plastic bag for lunch."; "It's good anytime you want something, but you don't want to interrupt what you're doing.").

Predispositions: Perceptions of (Brand)

In the talk about cold cereals, before selling statements are shown, and before the brand-focus of the panels is revealed, there is spontaneous discussion of (Brand). In the user-panels, (Brand) is mentioned as an example of what is "good" in a cold cereal.

Cold cereal is considered by (Brand)-users to be a "better" breakfast than non-users think it is ("I think it's a good thing to eat. When I've had my bowl of (Brand), I think I have done something good for my body."; "It really does stay with you. It's in there humming all morning—all day."; "...In the morning, I'm helpless. I write notes for myself at night so I won't think I have nothing to do. I have to get my act together fast, and I'm not up to much eating. (Brand) is ideal. It gives you a lot of charge for a small amount.").

The particular advantages of cold cereal which (Brand)-*users* mention, beyond *speed and convenience* and *lightness* are:

• *Nutrition*. Only (Brand)-users talk *spontaneously* about cold cereals as being nutritious. (For more discussion, see "Directed Perceptions of (Brand)", below.)

• *Compactness*. This is a near relative of *"lightness,"* but isn't identical. Mostly, they are talking about what is *in* the box, as a kind of magic pill ("I like the density. It's concentrated and you don't have to eat much. I guess I like to think of myself as not eating much, but it's really just right in the morning."; "The smallness of it is in keeping with my feeling of 'let's get going'."; "...I think there is some carry over from the astronauts, and the way their food has to be very compact. I think of (Brand) almost as space-food."; "I know somebody who runs the marathon, and he eats (Brand) before. You can literally eat and run.").

And then there's the *box*. ("It doesn't sound very important, but the size of the box. It fits on the shelf. We have other cereals that you have to put on their sides to get them in"; "I think of the box as easy to take along, and we do keep it in the car. I sometimes eat it out of the box, and it's a snack for the kids.")

• *Versatility:* Neither at this point, nor anywhere later in any of the discussions, is "versatility" ascribed to any other cold cereal. In the user panels, it is not surprising that—as long as the box is there anyway—they would try some "(Brand) recipes," and mention using it in salads, soups, casseroles, and desserts ("I wouldn't cook without it anymore than I would without flour."; "I do most of the cooking in our house, and I use (Brand) a lot, in casseroles. It adds flavor and nutrition, and doesn't load the thing up with salt.").

The mention of (Brand) *as a hot cereal* only surfaces once, in a non-user panel, but sweeps the board when it does, and leads to some third-person speculation about *versatility* ("I've never heard of using it hot, but I do know people who cook with it."; "Well, it's certainly great in ice cream, so it should make good desserts.").

Directed Discussion of (Brand)

In the two non-user panels, the intelligence that "we are especially interested in (Brand)" precedes any exposure to selling statements. They are asked to say what they think about it, from whatever experience they have had with it or with advertising, and who they think are (Brand)-users.

• Perceptions of (Brand). One male non-user is a sugar-freak, and will consider only cereals that are sugared and flavored. Favorite listings for the others are: Shredded Wheat, the various Chex cereals, Granola, and Raisin Bran. When asked to describe their favorite cereals, the descriptions sound very much like a purchase order for (Brand).

—*Concentrated*. ("I like a cereal that goes a long way and fights back and doesn't get mushy."; "A concentrated cereal (that) stays with you.")

—*Whole Grain*. ("A whole grain cereal...is more satisfying." "...nothing left out assures you you are getting the value of the wheat.")

—*Crunchy or Chewy*. ("I get sometimes a real hunger for crunch".; "I like a cereal that keeps me busy. I don't care if it talks to me. I want it to listen."

—*Pure*. ("I want a naturally sweet cereal, with no sugar added."; "I stay away from anything that lists salt or sugar on the box." ; "I don't want any additives or preservatives—not even any fortifiers.'')

When it is pointed out that they have, in effect, described (Brand) the question becomes *why are they not users?* Some have ready answers:

• *It doesn't seem light*. ("I suppose it is light, but it's this little tiny box that feels like a canon ball.")

• *It's expensive.* ("It really costs twice as much and you get half as much.")

• *It's too concentrated.* ("Concentrated is good up to a point, but when I eat, I want to sit for a few minutes. One big shredded wheat will take me that long to eat. You put the spoon in (Brand) and you're done.")

But more of the non-users have no particular reason for *not* eating (Brand). Most of the panelists in all four panels are first-person buyers of cereals. No matter who does the bulk of the shopping, these are people who buy their own cold cereal brands. One thing they suggest is that cereal-buying, like cereal-eating is semi-automatic, unpondered ("It isn't even so much a *choice.* You have to eat something, you grab cereal without thinking. The same way, you're in the store, you go to the same place and grab the same box. A new cereal can at least get your attention. But if you're used to not-buying (Brand) you'll go on not-buying it.")

Nutrition is raised as a focus, in the non-user panels, by the moderator. The panelists are alive to the issue, and think of the cereals they eat as being "healthy", "wholesome", "good for you" or "nutritious" ("You are always bombarded with fear. We are constantly informed that something else has been found to cause cancer. Your mental attitude enters in. You feel as if you've done your part—all you can do—if you eat something that's wholesome or healthy or good for you."; "...you feel better if you don't worry about your body. If you stuff it full of garbage, you worry."; "Food is comfort. Cereal especially, because you've always had it. I was so depressed last week all I wanted was some hot Quaker Oats. I knew it was safe for me. I finished the bowl before I could raise my head to see over the top of the box."). So *"nutrition"* has a lot of meanings. The panels recognize four main headings:

• *Wholesome* refers to purity. "It has no bad things in it." Wholesome is as close as you can come to grazing, in a box.

• *Healthy* refers to what *is* in the product more than what is *not* in it. If it doesn't have sugar, salt, additives, or preservatives, it's whole-some. If it *does* have all of the grain in it it's *healthy* ("That feels healthy to me. A whole grain of any kind is more satisfying. Your body doesn't miss anything and feels satisfied. That's when you have energy, and emotionally I feel light and buoyant.")

• *Nutritious* is close to "healthy", but is more detailed. It is the computer breakout on "healthy" ("...I think of nutritious as not only natural and if you're talking about cereal, whole grain. But it's a count of the vitamins and proteins and carbohydrates in it."; "...for some reason, I always think of a "nutritious" cereal as a laxative.").

• *Good for you* is the best of both *wholesome* and *healthy*. It has good things, hasn't got bad things. But it also differs in tone. It is more personal ("If it's good for me, I think that means for me personally. It's good for *me*."). It may also have *taste* overtones ("I know it doesn't really mean it's yummy, but the difference between "healthy" and "good for you" is, I would feel that the "good for you" one would be better tasting.")

When asked how we could make the transition from *"(Brand) is Nutritious"* (or "healthy", or "wholesome"—all of which they agree it probably is) to *"(Brand) is Good For You,"* they say that of course the answer is to make them feel more personal about it ("If I felt that somebody who feels the way I do would like it, I guess I'd like it too"; "...think 'oh, that person is like me', but I don't know who that could be. Somebody real, not perfect, for one thing.").

We then proceed to *identifying the person* (who is apparently not any of them) they now think of as (Brand)-user:

• *Age.* All of the non-users agree that the prototypical (Brand)-user is at least *adult*. Most of them specify that he is "over 45", and mention (Brand's spokesperson). The women are a little more general ("Not a child. At the earliest, 9th or 10th grade."; ..."any adult, right up to senior citizen."; "I think of silver-haired.")

• *Sex.* There is also general agreement about the fact that the (Brand)-user is prototypically male "...although there is no reason why it has to be."

• *Occupation.* Here, they are hazier. He could be blue-collar, white-collar, or athlete. Anything *except* "artistic" ("I don't know why. But I think of the person as more physical, and not a thinker or a person who dreams."; "...not a particularly sensitive person. Someone who doesn't communicate with you. Hard to know.")

• *Personality.* There is agreement that the (Brand)-user is a solid citizen—serious, stable and reliable. Most respondents also believe that "he" is independent and keeps his own counsel; a loner, who is shy or reserved. All find "him" more disposed to action ("...He's dynamic, active. Kinetic, is it?"; "Never quiet.... If he's talking he's also fixing something.") Most seem to agree that the user-person is a good friend, accepting and generous, but not at all "glamorous" or whimsical.

Net/net, although nobody actually says this, the (Brand)-user they have described is apt to be less attractive to these people than they are to each other. He is *not stimulating* (though he may be admirable), *not especially fun or quick-witted* (though he may be wise and give good advice), *not emotionally "free" or open* (though he may be good-hearted), and *not socially warm and accessible* (even though generous and accepting). If the goal is for these people to identify (Brand) with themselves, all of these lacks are *problems to be fixed*.

Reactions to Selling Statements

Three Selling Statements are shown to Panels I and II (the user-panels):

A. *"The Cereal that is the intelligent choice for people who give careful thought and demonstrate concern in everything they do and eat."* (The word "intelligent" is deleted for panel II).
   The reaction to this statement is negative, on balance. The written reactions are less lethal than the group discussions, but not a whole lot less.

   —*Pluses:* Respondents see that the statement is trying to position "this cereal" as healthy, and as a caring and cautious thing to put into one's own and one's family's bodies. They also see that it is targeted "above" the mass audience ("for educated, intelligent people.").
   —*Minuses:* Most of the brickbats tossed at this statement have to do with the "tone" which panelists read into it: the attitude which respondents *assume is behind the statement.* More than half feel that the statement is *condescending* or snobbish (It's patronizing. I feel as if they think they are conning me. It's 'Eat this and everybody will think you're intelligent.'"; "I like your word 'patronizing'. I said 'snobbish'.").

There are also overtones of *intimidation* ("...If you buy anything else, any other cereal off the shelf, you're not intelligent or concerned."; "If I use something else now, I'm stupid. How do I get smart? By eating (Brand)?").

The user-men are kinder to this statement, and a couple even say they might try, out of curiosity.

B.*"The Cereal for healthy, active people who get the most out of life."* The statement is felt to be "okay," with a generally upbeat tone, but rather featureless and innocuous ("It sounds like Wheaties."; "It doesn't really say much.").

—*Pluses:* This at least does not offend. The ideal of healthy, life-loving people is appealing. It suggests to them *energy,* which is one of the things they look for in a cold cereal, and it therefore offers some legitimate promise of *competitive goodness.* It arouses images of athletes ("Reminds me of Bruce Jenner."; "...Johnny Weissmuller"), and they would *"feel confident"* that they were putting something wholesome into their bodies.
—*Minuses:* Though inoffensive, they also feel that this statement offers no specific information that sets it apart from a dozen others. It is a pleasant but almost *generic* cold cereal promotion.

C.*"The Cereal for people who are rediscovering simpler lifestyles and are getting back to basic values."* This statement is seen by all four panels. But the responses are not strictly comparable for users/non-users, since the non-users see only this statement and have already been tipped-off that the cereal is (Brand).
For everyone, on balance, the statement has positive impact. In this case, the written comments are resoundingly positive, and the discussion is where we hear the quibbles.

—*Pluses:* All panelists, whether aware it is (Brand) or not, feel that the cereal being described is *"natural" and "healthy"* ("It's from the field straight to you.") It also resonates on the *ease/speed/convenience—in a word, simplicity*—which is a primary advantage of cold cereals ("...Simple, no junk, and it's easy. Grab it and run—like an apple or an orange.") It has some *specific identification* with particular people, who are "doing something about their lives" ("It would say that if you think about it, you will try it. The same thing they tried to say in the first one, but not insulting.").

—*Minuses:* There are some quibbles about advertising "hype" ("What does cereal have to do with ...getting back to basic values?"; "It says nothing about cereal. You could be advertising tennis shoes".;"What do they mean 'rediscovering?' Didn't we know about this?"). But my interpretation of the quibbles, based on the fact that they don't appear in written comments, and don't "ring true" in the discussions, is that this is the reflex kicking of consumers who-don't-want-to-be taken-in, and is not specific to the statement. Concepts always lack substance and particularity, but as concepts go, this one looks promising.

The (Brand) Reveal has the effect, in the two user panels, of making everything okay. All is forgiven (including a "patronizing" statement) because it is (Brand). But the new information also has the effect of reinforcing their choice of the third statement ("If you have to advertise, I like that one the best."; "The first statement could be Granola, and the second could be Wheaties, but this last one says (Brand)."; "All three statements I now think are true, but that 'basic value' one is more up-to-date. That's the way things are heading."; "It sticks in your mind."; "Could you really trust people who get the most out of life? What do they care and what are they *doing*? But the last one could apply to anyone, from you to your grandmother.").

Asked to elaborate on the meaning of *"simpler lifestyles"* and *"basic values,"* the discussion centers around three ideas: *Waste (Reduction), Pace* and *Accountability.*

• *Reducing Waste.* People who are "stepping up into less is more," our panelists say, are more *selective* consumers ("...you don't have to consume everything out there. Just pick a few quality things and use them for all they're worth."; "...the simpler lifestyle is to stop wanting always more..."; "It means getting your money's worth."; "...not wasting *time* or effort running after more than you really want."). Net/net: not spending the precious only time of a precious only life, or the *motion* or the *money* for more than you want, or for less than the best.

• *Pace.* "Simpler lifestyles and basic values" also implies a changed, slower pace ("Not getting stampeded into the race, and missing things along the way."; "...putting on the brakes and saying 'hey, wait a minute. What am I hurrying for?'"; "You have to accept pressure for it to bother you. It means saying 'sorry, you won't get it tomorrow.'"; "You take the lid off the pressure cooker before you get spareribs on the ceiling."). Net/net: you only "go after it" after you've quietly thought it over and decided it's worth running for.

• *Accountability.* "Simple" and "basic," the respondents insist, do not reduce everybody to homogeneous soup. They mean different things to each individual, and really foster uniqueness ("...not living according to set-by-the-clock standards. You're self-paced."; "There's no keeping-up-with-the-Joneses. What's good for them may not be good for you."; "'Simple' doesn't mean 'easy'. The easy lifestyle is to take someone else's formula for how to get somewhere. You may not be satisfied when you get there, but it's easy, and it's not your fault if you don't. ...But 'basic values' is figuring out what you want, and 'simpler life-styles' is figuring out the shortest way to it.") And I can't net/net better than that.

Reactions to Illustrated Copy

Three rough illustrations with copy are presented to the first two panels:

D. *("Bank President"—Real People): An executive opting for voluntary simplification, and including (Brand) as part of the prescription.* On balance, responses to this "execution" suggest that it could be both arresting and involving, but is, at the moment, far-fetched and lacks immediacy for most of these panel members.

—*Pluses:* The situation is *recognizable* ("Most of my friends are in that category. They have given up jobs as executives to go back to basics."; "It's too exaggerated. He wouldn't make that much of a jump."; "You are not supposed to take it literally. It's a way to *represent* a changing lifestyle."). It is also an *exciting* situation. ("What he's doing is important. He's changing his whole life: thinking it out, taking the pressure off, setting priorities--and eating right"; "For me, when I did that, it was a real adventure—fortunately, with a happy ending.")

And they can also recognize a *possible tie-in with eating habits* ("If you make that kind of change, you would also change the way you eat": "...the connection isn't made, but I can imagine a guy who would never stoop to cold cereal finding that he likes it."; "This kind of switch usually is to more natural, healthy ways of living. It...is an opportunity to plug a natural, healthy food like (Brand).")

—*Minuses:* The situation is *over-stretched for effect* ("It sure is flowered up. I don't believe anyone would do that."; "That's too much of a jump to be true. He should be less than a bank president, or else he should just move to a small branch office."). They also feel that *too little attempt has been made to understand the feelings* that would prompt that kind of switch ("If you are supposed to be happy at the end, something bad should be connected with the beginning, that would make him get out."; "I was president of my company, and making three times more than I am now. But it wasn't worth it. He should be more frazzled or sweating bullets in the first part."; "You don't know why he chucked the job?"). It could also be *frightening* ("It could be scary. You have to give up your job.").

E. *("Ice-Fishing"): A spartan and unusual recreation is given as an example of getting back to basics, offering Brand as another example.* This illustration/copy statement is not offensive, but not one person is drawn to it. It is simply foreign to anything they might enjoy.

—*Pluses:* None, except possibly shock value.
—*Minuses:* "It leaves me cold," repeated a number of times.

F. *("Our Town"): A slightly 'limboed' setting for a community that is getting back to basic values (and reliving earlier times?), and to (Brand).* This is not as dramatic as the bank-president story—also not as definite. But most of the panelists who see it like it pretty well.

—*Pluses:* Some people are getting *back to nature,* and they *don't* have to do it alone. ("The idea of working out a way for a town to live that way is sort of interesting."; "I'm sure a lot more could be done to make the places where we live more natural, closer to nature. And you wouldn't have to quit your job."). It plays right into the romantic, and wistful, *fantasies of these men who want to go back* and do it all again ("It seems... as if it were an earlier time. You could leave your office and go back to pioneer times."; "This is more permanent. It's not some two weeks in the arctic adventure. It's like a return to an earlier way of life.").

—*Minuses:* The most serious negative reacton is the suspicion of *phoniness* ("It's just too folksy, too apple-cheeked. They think we're idiots. It is just not respecting the people who do this."; "There's no need for it. They are doing it just as dress up. I'll bet there's a ticket-booth somewhere.").

—*Net/net:* For three trial-runs on a new course, the reactions of these people are encouraging (*if* the screening works and they really are "inner-directeds"). One of the copy/illustrations seems to have both grab and believability. Another is developable, and only one misses the target completely. And the "miss" is not a mile, at that.

But the reason for showing these boards at all is to gain information about next steps, i.e., to look for *general* guidance. The general hypotheses that should be tested later with numbers:

• People of this kind are ready to believe and identify with the transition to "less is more."

• No change in lifestyle is "too much" if a reason is given or suggested. Any change may be, without the reason.

• These respondents appreciate "texture" in people, at least as much as in cereal, and prefer someone who sweats, frowns, and is not too smooth (which may put a burden on casting).

• To prove that we know them, and to invite them to identify with what we are saying, we may get further if we understand what their lives are like everyday, and the ways they deal with recurrent problems than if we "catch" them at some arcane recreational retreat.

Panel "Scenarios"

Since the reactions of the user-panels to the three copy-illustrations are near consensus (and we may have learned all that is presently learnable from them), the two non-user groups are asked, instead, to *suggest* plots or situations for possible commercial development. One of the things they do is to invent the *executive drop-out,* which leads to showing them the *"Bank President" board,* about which they say, yes, that is the idea all right, but does the jump have to be so big?

In addition to second guessing us, they offer several other ideas (see more complete sketches in appendix, below):

- Houseboat
- Marathon Runner
- Corporate Lawyer/Antique Dealer
- Newsman/Novelist
- Condo owners/cabin builders
- Drop Out by staying put
- Scoutmaster on Wilderness Hike
- Lunchtime Kite Flyer
- Women's Lib in Reverse
- Middle-Aged Huck Finn (view of marina)
- Lady Chemist who becomes horse-breeder
- Broadloom-and-plant furnished apartment
- Fitness is a family affair
- Grandma does Yoga
- Tidying up "our" world
- Flower on the breakfast table
- Careful shopper
- Lunch at the Beauty Shop

They also produce some slogans—some of which tie in with some of the scenarios, and all of which are interesting.

- The cereal that lets you be yourself (you can drop pretenses)
- We're on your side (change is hard to do alone)
- Make Time (Nobody is going to give it to you)
- Fitness is a family affair (from the "script" of the same name)
- Whose world is it anyway?

APPENDIX: PANELIST "SCENARIOS"

Houseboat. Man gets electric bill, rent bill, and the elevator isn't working so he has to walk twelve floors. Suddenly whips out a catalog, and next thing you know, he's living on a houseboat.

Marathon Runner. Simple visual shows runner at the starting line, grabbing a quick bowl of (Brand). He is saying something about how running the marathon isn't just to keep his body fit, but to supply some kind of challenge, in a world "that doesn't have many frontiers."

Corporate Lawyer/Antique Dealer. He walks out of a board room looking whipped, goes outside, passes an antique shop window and the owner waves. The forefinger of God strikes him, and now he has an antique shop on Puget Sound.

Newsman/Novelist. An important person, or one who's accomplished something that enables him to make an independent decision. A newspaper man, who's had to write for someone else. He's now had his first book published. He's made an achievement for himself. He gets enough remuneration from that so he can pursue the lifestyle he really wants and write about what he chooses. He is sitting at an old Underwood typewriter and he's got a draft of a new book. There's a copy of the book he's just written. He's smoking a pipe and the ashtray is dirty. The cat is sitting (I *think* that's what he said) at the typewriter. He's his own person. (Care to work that into 30 seconds?)

Condo Owners/Cabin Builders. A couple, building a cabin from scratch. Doing everything. They arrive at the site in their car, put on overalls, work awhile, go and get a quart of milk from the country store and have a (Brand) picnic.

Dropping out by staying put. A man in his office. Says that by this time he thought he'd have the big one across the hall, "and they offered it to me. Know what? I didn't take it. I like what I'm doing. What do I need with two secretaries and an ulcer?"

Scoutmaster on Wilderness Hike. No script.

Lunchtime Kite Flyer. Boss asks man to have lunch. He says, "Sorry, JB." Picks up large flat portfolio. Sprints into the hall. Goes down in elevator. Fights for a cab. Gets in and says, "Golden Gate Park" (or whatever). Gets there and pulls kite and small pouch of (Brand) out of portfolio.

Women's Lib in Reverse. Woman in typical housewife milieu. Says "I've liberated myself. I don't really *have* to be a nuclear physicist. Taking care of my kids is what I really like."

Middle-Aged Huck Finn. A man sits at his desk, with his slide rule, and looks out at the marina. Then a lightbulb lights over his head, and in the next shot, he's on a boat.

Lady Chemist/Horse-Breeder. This was suggested by another panelist, hearing the woman who said "I am too lazy to become a really great chemist, and I didn't want to be a mediocre one, so I stopped. I love raising horses."

Broadloom-and-Plant Furnished Apartment. Maybe you can't stop living in the city, but you can quit reupholstering chairs and dusting bric-a-brac. Coming to *my* apartment keeps my friends limber. (Show apartment entirely furnished with a wall-to-wall or to-ceiling carpet, and a window full of plants. A stack of cushions is the only furniture.)

Fitness is a family affair. Father (and mother?) and kids running together.

Grandma does Yoga. No script.

Conestoga. There's this park where you can actually rent a covered wagon. You could show somebody driving up in their car, and getting out—a whole family—and getting into a Conestoga wagon.

Tidying up "our" world. Kids—some big, some little (maybe scouts)—cleaning up a beach after an oil spill.

Flower on the breakfast table. "Make time to smell the roses."

Careful Shopper. Show people really checking automobile, and buying small car instead of Cadillac. Show someone inspecting the seams in a garment. Pull back and the garment is blue jeans. Show some person (people) in grocery store, reading label and picking (Brand).

Lunch at the Beauty Shop. A very important woman (lady senator, movie star) has come in to get her hair done. She's under the drier and pulls out her little bag of (Brand). The operator has gone back into the employee rest room, and is pouring milk into *her* bowl of (Brand).

Index

A

Accountability, 91
Advertising, acceptability of, 92
AIO (Activities, Interests, and Opinions), 60
Alpha error, 115
Appendix A, Six-Week Schedule for a
  Focus-Group Project, 233-35
Appendix B, Qualitative Research
  Proposal for *Sales & Marketing
  Management*, 237-39
Appendix C, Sample Screening Device
  for Selecting Focus-Group
  Panelists—*Sales & Marketing
  Management*, 241-43
Appendix D, Discussion Guide for *Sales
  & Marketing Management*, 245-49
Appendix E, Sample Introduction to
  Focus-Group Panelists, 251-54
Appendix F, How to Score the Buzzword
  List, 255-59
Appendix G, Short Report Exploration of
  Consumer Responses to Introductory
  Concepts for Cocktail Mixers, 261-75
Appendix H, Full Report, 277-310
Apprenticeship, 181-82
Assumptive mode, 13

B

Believability, 78
Beta error, 115
Biases, 6-8, 214
Blind screening, 24, 104
Brand name(s). *See also* Product(s)

  bonding of the manufacturer with a,
    155-57
  commitment of panelists to, 152
Broadeners, 24
"Butterflies," 132-33

C

Chart entries, 121
Client
  assessing prospective moderators by
    the, 189-91, 194
  input during an interview, 200-202
  matching the moderator and the,
    187-92
  "pre-game warmup" of the, 199
  qualifications for the ideal, 188-89,
    201-2, 205-6
  sensitivity to potential problems, 214
Client-moderator relationship, 108-11,
  214-16
Client-to-client relationships, 83
Communicative channel(s), 71
Competitive bids, 12
Confidentiality in focus-group interviews,
  104-6
Copytest procedures, 135
Corporate image, research centered on
  the, 155-56
"Couple decisions," 22

D

Data
  accessibility of focus-group, 143

reliability of, 112
validity of focus-group, 112-16
Demographic questionnaire, 24, 31
Dichter, Earnest, 63
Discussion guide, 15-20

E
Earphone system of client-moderator
    contact, 200
Embeddedness, 77
Emotional motivations, 53-59
Errors
    alpha versus beta, 115
    in the field, 213

F
Farley, Jane C., 139
Figure drawings, instruction sheet for, 24, 31
Focus-group interview(s), 11-36
    afternoon versus morning, 27
    applicability of, 144-45
    as the basis for marketing decisions,
        162
    believability of, 144
    casting, 149
    confidentiality of, 104-6
    controlling, 173-74
    in conjunction with a new research
        effort, 148, 192-95
    for creative purposes, 126-37
    credence in, 106
    deciding the specifications of, 169-71
    defining, 3-8
    depth of expression and understanding
        in, 172-73
    error in, 150
    ethical considerations in, 104-8
    exploratory, 147-48
    goals for, 146
    hostess functionaire in, 218-19
    as an interpersonal event, 83-97
    interpreting, 74
    to introduce new marketers to a
        product, 147-49

moderating, 45
the myth of "quick, easy, and cheap," 7
need for clearly defined goals in, 146
planning, 170-71
problem, 211-228
the quick and cheap myth of, 145-46
reactions to presented materials during,
    135-37
review of taped, 122-24
rules of order for, 14-15
scheduling, 24-28
the setting for, 219
in studying creative concepts and
    executions, 160-62
the technical evolution in, 39-50
the theoretical concept of, 53-64
as tools of exploration, 145-53
transcripts of, 121
used for show, 158-60
video taping of, 12-24, 144, 158
wrap-up, 31, 75
Focus-group panel members
    broadening the sample of, 21
    casing, 128-29
    characterized as "butterflies," 132-34
    characterized as "sponges," 131-32
    chemistry problems between the
        moderator and, 221-23
    choosing, 167-82
    communicative range of, 21
    counterfeit, 216-17
    energy problems among, 220-21
    the flake among, 226-27
    freshness of, 104
    gender consideration in the selection of,
        21-22
    the joker among, 224
    level of personal revelation of, 73
    level of private acknowledgement of, 72
    level of public affirmation of, 72
    narrowing the ages of, 21
    no-show, 218
    number of, 171-74
    personal-motivational context of, 133

personal revelations of, 73
problem of best friends among, 224-25
professional, 217
respect for the responses of, 106-8
sample screening device for selecting,
 241-43
selection of, 167-69
tone of the discussion of, 108
Focus-group panel(s)
 coping with inherent natural vice in
  either the moderator or members of,
  227
 coping with problem, 211-28
 homogeneous/heterogeneous issue in the
  composition of, 174-80
 psychopaths as members of, 179
 salesmen as members of, 178-79
 sample introduction to, 251-54
 size of, 176
 teachers as member of, 179
Focus-group project
 the assumptive mode of the moderator
  as an obstacle to the planning of a,
  13
 competitive bids for a, 12
 confronting fallibility in the field during
  a, 216-19
 as a microcosm, 97
 planning a, 12-26, 192-95
 proposal for a, 11-12
 sample schedule for a, 233-35
 stages in the development of the,
  185-87

G
*Golf and Limerence: Romancing the
 Game*, 135

H
Hawkins, Del I., 64

I
Impression-management by the moderator,
 223-24

Independence of verbal and written
 responses, 80
Influential innovator (I.I.) as a panel
 member, 180
Interaction climate, 128-29
Interaction facilitating group, 88-89
Interpretation of a marketing message,
 79-80
Interviewing, depth of, 45

L
Lazarsfeld, Paul F., 63
Liking, 78
Limerent feelings, 35

M
Marketing researcher(s)
 infatuation of marketers with focus-
  group interviews as viewed by, 144
 origin of focus-group research and
  conflict with, 39-44
Mini/maxi panel-size dispute, 171-74
Moderator(s). *See also* Rapporteur(s)
 academic training recommended for a,
  48
 activities performed during the
  interview by, 87
 acts of God that cause problems for the
  focus-group, 219-28
 apprenticeship for a, 48-49
 assumptive mode of the, 13
 basic tools and techniques which can
  help, 86-87
 coping with inherent natural vice in
  either focus-group members or the,
  227
 conceptual tools of, 101-3
 dress code for the, 84-85
 enhancing the recall of the, 122
 as facilitator, 45
 ideal, 187-98, 205-6
 impression-management by the, 223-24
 the in-group, 225-26
 interview self of the, 88

as partner, 92
physical qualities of, 195-96
primary relationships of the, 84
as prime mover/participant
resolution responsibility of the, 89-90
topic bridging by the, 89
Moderator/client hazards, 213-16
Motivation, 136-37

N
Newness panic, 110

P
People boxes, 60-61
PGSRs (psychogalvanic skin response),
    61-62
Planning
as a goal for focus-group projects,
    192-95
client staff participation in focus-group, 14
a focus-group project, 12-26, 233-35
rules of order for focus-group, 14-15
Plethysmographs, 61
Post mortem, The, 31-33, 45, 75,
    200-202
Predisposition discussion, 30, 129-30
Private acknowledgement of panel
    members, level of, 72
Product(s)
brand-history of, 152
comprehension in the promotion of, 76
focus-group exploration in the
    marketing of new, 147, 149-53
heterogeneity among consumers in the
    usage of, 176-80
use of focus groups for the new
    positioning of existing, 147
panelists' brand commitment to, 152
repositioning of, 153-55
Proposal(s), 11-12
client's choice of rapporteur in
    consideration of the, 191- 92
Public affirmation of panel members,
    level of, 72

Purchase decision
behavior, 59-60
motivational operations of the, 136-37
simplifying the, 61-63

Q
Questions
avoidance of direct, 68-70
"blind" or misleading, 24
Quorum fallacy, 13

R
Rapporteur(s)
client assessment of the, 191-92
expertise, 71
multiple, 180
task of the, 46-49
Report
"Background and Purpose" section of
    the, 122
framing the, 120
"Implications" section of the, 123
"Methods and Procedures" section of
    the, 124
numerical representation of data in the,
    120-21, 137-39
oral presentation of the, 203-5
"Predispositions" section of the, 125
preparation period, 202-5
preparing the data for the, 120-21
"Reactions to Presented Materials"
    section of the, 135
"Sample" section of the, 123
"Summary" and "Implications" section
    of the, 124-35, 137
writing, 119-42
Research facilities, client-oriented, 93-94
Researcher
as contractor, 90
relationship of client to, 90-91
Resolution, 89
Responses
autonomic, 62
quantification of, 137-39

Riesman, David, 39, 49
Ringer-concept, 162
Rules of order, 14-15

S

Salesmen as members of focus-group
    panels, 178-79
Sampling decisions, 22-23
Scheduling, 24-28
Screener, The 15, 20-24, 241-43
Screening, blind, 24, 104
"Sponges", 131-32
Sponsor, use of focus groups by a new
    product, 148
Stanford Research Group, 60
Summary report, 44, 139
Supplier-to-client relationships, 883
Supplier-moderator relationship, 96-97
Survey questions, translation into target-
    ese of, 157-58
Synectics technique of analogy-
    substitution, 207

T

Teachers as members of focus groups,
    179
Topic bridging, 89

Toplines and full reports, 33-36
Total immersion process of learning, 123
Tull, Donald S., 64
Two-sided response, 161

U

User personality categories, 61

V

VALS (Values and Lifestyles) categories,
    60
Video taping
    of focus-group reports to obtain venture
        capital, 158-60
    used in focus group facilities, 144
"Vocational monologuists," as focus-
    group panelists, 179

W

Warm-up period, 30
Wells, William G., 8
Wrap-up of an interview, 31, 75

Z

Zikmund, William G., 8